Metropolitan Intimacies

CULTURE, HUMANITY, AND URBAN LIFE

Series Editors
Jessica Bodoh-Creed (California State University)

Melissa King (San Bernardino Valley College)

Mission Statement

How are urban processes entangled with human experiences? In the *Culture, Humanity, and Urban Life* series, scholarly monographs and edited volumes explore this question and illuminate diverse forms of such entanglement through empirically based research. This series emphasizes anthropological approaches to the study of human life in relation to the urban. It seeks to illuminate experiences and effects of urban cultures and situate specific cases in a comparative set. By exploring the intricacies of human-urban relations, this series contributes to better understanding of the ways that humans particularly conceive of and experience nature, personhood, ethics, culture, and social life.

Books in Series

Metropolitan Intimacies: An Ethnography on the Poetics of Daily Life, by
    Francisco Cruces
The Belfast Imaginary: Artists and Urban Reinvention, by
    Katherine Keenan
*The Everyday Life of Urban Inequality: Ethnographic Case Studies of
    Global Cities*, edited by Angela D. Storey, Megan Sheehan, and Jessica
    Bodoh-Creed
*Urban Mountain Beings: History, Indigeneity, and Geographies of Time in
    Quito, Ecuador*, by Kathleen S. Fine-Dare

Metropolitan Intimacies

An Ethnography on the Poetics of Daily Life

Francisco Cruces

LEXINGTON BOOKS
Lanham • Boulder • New York • London

Published by Lexington Books
An imprint of The Rowman & Littlefield Publishing Group, Inc.
4501 Forbes Boulevard, Suite 200, Lanham, Maryland 20706
www.rowman.com

6 Tinworth Street, London SE11 5AL, United Kingdom

British Library Cataloguing in Publication Information Available

Library of Congress Cataloging-in-Publication Data

Names: Cruces Villalobos, Francisco, author.
Title: Metropolitan intimacies: an ethnography on the poetics of daily
life / Francisco Cruces.
Description: Lanham: Lexington Books, [2022] | Series: Culture, humanity,
and urban life | Includes bibliographical references. | Summary: "In
Metropolitan Intimacies: An Ethnography on the Poetics of Daily Life,
Francisco Cruces examines intimacy and meaning-making in metropolitan
residents' daily lives"—Provided by publisher.
Identifiers: LCCN 2022014800 (print) | LCCN 2022014801 (ebook) | ISBN
9781793633217 (cloth) | ISBN 9781793633231 (paperback) | ISBN
9781793633224 (ebook)
Subjects: LCSH: City and town life. | Sociology, Urban. | Meaning
(Psychology) | Intimacy (Psychology)
Classification: LCC HT119 .C78 2022 (print) | LCC HT119 (ebook) | DDC
307.76—dc23/eng/20220411
LC record available at https://lccn.loc.gov/2022014800
LC ebook record available at https://lccn.loc.gov/2022014801

Contents

To the memory of María de los Ángeles Villalobos Rodríguez,
Antonio Cruces López,
and Margot Hernández de Guaderrama.

LIST OF FIGURES AND TABLES

x

ACKNOWLEDGMENTS

The last thing I would want is to bore readers with a never-ending list of debts of gratitude owed to the many people, places, and institutions that made this work possible. To be frank, I can barely recall them without faulty omissions. But this is a book on intimacy. And debts—the recognition of a circuit of gifts to which one inescapably belongs—is what intimacy is all about.

My first acknowledgment must be to Jorge Moreno Andrés, a great Spanish visual anthropologist. Jorge has certainly been the cocreator of a good deal of the data, ideas, and images presented here. I am indebted to his expertise as well as to his merry companionship throughout our fieldwork in Madrid, Mexico City, and Montevideo.

A second mention is obliged to Cultura Urbana, the study group founded by me and other peers at Universidad Nacional de Educación a Distancia (UNED) in Spain in 2006. In its various arrangements through the years (featuring Honorio Velasco, Ángel Díaz de Rada, Luis Reygadas, Karina Boggio, Héctor Fouce, Gloria G. Durán, Romina Colombo, Fernando González de Requena, Fernando Monge, Sara Sama, Montserrat Cañedo, Nuria Esteban, Nadja Monnet, María Brea, Livia Jiménez Sedano, Katarzyna Porada, Sandra Fernández García, Mar Ocaña, Rubén Corchete, and Trinidad Arribas), this group has nourished my interest in contemporary, emerging practices with rigor and imagination.

An exhaustive list of the participants in the exploration workshops that ground this project is beyond my reach. I feel obliged and grateful to all of them for trusting me with precious confidences. A special mention is due to the handful who agreed to appear in our movie, sometimes even with their dear ones: Christian, Natalia, Patricia, Daniell, Karla, Martina, Carolina, Penélope, Beatriz, Nahiara, Rosario, Isabel, Ana Laura, Carla, Miguel, Néstor, Jakob, Ismael, Noemí, José Luis, Antonio, Sara, Irene, Fabio, Linda, and Iván.

Medialab Prado (Ayuntamiento de Madrid), Designit, Off-Limits, and CSA La Tabacalera de Lavapiés hosted our workshops in Madrid. Centro Cultural de España, Facultad de Psicología de la Universidad de la República, and Centro de Investigación CEIS did the same in Montevideo. The Department of Anthropology at Universidad Autónoma Metropolitana-Iztapalapa and the media center at CENART hosted workshops in Mexico City. I am grateful to the persons who opened these gates for us: Marcos García, Patricia Larrondo, Karina Boggio, Maria José Bagnato, Antonio Zirión, Nancy Flores, Valeria Cuevas, and Enedina Ortega.

Premieres of our documentary, *The Order I Live In. An Indoor Symphony*, were held at UNED-Ateneo Español (Mexico), Centro Cultural CentroCentro

(Ayuntamiento de Madrid), and Centro Cultural GOES (Intendencia de Montevideo). Other venues made the screening possible in several locations: Cineteca de Madrid, Filmoteca de Andalucía, Designit, Escuelas Pías UNED, Twelfth SIEF Congress, Fifth AIBR Congress, ENSA Marseille, Universidad de Sevilla, CLAS (UC Berkeley), CILAS (UC San Diego), and Center for Ethnography (UC Irvine).

This fieldwork was financed by the collective research projects *Prácticas culturales emergentes en el Nuevo Madrid* (CSO2009–10780, MICINN of Spain), *Madrid Cosmópolis. Prácticas emergentes y procesos metropolitanos* (CSO2012–33949, MINECO of Spain), and *Jóvenes, culturas urbanas y redes digitales. Prácticas emergentes en las artes, el campo editorial y la música* (Fundación Telefónica/UAM-I/UNED), the latter in coordination with a Mexican group led by Néstor García Canclini. I also benefited from periods as visiting scholar at Institut Français d'Urbanisme (*Procesos de metropolización y esfera íntima. Una aproximación comparativa*, PR2009–0160, MEC of Spain), the Department of Anthropology at UCSD (*Metropolization and the Sphere of Intimacy. A Comparative Exploration*), and the Department of Anthropology at UC Berkeley (*The Poetics of Daily Life: A Visual, Trans-urban, and Collaborative Ethnography*, PRX19/00099, MECD of Spain). I received two visiting grants from the Uruguayan CSIC and the Faculty of Psychology at Universidad de la República. Karina Boggio, Stanley Brandes, Jérôme Monnet, John Haviland, George Marcus, Rihan Yeh, and Jocelyne Guilbault were our most gracious hosts during these stays. I am also grateful for the continued support from my own institution, the Faculty of Philosophy at UNED, personified in the deans Manuel Fraijó, Jacinto Rivera de Rosales, and Jesús Zamora.

Whether quoted or not, Honorio Velasco, Néstor García Canclini, Jose Luis García, Jesús Martín Barbero, and James W. Fernandez will find here many of their teachings—or at least my efforts to follow paths cleared by them. I have also benefited from ideas from Ruth Finnegan, Gerd Bauman, Boris Shoshitaishvili, Jaida Samudra, Martha Radice, Susanne Österlund-Pötzsch, María Moreno Carranco, Ana Rosas Mantecón, Miguel Ángel Aguilar, Rosalía Winocur, Ángela Giglia, Renato Ortiz, Germán Rey, Gemma Lluch, Remedios Zafra, David Teira, Ramón del Castillo, Jordi Claramonte, María García Alonso, Manuela Cantón, Amparo Lasén, Antonio García, Francisco Ferrándiz, Wenceslao Castañares, Gonzalo Abril, Cristina Peña-Marín, Ana María Ochoa, Ana Ullán, and Silvia Martínez.

Orvar Löfgren, Jean-Claude Kaufmann, and Arlie Hochschild, who inspired much of the first chapter of this book, offered me generous feedback.

This text was copyedited by Alexander Melczer with extreme patience and professionalism. Maritza, Octavio, Darío, and Luis Fernando contributed to its termination with irreverent jokes and warm company.

Intimacy is a never-ending process of self-understanding, where the others emerge entangled and revealed. The experiences of intimacy recounted here reminded me again and again of my mother, María Ángeles, and my father, Antonio, as well as my mother-in-law, Margot. They left behind a legacy of memories that help me make sense of both my own life and that of others. I dedicate this book to their benign and indelible presence.

Introduction

SOMETHING TOO GOOD TO BE FAKE

Camilo is a fortysomething designer from Uruguay.[1] When we first interviewed him a few years ago, he was sharing a modest apartment with a friend of his girlfriend—who at the time was living with her two daughters nearby in the same neighborhood. As soon as he opened the door for us, he confided, "A weird situation." El Parque is a beautiful modernist area in Montevideo, Uruguay, with shady avenues and unique houses built in a variety of styles from the twentieth century.

We met Camilo for the first time during a workshop at the Spanish Cultural Center in Ciudad Vieja. Feeling at Home was a collective exploration in which around fifteen people engaged in open participation, sharing experiences on the topic of intimacy. Camilo had very clever insights about his personal habitat and a relaxed disposition toward sharing details. A professor of design, he was capable of accurately translating reflections about the everyday into words. For instance, he began by sharing the unconventional situation of living in "at least three different homes at the same time": the first, a shared apartment; the second, his fiancée's house, where he slept most nights; and the third, a weekend beach house that he co-owned with his brother. Hence this witty definition: "Home is any place where I don't have to ask permission to open the fridge."

There was a history behind this. While studying architecture, Camilo had dreamed of building his own house. But more than twenty years passed before he could find the right place, buy it, and completely remodel it. During this lengthy period, he had experienced both living alone and with his girlfriend. A short time after they split up, he finally moved in to the newly remodeled house alone, only to discover that he was not happy in the home he had so carefully planned and executed. He could not stand so much loneliness. After a while, he rented out the house and moved to a more modest place.

Camilo's story is one of life lessons and surprises. Are we the masters of our fate? Does everything we expect from life necessarily happen as we imagined it? Our plans, once executed, may lead to deception or even nightmares. This moral bearing was hinted at in other minor episodes of the story, such as a disappointing first dinner he had in an empty house or his being kicked out of the very "club for singles" that he himself had founded.

Camilo's story was, as a parable, solidly built on narrative resources. What does it speak about? On the one hand, it recounts a modern subject's quest for a life and a space of his own. The outcome of this quest cannot be taken for granted. Life might be serendipitous. Nothing is set in stone. The stream of life takes unexpected turns. Our resulting timeline is made not only out of the fulfillment of desires and plans but also happening, surprise, and mystery. On the other hand, the telling of such a quest allows one to gaze at it from a certain distance, reflecting on its obstacles, twists, and ironies. The art of narrating life is part of the art of living. Not everyone masters both (living and recounting) equally well. But we are all doomed to doing both.

Intimacy is about striving for a good life and about imbuing it with sense. It is the place where life and story come together.

A BOOK ON INTIMACY MADE OF STORIES

Our life is made from little stories: routine, trivial, funny, astonishing, incomplete. Whether boring or exciting, shocking or predictable, lewd or tame, they speak as much about the self who authors them as of the "we" that emerges when they are shared. And implicitly they also speak about others, who are either excluded or made the focus of the conversation. The workday, the commute, the TV news, the laundry, the kids' homework, unfinished chores, expected or remembered circumstances: all these things may appear to be unimportant or trivial. But they shine when, under the light of a good story, they take an unexpected turn that leads us into the more ambitious territories of the beautiful, the embarrassing, the compassionate, the nostalgic.

Everyday microstories are a port of entry to affects and to underlying cultural and personal keys. Their meaning is never fixed. Instead, they are open to the demands of the action, the flow of conversation, and the situated interpretation of the participants. Yet they respond to a persistent, stubborn search for meaning. It is through stories that we unravel the ultimate sense of our lives, the coherence of the world, and our place within it. They help glue together the fragments of our precarious existence. Little stories matter.

This book is an ethnographic exploration of the poetics of microstorytelling in contemporary urban life. More specifically, it stems from an experimental, visual, collaborative, transurban ethnographic research project conducted from 2010 to 2017 in Madrid, Spain; Mexico City, Mexico; and Montevideo, Uruguay, which documented and analyzed current processes of metropolization of the intimate sphere.[2] In this project, microstories were the medium of research; intimacy, the object; metropolitan processes, the ultimate variables we need to keep in mind in order to make sense of the whole.

Our corpus somehow fits in between the formal definitions that sociolinguists have given to the ordinary talk genres, particularly the "oral account of personal experience" (cf. Labov and Waletzky 1967; Ochs and Capps 2001) and what folklorists have studied as the "personal narrative" (Stahl 1989; Bauman 2004). Certainly, not all the resulting material has a narrative form. And many of these exchanges were of an unpolished and improvisatory nature, as most conversations are. But, as a matter of fact, many of the most enlightening interventions by participants and interviewees actually took the form of very good stories that were poetically arranged, "twice-told," rich in structure and artistry. They appear embedded in dialogue or intertwined with other sorts of utterances. In this sense, they fit the narratologists' idea of a "minimal story": a verbal account gathering the basic temporal elements of narrative structure, functioning as a source of logical connections and inference, to be flexibly used during a conversation (cf. Prince 1973, 22; Herman and Vervaeck 2005, 13).

Our microstories are samples from a broader exchange of anecdotes, comments, and dialogues that took place across circa forty collaborative workshops and thirty filmed interviews with several hundred participants, on topics like household appliances, singing in the shower, grooming practices, personal objects, family albums, ways of reading, household chores, parenting, furniture, heirlooms, kitchens, urban transit, and practicing music. Random as this collection may seem, it depicts the core of our research: the somehow mysterious—even unintended—emergence of one's own order in everyday life.

In fact, *The Order I Live In* is the title of the documentary film we produced (Moreno Andrés and Cruces 2018). In it, the best of these stories was captured on camera. Twenty dwellers introduce us to the spaces they live in, the stuff they love, the trifles that move them. The resulting account counterpoints the classical urban symphonies—with their aesthetics of crowds, machines, and busy public places. Here, the emerging collective voice instead dives into what George Perec (1989) called *l'infra-ordinaire*: little events, ambient sounds, confidences. It is only through singular, concrete microstories that we get a glimpse of the whole existence of the ones doing the telling.

Some of the questions raised by the film were left unanswered: the fate of "intimacy" nowadays, the role of narrative in daily life, the promises and limits of ethnographic collaboration. Would it be possible to understand today's urban life without the rise of the intimate sphere? What are the intimate, the ordinary, and the domestic made of? What is the fate of the ongoing metropolization of urban dwelling? Can we record intimate life without ruining it? How can intimacy be properly narrated?

This book deals with these questions with a kind of depth that cannot be attained on film. Departing from an analytical look at stories, the text aims to place them in the broader context of a body of recent research, from diverse geographic and disciplinary provenances, shedding light on the intimate sphere and questioning the processes responsible for its constitution and transformation.

The argument of the book, then, is twofold. It contains a narratological statement: the poetic force of intimate storytelling and its performative, practical, and material consequences. Second, it holds an urbanological one: the emergence of the intimate sphere as an epochal, global phenomenon that deeply transforms long-held ideas on urbanity, the "urban common sense" passed down from the earlier experience of first modernity. We see these two arguments converge when granting the poetics of daily life its due place among a number of other formative forces responsible for the metropolization of dwelling in late modern societies: reproduction, reform, community, commodification, individualization.

THE RISE OF INTIMACY

Defining the intimate realm is by necessity a slippery issue. On the one hand, intimacy is commonly understood in contrast to the notion of a public sphere: a socially regulated and open space for economic exchange, productive activity, political decision-making, administrative processes, the flow of people and goods, and deliberative discourse. The development of this public space has often been considered a key dimension of modern urban societies (Weber 1969; Habermas 1989; Sennet 1969; García Canclini 2010a; Ascher 1995, 2001).

However, within the idea of intimacy, there is much more than merely what is not public. Actually, the nonpublic realm of our lives is also usually described as a mix of private, domestic, everyday, and indoor dimensions. Yet the category of intimacy adds something essential to these notions: the idea of subjectivity. Intimacy has to do with the self and with the spaces for its care and development. The spatial boundaries of subjectivation can be mapped in many different ways: legally (as privacy), physically (as house or habitat), morally and emotionally (as home), functionally (as domestic life), temporally (as everyday), or phenomenologically (as life-world). What the concept of an intimate sphere does is to bring together these disparate definitions, placing the self at the center of a real entanglement that embraces habitat, living with others, privacy rights, housekeeping, familial memory, personal secrets, everyday routines: all that encompassed under a singular, unique biography. Instead of adopting a rigid definition from the onset, the ethnography presented here explores this entanglement by chasing people's own definitions down the path of complexities and contradictions they may entail.

The rise of intimacy is an epochal phenomenon, one of the defining events of our times (Giddens 1991, 1992; Hochschild and Machung 1989; Hochschild 2003). Classical conceptions of urbanity subordinated this realm, rendering it secondary, as in commonsensical couplets like public/private, world/home, and production/consumption. In all these dichotomous pairs, the second term is the unmarked, weak, or subordinated one. Yet in late modernity, intimacy has become a crucial concern, both in the public arena and in the discourse of social sciences. Contested, theorized, visibilized, interrogated, and even mystified, intimate life has become a focus of attention. Also, an object of desire—*intimate* sounds sexy nowadays—and an incredibly strong drive for commercial, political, and social demands. In this day and age, we expect intimacy for everyone, an amazingly powerful universal claim.

Phenomena testifying to this attention are easy to find: from women's massive demand for equal treatment in the labor market to work-family conciliation policies; from the expansion of telecommuting to the growth of a new market of personal services like babysitting, coaching, catering, take-out food, and personal shoppers; from the global success of IKEA to the corporate redesign of the workplace, following hospitable criteria intended to turn it into a second home; from the triumph of self-help and how-to books to the selfie as a favorite online expression for generations new and old; from the self-centered ethics of informality (being *cool* as a calculated detachment from the rigidity of any grammar of politeness) to the hyperreal aesthetics of the reality show (a TV genre that not only exhibits but produces real forms of intimacy live). Symptoms are everywhere. They pertain to all levels of social life. Public interests ceased monopolizing serious matters decades ago.

It can be argued that this was always the case. Back in our grandparents' times, private affairs were also publicly discussed, and a sense of the value and uniqueness of intimate life did indeed exist. The difference is one of legitimacy. Today's rise of intimacy involves a public and general recognition of its value. Nowadays, the cultural sanction given to the ordinary, everyday life, and intimate relations is hardly ever questioned, if at all.

Likewise, these topics have also gained prominence as theoretical interests. In nearly all the disciplines of the humanities and social sciences, subfields have appeared around the study of domestic, private, intimate, and everyday life. Such cross-disciplinary convergence by historians, sociologists, ethnologists, geographers, psychologists, and urbanists has a distinct flavor of antidisciplinary revolt, for it challenges not only the conceptual and practical dominance of the public sphere but also the fragmentation imposed on the intimate experience by an artificial, scholarly division of labor that cuts it into pieces, each one under the rule of a separate discipline.

Outstanding figures of sociological thought like Simmel, Benjamin, Lefebvre, Bachelard, Schultz, Elias, and De Certeau showed interest in the topic of intimate life. In this book, we will not delve too deeply into their works. Among these classical authors, the interactionist approach by Ervin Goffman (1959, 1967, 1981) stands out for its pertinence in the present. Notwithstanding the strong academic trend toward posthumanist, post-structural, and deconstructional critiques of the self (be it in a Foucaultian, Harawayan, or Derridian way), I feel more at ease with the analytical benefits that a dramatological and interactionist view may render, grounding an ethnography of the presentation of the self in the context of social encounters in daily life. I have also followed the recycling of frame theory in a number of constructivist and reflexive epistemologies within sociological, communicative, and psychosocial traditions (Giddens 1991, 1992; Kaufmann 2004; Beck, Giddens, and Lash 1997). Thus, my toolbox borrows from a variety of readings I find of good analytical use. Specifically, in chapter 1, I will mention a few authors who, ever since the 1990s, have successfully thematized the realm of intimacy from different angles. I have benefited from the long-standing work by Arlie R. Hochschild, an American sociologist of emotions, domestic work, and gender (1997, 2003, 2012; Hochschild and Machung 1989); from the cultural history of everyday life by Swedish ethnologist Orvar Löfgren (2014, 2015a; Frykman and Löfgren 1989; Ehn and Löfgren 2010; Ehn, Löfgren, and Wilk 2016); from the cognitive sociology of boundary-making by Christena Nippert-Eng (1995, 2010); from the details about laundry, romance, new forms of dating, and quarrels between spouses so wittily commented on by the French sociologist Jean-Claude Kaufmann (1997, 1998, 2009); from the aesthetic insights on taste and dwelling by the British cultural studies theorist Ben Highmore (2002, 2011); and from the lucid critique of privacy by the Spanish philosopher Jose Luis Pardo (1996). They all share a constructionist conception of the human subject, a holistic gaze, and an ethnographic appreciation for nuances of characters acting in situated ambiances.

The reader will also find a narratological approach here. Ruth Finnegan's book *Tales of the City* (1998) paved the way for that. She showed how fertile a narrative analysis can be when applied to various scales of urban discourse. In her monograph on the British city of Milton Keynes, the big tales of urban theory are juxtaposed against those of the planners' and officials' bird's-eye views, as well as to the more modest narratives of the local chronicle and the daily anecdote. This kind of narrative analysis has been systematically practiced in various sociolinguistic, semiotic, and folklore schools and applied to many kinds of objects and genres.

METROPOLITAN PROCESSES

The current metropolization of everyday life is the proper interpretive horizon to reflect on intimacy. Geographers use the term *metropolization* to refer to the process by which a city becomes a metropolis: an economic, political, and cultural center for distant territories (Ascher 1995, 2001; Kasinitz 1994). For centuries, and particularly during the second half of the twentieth century, an accelerated globalization turned the world's cities from capitals of their regions into nodes within a worldwide network of exchanges and interdependences, deeply reconfiguring their morphology and functions (Sassen 2000; García Canclini 2010a; García Canclini, Cruces, and Urteaga 2012). Whereas metropolitan processes have been fully documented in demographic, economic, technological, political, and communicational terms, their inner, more intimate facet has been less explored. Yet an obvious link exists between the more general processes of metropolization and the rise of intimacy. A "metropolis of individuals" (Bourdin 2005) is the result of the universalization, democratization, and globalization of specific forms of dwelling. Today, the most important events in our cities are happening at home.

What is the pertinent temporal scope of this rise of intimacy? Of course, the origins of this process can be traced as far back as to the slow ascent of the individual in Western societies (cf. Dumont 1985; Ariès and Duby 1985; Elias 2000). A genealogy of the concept from literary sources finds a foundational moment in the nineteenth century, with Romantic creations like the romance novel and the personal diary (Coudreuse and Simonet-Tenant 2009). At the dawn of the twentieth century, a conventionalization of rituals of hospitality and hosting of guests in the bourgeois home became codified in guides of *art de vivre* for housewives as well as in the very floor plan of the buildings (Eleb and Debarre 1995). Another foundational moment can be identified between the two world wars, when the sociological canon for the study of the metropolis was established. The ideal type of city life by the German and Chicago schools reflects the legal and cultural frameworks of a first modernity. After World War II, such structures, with the couplets of oppositions that grounded them (public/private, work/home, production/consumption), have become increasingly eroded and questioned under the globalized conditions of a second, advanced, and reflexive modernity (Beck, Giddens, and Lash 1997). During the last four decades, the successive computational, Internet, and cellphone revolutions have produced further waves of disruption. Regarding intimacy, the effects are paradoxical and still to be fully assessed. On the one hand, these mutations have globalized, democratized, and universalized the demands for intimacy. On the other, they tend to undermine some of the classical conditions for bourgeois privacy and intimacy as we knew them throughout the twentieth century.

Conventional wisdom tends to place this discussion on the societal versus communal axis, following the Tönnies classic vein gemeinschaft versus gesellschaft. It is clear that, in a "post-gesellschaft" society (Lyon and Driskell 2011), this dichotomic conception has reached a dead end: our problems at home have proven to be, inextricably, societal and communal. On the other hand, a Marxian perspective on the critique of everyday life has always stressed notions like work, alienation, and reproduction, unveiling the conflicts and structural contradictions associated with the private realm as an extension of the public worlds of economic production, political struggle, and class conflict. The best example of this kind of reasoning would be the cold-hearted Marxian definition of the home as "the place for reproduction of the labor force." Insightful as it may be, such a definition does not allow much room for a caring, detailed understanding of the stakes at play in intimate life. When speaking of home, Marxians like the Lefebvre of *Critique of Everyday Life* (2004a) do not seem to differ much from other modernist reformers, like the hygienists or the utopian urbanists, in their advocacy for a reform of mores that must always come from the outside. Intellectuals are always prone to reform others' intimacy, when what is really needed is for it to be understood. For such understanding, sometimes it is better to rely on artistic and literary sources. Be that as it may, the history of intimacy has been traversed by movements of hygienization and rationalization that drastically reformed both the architecture and the social organization of bourgeois and working-class dwellings between the final decades of the nineteenth century and the first ones of the twentieth (Frykman and Löfgren 1989; Eleb and Debarre 1995; Eleb and Bendimérad 2010). This movement of reform continues today in the massive and intensified intervention by expert systems in the current making of our habitat: from architects and promoters to interior designers, furniture companies, pediatricians, educators, housekeepers, and a host of other professionals in charge of externalizing functions from the domestic core to the market and state agencies.

Considered at a macro level, metropolization processes are deep abstractions. Globalization, delocalization, cosmopolitanism, individualization, gentrification, dualization, tertiarization, reproduction, commercialization, digitalization, and mobility are indeed essential concepts for describing our current way of life. But they are, to the same degree, hard to grasp on-site in tangible terms. How do they incarnate in the stories of common people, becoming flesh and blood? I have been literally haunted by the challenge that this question poses for an ethnography of the intimate space. Does intimacy not consist precisely of the singularity of every life-world? Is the quest for individuality not one of the main aspirations that everyone has for their home? Something truly unique—and therefore very difficult to translate—appears in every indoor atmosphere and in the sinuous path followed by every biography. The ethnographer would want to convey this to the reader, making interpretive justice for the infinite ways of building space, managing relationships, and telling one's own tales.

The very idea of a home is relational. What we call a home is never a collection of disparate elements but rather a stabilized ecology and a system of relations, perhaps not so much as a self-contained microcosmos but at least as something akin to a constellation. Intimacy is the locus for an integrative, synesthetic experience. It emerges from some subject's irreducible form of linking time and space. "Feeling at home" is inhabiting a place that connects us both to a lived past and to a future of possibilities. That is exactly what we imply by the expression "to have a memory": a unique arrangement between time and place. What an ethnography of the intimate should offer is a modest but pertinacious chase after the traces and meanders of personal memories and potential for growth, entangled in singular places.

The metropolization of intimacy is therefore the locus of a constitutive tension between societal forces and individual development. On the one hand, intimacy as we understand it today is the result of a long evolution, paralleling the rise of the public sphere during an earlier phase of modernity (Giddens 1991, 1992; Coudreuse and Simonet-Tenant 2009). Such forces can only be grasped in holistic terms, as they are structural, institutional, and deterministic processes involving rationalization, commodification, mobility, and individualization. On the other hand, the outcome of the convergence of such processes is the very subject that becomes individualized—both in the positive sense of being freed to make one's own decisions and in the negative one of becoming partially detached from protective bonds of family, class, religion, ethnicity, and locality. It is due to the structural action of universalist institutions (the market, the state, the school, the media, and the technoscientific agencies) that a subject becomes plainly "individualized." To be an individual means, paradoxically, to be institutionalized (Bott 1957, 315; Beck and Beck-Gersheim 2001). This epochal and contradictory condition—being pushed to become a full individual—sets the stage for the drama of intimacy. To invent yourself, to set a place of your own, to joyfully—and painfully—discover an invisible order in the home you make and the life you live, to express such order in idiosyncratic forms of discourse and practice: all that has become the dominant theme in everyone's life.

THE POETICS OF DAILY LIFE

This drama has an inescapable discursive dimension. Intimacy is made with words. It is molded by words—for example, the fact of being named long before our births. It is registered through words, as we can sense in the routine of talking about our days at the dinner table. It is projected into the future by words, in the ceaseless reflexive activities of planning, anticipating, and fantasizing—endeavors that Giddens (1991) cleverly called "colonizing the future." This is so because intimacy is nourished by sharing experiences with close ones, building a coherent discourse on the self, commenting on the ordinary, bridging gaps in the flow of events, and weaving together the strands of that constant struggle that is becoming an individual. In the inspiring words of Jose Luis Pardo (1996, 29), intimacy "resembles the art of telling life." This does not mean that intimacy is merely a narrative thing. The discourses of the self have their place among corporeal, sensuous, and material aspects. They are never disconnected from practical activities and feelings. What it does mean is that intimacy contains a discursive dimension imbued with a poetics of its own. And that it is integral to life itself. "It might be possible to live a life without intimacy," Pardo (1996, 30) remarks, but such a life is not really worth living.

For these reasons, this book stands behind a poetic approach to intimacy. Could intimacy be anything but poetic? It goes without saying that, in this context, "poetics" does not have to do with poetry but with *poiesis*—with the emergence, creation, and reproduction of cultural and personal meanings (Stewart 2005). More specifically, it has to do with the deepest sense embedded in our actions, relationships, and experiences. Such a sense does not exist positively as a given, in a timeless, stabilized manner, frozen or hidden below the discourses and practices under consideration. We should not take it for granted. Meaning is always a problematic thing. It is the object of a permanent quest, the mutating and hazardous outcome from intermittent peaks of excess and scarcity, gains and losses, continuity and breakdown. The key to the social life of meaning lies in its itinerancy, in the fact that it is never fixed (Hall 1997). By definition, meaning has to be tirelessly retrieved, invented, and rebuilt. Poetic processes are at the heart of cultural generativity and individual agency.

The main contention of this book is the need to place life poetics in the context of other metropolitan processes. Our ethnography shows how the poetics of daily life, far from being a minor detail, constitutes the core of the intimate sphere. It is an essential process that depicts the ceaseless, creative, and agonistic activity of people precisely in the matters they cherish most. It accounts for the vitality, visibility, and power of this sphere.

Nowhere do we observe the assertive agency of subjects better than in their poetic use of the living word within everyday spaces. This same argument can be made a fortiori, when considering those places where intimacy has been canceled or foreclosed and people are forced into homelessness, out in the open, or under the harsh surveilled and depersonalizing conditions of total institutions (in places such as detention centers, hospitals, and asylums). In both cases the microethnography of personal encounters documents, again and again, the stubborn flourishing of an emergent sphere of mutuality and identity, even if it is forced to take the deviant forms of smuggling, hoarding, or other transgressive behaviors.

The analysis of the emergent order in everyday life calls for the crucial function of language that Jacobson (1960; Fernandez 1986) named "poetic." The poetic function refers to what happens when the informational and representational powers conventionally coded in natural language are diverted to unconventional objects of reference and meaning. As every new context of usage brings slight changes, adjustments, and wanderings, both into the specific utterances and their meanings, we could say that the poetic dimension is always present in human speech. Strictly speaking, no use of words could be considered fully "literal." The linguistic consequences of this will be further examined in chapter 5, implying a gradualist conception of conventionality that underscores the figurative potentials of language. Poetic analysis defies univocal attribution of fixed or structural meanings to particular signifiers— a vulgar sense of interpretation broadly debased after the linguistics of use, constructivist epistemologies, and dialogical approaches to human communication. Instead, it invites us to enter a productive conversation with the nuances and connotations of the analyzed discourse.

Language at home typically fits that description. Everyday interaction generates its own idiosyncratic patterns that can greatly deviate from any standard public grammar. People living together produce a common horizon of routinized assumptions by the simple fact of their movements, actions, and exchanges, which become naturalized across time. Every novelty—any new comment, dialogue, object, movement, action, or utterance—will necessarily come to be contrasted against this dense background, becoming meaningful and subject to interpretation. In this sense, the poetic dimension overlaps with aesthetic and ethical ones.

In order to account for the minimal story as a genre, I will resort to four semiotic resources or effects of meaning: signature, displacement, closure, and reverberation. Signature is linked to the intrinsic indexicality of discourse. It imprints both the original story and any mediated one with marks of authorship. Displacement (semantic and physical) accounts for the materiality of stuff as well as for deviations in meaning. The continuous transit of objects and persons in the densely populated space of the home provides a mold for semiotic loops, where objects become agents and signifiers are turned into signified and vice versa. In this way, the affective and semantic thickness prototypical of the intimate realm is closely related to the trajectories, rhythms, and circuits of these slow-paced dwelling activities and their recurrence. Closure indicates a search for form: a will for style, which the storytellers in our corpus abundantly proved. It manifests itself in the stylization of the structure of the story, with the deployment of the characters, the refinement of the plot, and round endings. It can also be appreciated in the care and beauty of its performance. What is important here is to note that the formal stylization of a narrative and its moral impact on the listener are closely linked. Telling a story always carries aesthetic and moral consequences, for example, in terms of credibility, veracity, emotion, and belief. Finally, the principle of reverberation or resonance denotes the basically narrative character of the receiver's account. It entails that the authorship of the minimal story is always shared. A performance and its meaning are grounded in a mutuality built on empathy and common concerns (Abrahams 2005, 2, 9). In the articulation of these four principles, we get clues about their emotional power to move the audience. They make us believe that "someone's stories" are "everyone's stories."

These four principles also apply to any analytical discourse elaborating on the informant's narratives. To that degree, ethnographic, literary, and historical accounts of others' intimacies should always be understood as stories made of stories. If the primary object of discourse can be called its "reference," there always exists a second order of metadiscourse that demands interpretation (Barthes 1957). It is this second order of meanings around which poetics revolves and where one can dive into a thick description of intimacy.

AN OVERVIEW OF THIS BOOK

This book is organized in three parts. The first part introduces the overall argument, builds its theoretical framework, and presents the design of the research project. The second part provides the empirical evidence mostly in the agreeable form of narratives originated in workshops and interviews. The third part is devoted to the discussion of this material, highlighting the important place of poetic processes in the constitution of intimacy.

In this introduction we have put forward the main arguments of the book. In the first chapter, a basic analytical tool kit for the endeavor will be sketched out. What do we need in order to make sense of someone else's intimacies? The work of the authors mentioned above inspires a frame with ethnographical, historical, sociological, and linguistic insights. I will discuss a tentative definition for intimacy as a domain of experiences of closeness and familiarity linked to the deployment of the self, and I will summarize some of its current trends of transformation.

Chapter 2 deals with the genesis of the project and its decade-long development. It focuses on a methodological invention we called the collaborative exploration workshop, providing an explanation of its operating rules, the themes addressed, and their implementation in the three cities studied. It also reports on the interviewing and filming that followed as well as the subsequent screening of the film, with many of the participants in attendance.

Chapter 3 analyzes the bulk of the stories, together with some other materials from workshops and interviews. The emphasis here is narrative. How could it be any other way? Personal narratives want to be listened to; the first duty of the transcriber is to make sure they can keep speaking on their own. The interviews portray the singularity of persons and homes, while those stories created in workshops are readable in a more collective key. Our analysis underlines the search for style, the invisible conventions of modern life, and the starring role of ego in a plot governed by the agonistic task of making a space of one's own.

Chapter 4 offers a brief detour through IKEA's showroom, its captivating mise-en-scène and the strong impact it has had on Spain's indoors since the 1990s. This ethnography was initially thought of as an observational exercise on the materiality of home. But it brought us farther, as far away as France and California, to compare shopping malls and their atmospheres. It also took us inside this large transnational corporation to inquire into its trade with the department of interior design of IKEA Spain, discovering the centrality of storytelling for a global business with great impact.

The final part of the book is devoted to discussing these findings. Chapter 5 places poetic processes in the more general context of the rise of intimacy. It weighs the narratives of the self against the background of broader deterministic processes, which I singularize as reproduction, reform, community, commercialization, and individuation. Cultural and personal *poiesis*, understood as the generation of and search for meaning, accounts for what can be deemed more distinctive and deeper in the intimate realm. Signifying practices as micromoves, routines, rhythms, and rituals of daily life are particularly distinctive of such a sphere.

Signature, displacement, closure, and reverberation will be specifically thematized as operating principles of such poetics. I will also explore to what degree they apply to second-order narratives, such as the ethnographic writing and the filmic edition, which elaborate on vernacular ones.

In the form of a short epilogue, the conclusion evaluates the futures for intimacy in a context in which old notions of urbanity find themselves in a predicament as new figurations of urban life develop. It also summarizes some of the learnings on subject, knowledge, and language that can be extracted from the stories presented here. Finally, it brings a methodological reflection drawn from this ethnographic journey. Collaboration, dialogue, and remembrance are the basic skills mobilized in the process of learning about someone's intimacy. The effort to provide these stories with a second life has also been a source of knowledge about myself. Research on intimacy is as personally enriching as it is epistemologically intriguing.

TOO GOOD TO BE FAKE

Norma, an anthropology student in her thirties, was living in Colonia Narvarte, a middle-class neighborhood in Mexico City. We had met her in Personal Belongings, a lively workshop about favorite objects. Norma, having been recently diagnosed with a rare form of diabetes, had chosen to bring an insulin kit she was forced to carry with her at all times. Colorful stickers customized the little case in an effort to dress up its gloomy aura with a kind of childish optimism.

When we visited her home, we talked extensively with Norma about the domestic routines she shared with her two roommates, the street noises that entered through the window at night, her research on film audiences, her cherished collection of volumes of *Le petit prince* in various languages and formats, the calculated disposition of furniture in her austere bedroom. In the end, all this seemed to revolve around one fact: she had been changing homes, one after the other, throughout her entire life. Born in Guanajuato, Mexico, she had also lived in Veracruz, Querétaro, San Luis Potosí, Xalapa, León, and Mexico City. One story in particular brought together a number of aspects of this biography of intense mobility:

> We began to move a lot, from city to city, from house to house. I don't know why and never tried to ask, anyway. But the point is that so much movement gave me the feeling that I was about to vanish. A kind of fear of disappearing. In León—our second home—I couldn't wait to sign my name on a wall, so others would know that I had been there.

> Whenever we arrived at a new home, I noticed the marks on the walls. This made me wonder who these people were, what was this house like before, who were they, what were they like. I also wanted to leave my name, so the next family could wonder about me.

> Then, to avoid being severely scolded, I went inside a closet with a piece of chalk . . . and wrote my name in blue as deeply as I could. I felt so good! So, I did it again in the next house. And then in every new one. Afterward, this sort of evolved. Now I was also writing the dates when I moved in and out. Dates

became important: I wanted to be sure about what had happened and when. The first time I moved to León, it was the sixteenth of October. I was six years old. Xalapa on August the fourth. And so on.

Years later, there is an unexpected turn of events. A young Norma goes to a house party in León. It is now the second time she has lived in this city. For no apparent reason, she begins to feel uneasy with the place. Sitting in an armchair in the living room, she takes in the whole scene. An uncanny feeling, somewhere between familiarity and awkwardness, overcomes her in a kind of dejá vù. "It was not something odd enough to ask about, but I couldn't ignore it either," she says. All of a sudden, the penny dropped: she and her family had lived in that very house many years ago, during the 1995 economic crisis. She envisions herself as a little girl lying in her parents' bed with the flu. Rushing upstairs, she enters the bedroom and opens the closet. There it is: the first signature she ever made.

Folklorists have called poetic justice a closing narrative resource, common both to modern urban legends and traditional storytelling, by which a surprising turn in the story rounds it off, giving the narrative structure a formal, stylized ending. Such stories are, in Brunvand's (2001) merry expression, "too good to be true": too well structured, too round, too allegorical. The component of justice is important here, since what leads the listener to grasp something of moral weight from the characters, their motives, and the consequences of their actions is precisely such a playful, circular, and satisfying form of the plot. Good stories beg for good endings—though not necessarily happy ones.

What characterizes the discourse on intimacy is its open, tentative style. In everyday talk, characters are not necessarily archetypal as is the case with mythical heroes. Plots need not be arranged in a threefold plan of action as in classical theater. And no generic conventions exist for their performance as readily recognizable and taken for granted as those accompanying the oral texts of tradition. Everything in the art of telling daily life seems negotiated, brittle, and ephemeral. The rules of this art seem fuzzy, situational, and deeply personal, penetrated by all kinds of other genres, media, and means of communication. If anything defines minimal stories, it is the fact that they are porous to the timing of routines, the demands of action, and the flow of conversation.

Yet we find a resolute will for form in stories like the ones I am presenting here. Brunvand's poetic justice states that, if something is too beautiful or too perfect, it cannot be true. But the search for style in everyday storytelling beautifully contradicts this idea. On the contrary, in these minimal stories good form must be read as a metacommentary stating that they are too good to be fake. They are beautifully told because they are real. Their poetic justice lies in the fact that they have happened to someone in real life. They say something important about who we are, about how our lives have been.

Intimacy is too good not to be true.

NOTES

1. Most of the people mentioned in this book appear under a pseudonym.

2. Parts of chapters 2 and 3 previously appeared in Francisco Cruces, 2016, "Personal Is Metropolitan: Narratives of Self and the Poetics of the Intimate Sphere," *Urbanities—Journal of Urban Ethnography* 6(1): 8–24, as well as in Francisco Cruces, 2016, "Intimidades Metropolitanas," in *Cosmópolis. Nuevas maneras de ser urbanos*. Barcelona: Gedisa, 315–346. They have been reprinted in a modified form with permission from the publishers.

Chapter 1

Getting Inspired

THE RETURN OF THE SUBJECT

In a famous essay titled *L'infra-ordinaire*, first published in 1973, the French writer George Perec outlined a peculiar research program on everyday life. "Question your teaspoons," he prompted. "What is behind your wallpaper? How many movements do we need to dial a phone number?" (1989, 13). If the questions appear trivial to the point of eccentricity, precisely this would be indicative that they are essential for a quest in which we are invited to interrogate "bricks, concrete, glass, our table manners, our utensils, our tools, our use of time, our rhythms. Questioning whatever no longer surprises us,"(1989, 12). Unlike the sort of extraordinary events reflected in the news ("Trains only come into existence when they are derailed, and the more passengers dead, the more they exist"), what Perec (1989, 11) urged us to unveil was the unnoticed actions, events, and objects that make up the backstage of daily life: "that which happens and returns every day, the banal, the quotidian, the evident, the common, the ordinary, the infra-ordinary, the background noise, the habitual." He carried this endeavor out in a literary way all his own, applying idiosyncratic techniques like listing things, making obsessive inventories, registering, and chronicling. Such a project promised nothing less than "to finally establish an anthropology of our own: one which will speak about ourselves, looking inwards for what we have been pillaging from others for so long. Not the exotic anymore, but the endotic" (Perec 1989, 12).

The idea of the infra-ordinary springs up as a kind of epiphany. The infra-ordinary encompasses the repetitive and routine—the small, banal, and invisible as well as the absurd, casual, and random. It highlights the silent character of quotidian things. The uncharted world of ordinary things is opposed here to the spectacle of breaking news constructed in the media through the coverage of plane crashes, train derailments, accidents, deaths,

17

and scandals. These work as allegories of the space-time of the national sphere and of an exocentric anthropology.

This dissatisfaction with conventional definitions of "reality" reflects a state of mind prevalent in the 1970s and 1980s. It is not by chance that whole new realities were making their way simultaneously in many realms around that time: a planetary urbanization, the increased visibility of women, racial issues, the impacts of scientific and tech expert systems, the entrance into representation of the ex-colonies, the world-scale mundialization of youth culture. These changes stimulated new fields of study that challenged conventional walls dividing disciplines such as gender studies, cultural studies, ethnic and race studies, urban studies, and social studies of science and technology.

In those new areas, traces of a revolt against the parcellation and fragmentation of the experience of the subject can be noticed. The disciplinary tendency to compartmentalize knowledge splits the lived world into a myriad of overdeveloped fields: time for the historian, space for the geographer, society for the sociologist, music for the musicologist, behavior for the psychologist, text for the semiologist, difference for the ethnologist, the house for the architect, the city for the urbanist, and so on. In this process, something of primary importance is lost: the subject themselves and their unique and integrative experience. Hence the concluding remark in Perec's manifesto: "How to give them [all these things] a meaning, a tongue, to let them, finally, speak of what is, of what we are," (1989, 11).

An increased interest in domestic, private, intimate, and everyday life was part of these dynamics. Unlike what happened in those other areas, the result was not a new label: such a thing as intimacy studies never took on an institutionalized form. It is a matter to be divided among a geography of domestic space, a history of private life, an anthropology of the home, a sociology of everyday life, a phenomenology of the life-world, a psychology of the self, a sociolinguistics of the oral account, and a variety of literary, folklore, and discourse studies on ordinary genres and styles of expression. Yet these labels, and still a few others, denote the interdisciplinary convergence of gaze upon a shared topic that up until that moment had been insufficiently thematized.

The topic as such was not, of course, new. Along with artistic movements like surrealism and situationism, some of the big names in cultural theory also dealt with it in one way or another. Simmel, Lefebvre, Benjamin, Bachelard, Langer, Schütz, Elias, De Certeau, and Goffman are among the authors who set essential milestones in this domain (for a review, see Highmore 2002).

What the 1980s brought were collective and systematic efforts to draw attention to a unified object of research whose agenda was rapidly gaining recognition. Landmarks of this interest are the collective volumes of *Histoire de la vie privée* (Ariès and Duby 1985) as well as monographies like *A casa e a rua* (Da Matta 1984), *The Second Shift* (Hochschild and Machung 1989), *Kitchen-Table Society* (Gullestad 1989), *Culture Builders* (Frykman and Löfgren 1989), *The Transformation of Intimacy* (Giddens 1992), and later titles like *Home and Work* (Nippert-Eng 1995), *L'invention de l'habitation moderne* (Eleb and Debarre 1995), *La intimidad* (Pardo 1996), *Le coeur a l'ouvrage* (Kaufmann 1997), *At Home* (Cieraad 1999), *The Perception of the Environment* (Ingold 2000), *Espaces domestiques* (Collignon and Staszak 2003), *Home Truths* (Pink 2004), *The Comfort of Things* (Miller 2008), *La intimidad como espectáculo* (Sibilia 2008), and *Pour une histoire de l'intime et de ses variations* (Coudreuse and Simonet-Tenant 2009).

Notwithstanding the heterogeneity of the fields and geographical provenances of these contributions, a common agenda can be drawn. Two main ideas are of particular value. First, they call for the rescue of the unified experience of the subject, beyond artificial parcellations. They invite the exploration of the specific forms of productivity and agency that are generated in the act of dwelling, the integrative (synesthetic, synkinetic, holistic) character of practices and atmospheres, their poetic and aesthetic values. They set their gaze upon the circular relationship between dwellers and their habitats. For that reason, they often circumvent customary oppositions like practice versus discourse, material versus symbolic, and production versus consumption. We do not need to either fix or dissolve such oppositions but to articulate them. In the end, articulation is what constitutes intimacy as such.

A second consideration is that explorations of this kind usually defy the taken-for-granted subordination of the intimate realm to categories and agendas imported from the public world—what I have called above "the primacy of the public space." Such a primacy is not gender-neutral but is rather male-oriented. In the words of the geographers Béatrice Collignon and Jean-François Staszak (2003, 6),

In a masculine system that values public space, domestic space is, both for the common representations as for the scientific ones, a minor, secondary space. We can put forth the hypothesis that the former is taken to be nobler as a scientific object, and therefore reserved for and appropriated by male researchers, while the latter is relegated to their female colleagues. This would explain why in this colloquium women have outnumbered men. Following a parallel hypothesis, we must assume that such an imbalance must be interpreted as an infra-representation of the masculine. Women seem to have anticipated the scientific interest that domestic space harbors, partly because they know and have managed this space beforehand.

A single, unified concept does not exist to refer to such a place. Of course, it can be properly represented as domestic but also as private, intimate, or everyday space: a "home," an "interior," a "habitat." This is a definitional labyrinth that I will address later in this chapter. The point here is that the subordination of these terms to the public space, understood as the strong, marked pole of a dichotomy, has historically tended to diminish, segregate, and render invisible the other pole. Locus of the dominant political, economic, and productive forces, the notion of a public space (and its abstract projection, the "public sphere") has been foundational to the project of modernity (see Weber 1969; Sennet 1969; Habermas 1989; Giddens 1990; Elias 2000; Bauman 2001). It has been metaphorically figured through spatial synecdoches and metaphors of totality, like the skyline, the city walls, the democratic agora, the factory, the lab, the street, the road, the human body, the assembly line, the city square (Cruces 2012, 61). By spatializing its rather abstract political, economic, and legal definitions, such images help to render them concrete and tangible. They convey the key principle of the subordination of private interests, domestic tasks, and intimate wishes to the social factory of the public domain. For that reason—as paradoxical as it may seem—any incursion in the terrain of intimacy must, by necessity, begin and end by taking into account the public space.

Being "the first revolution of modernity" (Giddens 1991, 3), the public space enjoys both a temporal and conceptual precedence over everything beyond its sway. It is also clear that the rise of intimacy during the second half of the twentieth century has entailed a deep transformation of the former cultural regime of modern urbanity, which has begun, since then, to visibilize, value, and politicize such a subordinated sphere.

I was doing fieldwork in Madrid a few years ago when I first came upon Perec's *The Infra-ordinary*. One of the participants in our workshops read a fragment of it out loud. Since then, it has been literally meeting me at every turn. I found it quoted in a piece on contemporary art by Ben Highmore (2005). Then a colleague introduced us, during a seminar, to the amusing exercise of the "time bomb" (Perec prompts the reader to put tickets, newspaper clippings, or little objects inside an envelope so that, twelve years later, one can open it). After that, I have found persons from places as distant as France, Finland, and Mexico who declare themselves fans of *Penser/classer* (1985), *Espèces d'espaces* (1974)—with his fabulous "*Voyage au bout de la lit*," in which the world is contemplated from a bed—and other works by Perec.

What does it mean that a programmatic vision of the 1970s has become common currency in our days? Is it not, in the end, the history of a triumph? In Perec's days, these ironies were wielded as a literary manifesto against the masking of reality by the media, political conformity, and the inertia of taking for granted—as dull, subsidiary, and uninteresting—the whole unquestioned world of life. Today, on the contrary, what we see in his outline is not transgressive provocation but some of our current and deeper concerns as late modern dwellers. The value of intimate things. The need to care for them. The urge to account for them. The fact that they are complex and construed. The fact that, in turn, they make us who we are. Whoever we may be, we owe it to them.

Perec interpellates today's reader. Is it because the state of things he was fighting is still in place? Or, quite on the contrary, is it because a broad change in sensibility has already happened? It could very well be that the old predominance of the public sphere, with its spectacularization of "now-ness" and the comparative derision of all quotidian things, is in frank retreat. This is what is entailed in the process that Giddens (1991) called "the rise of intimacy" and Hochschild and Machung (1989) described as "a working revolution." The revolution at home.

IS SELF-IDENTITY A MODERN THING?

I have selected contributions from Anthony Giddens, Arlie Hochschild, Orvar Löfgren, Christena Nippert-Eng, Jean-Claude Kaufmann, Ben Highmore, Jose Luis Pardo, and Ruth Finnegan as significant examples of this cross-disciplinary convergence that has grown from the study of domestic, private, intimate, and everyday life for over forty years. They are hetero-geneous in scope, yet they have inspired the construction of intimacy as an object for research. They introduce the definitional difficulties and nuances regarding the private versus public domains and help to characterize the rise of the intimate sphere and its mutations.

One early inspiration for my research came from several books by Anthony Giddens. Years before starting this project, we had already taken from *The Consequences of Modernity* (1990), one of his best-known works, some leading ideas to inform a multisited Spanish ethnography on risk and trust in institutions. *La sonrisa de la institución* (The Institution's Smile) was a collective effort by six ethnographers to describe the ongoing processes of institutional repersonalization and rescue of the subject that could be found in expert systems like hospitals, banks, airlines, customer service departments, neighbor committees, and city councils (Cruces et al. 2002; Velasco et al. 2006; Díaz de Rada et al. 2002). Following Giddens, the notion of the expert system refers to complex systems of knowledge based on a highly specialized division of labor. Such systems tend to be abstract, universalist, and disem-bedded from local conditions of copresence. The concept of disembedding is key in this theorization. It highlights how technoscientific knowledge oper-ates by extracting certain cultural forms from their original setting and reas-sembling them in distant temporospatial coordinates. Using points of access to expert systems as ethnographic sites, our research revealed the coexistence in late modern institutions of a bedrock of technobureaucratic, instrumental rationality (based on notions of efficacy and maximization of results) and an alternative, softer, and more recent regime or code oriented toward a holistic reconstitution of the subject—the very same subject previously anonymized, numbered, objectified, fragmented, commodified, and handled by mechanistic, technoinstrumental, or bureaucratic procedures. This second code or layer of institutional reflexivity was also aimed at caring for and repairing the personal bond with citizens, clients, users, neighbors, and patients, a task accomplished by means of a figurative work governed by metaphors of proximity, transparency, and trust. The trope "trust in institutions" was the master narrative. Thus, such points of access constituted a privileged arena in which to observe both encounters and clashes between, on the one side, the disembedding and calculative rationality of technoscientific and administrative systems and, on the other, the cultural reflexivity of lay agents on the ground. Our societal life is made of that inextricable amalgam.

The Consequences of Modernity not only stated the relevance of expert systems in contemporary social life but also established a dialogue with notions of trust and risk developed in German sociology, as well as with a broader tradition of psychosocial concerns about the formation of the self and its relation to society. On the one hand, interest in trust as a foundation of modern institutionality goes as far back as George Simmel's (1990) writings on "deep" and "systemic" trust. It is continued by Niklas Luhmann's (1979, 1988) theory on the systemic relation between trust and power and the works on globalization by Ulrich Beck, in particular *Risk Society* (1992). Trust and risk are conceptually interlocked. Risk implies the decision by a certain agent to assume the potential consequences of their actions in a given scenario of probabilities. Trust, meanwhile, is a decisional calculation to rely on the actions and decisions of others. Different modalities of trust (from deep confidence to mere cooperative coordination) may be more or less demanding with regard to a partial or total suspension of surveillance of the counterpart's behavior. The weight of the argument is that trust (and not some blindly calculative disposition) is what nourishes the modern agent's capacity to engage in risky decision-making in the complex arenas of market, state, and civic organizations. Contemplating industrial society as a result of uneven processes of collective and individual assumption of technological, environmental, and institutional hazards entails an important methodological consequence: it must, by necessity, take into account the subjective world of the agents as a key variable. No holistic, structural, or determinist shortcut may be applied in order to explain the functioning of a system, or society as a whole, without focusing on the purposeful agency and reflexivity of the agents involved.

This is the foundation of a reflexive view of modernity, hence Giddens's and other theorists' growing interest in diving into the psychosocial literature having to do with subjectivity, the formation of the self, and its roots in confidence, trust, and other forms of primary bonds. Giddens (1991, 1) explains,

> Modern institutions differ from all preceding forms of social order in respect of their dynamism, the degree to which they undercut traditional habits and customs, and their global impact. However, these are not only extensional transformations: modernity radically alters the nature of day-to-day social life and affects the most personal aspects of our experience. Modernity must be understood on an institutional level; yet the transmutations introduced by modern institutions interlace in a direct way with individual life and therefore with the self. One of the distinctive features of modernity, in fact, is an increasing interconnection between the two "extremes" of extensionality and intentionality; globalizing influences on the one hand and personal dispositions on the other.

Surprisingly enough, what begins as a theory of modern society becomes a theory of subjectivation. The underlying hypothesis states that the self, as we understand it today—as the right and duty "to have an identity," to forge a personality and life story of your own—is something basically modern, problematic, and institutional. Modern, because quick processes of societal change and mobility weaken older ties of kinship, religion, ethnicity, class, gender, and locality and set the individual off on a quest for their own "identity." Problematic, as the taken-for-granted signals that used to link an individual to fixed positions in terms of belonging (a social destiny) become affected along the process. To say who is who in a world of changing and mobile positions becomes harder. Institutional, because the intervention of administrative, labor, educational, and other formal agencies is strategic in producing individuality by disciplining the subject and drawing them out of their origins. The individual and the institutional are not opposing terms but two sides of the same coin.

Of course, this view of the issue constitutes a thought-provoking challenge. It aggressively contradicts both the common sense that sees the individual as something given and natural (a person) and the anthropological and psychological notion of the basic unity of humankind, according to which the self would be primarily a matter of universal human consciousness, not restricted to any particular society or culture. It would take a whole book to cope with such a gigantic issue, and I do not intend to do it here. Let's just take note of the three following points. First, this strong hypothesis is grounded in a discontinuist vision of modernity, contrasting it against the background of all previous forms of traditional culture and civilization. Second, this kind of view is exposed to the critique of being evolutionist, modern-centric, and institutionalist. Third, in multiple tones and versions, much of the current sociological thought partakes in this kind of discontinuous diagnosis regarding the intimate link between late modernization and the development of the self.

Three texts by Giddens pull together in that direction: *The Consequences of Modernity* (1990), *Modernity and Self-Identity* (1991), and *The Transformation of Intimacy* (1992). As we have seen, the first one explores modernity as a result of systemic mechanisms based on risk and trust and the development of confidence as its psychological foundation. The second investigates self-identity as expressed in discourses, practices, and representations of the self (like the life story), presenting individual self-consciousness as a logical correlate of other systemic transformations of modern society. The third of these books characterizes the intimate sphere as a space for the deployment of a person's subjectivity, with an emphasis on love and sexuality as its core phenomena. It shows the gradual visibility, legitimacy, and appeal of this intimate sphere throughout the twentieth century in what he calls a "second modern revolution" after the emergence of the public sphere from the Enlightenment.

What learnings can be taken from these books? They connect institutionality, individualization, and intimacy, showing them as different facets of the same evolutionary process. Modernity as a whole cannot be understood without the ascendent role of the individual. And this one is associated with particular modalities of subjective formation. Becoming an individual cannot be reduced to just a matter of rights and obligations. It is also about identity, loving relationships, and ways of self-expression. When speaking of intimacy, all these things come together.

EMOTIONAL WORK

One of the contributions that Giddens discussed is Arlie Hochschild and Anne Machung's *The Second Shift* (1989). This is a lucid and influential ethnography about American couples from different social classes and ideological types (from "traditional" to "egalitarian" and some transitional forms in between). The book focuses directly on their domestic chores and on the arrangements arrived at by these couples regarding who does what. The ideological definition did not necessarily run parallel to practical reality. There was, for example, one egalitarian couple who held a de facto, and noticeably unequal, distribution of work between the spouses. Conversely, a working-class couple had made their conventional expectations of the husband being the sole economic provider of the household more flexible in order to better adapt to employment and reproductive opportunities. The distribution of tasks at home is strategic when depicting the insertion of the domestic unit in encompassing social processes. These include the pressures undergone by young working women, invariably caught between the demands of their job and an ever-expanding domestic load; the tensions between married professionals regarding their asymmetries in career mobility, rhythms, opportunities, and sacrifices; and the enormous consequences of all this on the moral economy of the home. The "shift" in the title refers to the workload waiting at home after these women had finished their first, literal shift at the workplace. The subtitle of the book was equally telling: *Working Parents and the Revolution at Home*. If Giddens calls the rise of intimacy "a second modern revolution," Hochschild calls it a "stalled," incomplete revolution. What this process was disrupting were the roles within the family inherited from a previous phase of modernity. This is a seismic shift of historical proportions that is far from over.

The division of labor in the domestic unit is a hard fact. Without it, intimate life would be mystified and misunderstood. This line of reasoning had precedents such as the classical study by Elizabeth Bott (1957) about urban families in London. She documents how the inner structural core of the family (the division of roles between the spouses) is tightly related to the external links that the group maintains with the outer world, in the form of a social network. Arlie Hochschild focuses, as Bott did, on a selected sample of families and follows them closely. Although the research design takes the form of a comparison, every case is exquisitely understood on its own terms as a singular, complex situation. Her writing takes on literary values without losing sociological rigueur. One gets hooked in to a narrative thread of everyday routines, interactions, and events. The text gives the reader the poetic enjoyment of being part of other peoples' hopes and sorrows.

For over four decades, Hochschild has been tracking links between what happens inside the home and major societal transformations. The causal direction is two-sided: from home to work and vice versa. In an earlier book, *The Managed Heart* (1983), she addresses the deep redefinition of the workplace brought on by the commercialization of feeling, which was a result of, among other factors, the massive incorporation of women into the labor market in postwar America (she singles out the management of emotional labor in two particular categories of workers: flight attendants and bill collectors). A reframing of this topic returns in *The Time Bind: When Work Becomes Home and Home Becomes Work* (1997). Here, the corporate/home connection is explicitly explored. The research project had been entrusted to Hochschild by a big American industrial company willing to inquire into a mysterious organizational failure. Following a "total quality" philosophy, management had implemented flex-time opportunities. Why were female workers not applying for it? Hochschild's answer to the enigma is nuanced. It points to a process connecting the conversion of the workplace into a "second home" and, conversely, the corresponding taylorization of the household.[1] Time is the variable that binds the two. For a majority of the employees, the more they invested professionally and personally in the workplace, the more mechanized and undervalued—"taylorized"—the time spent doing family chores became. A taylorized model was particularly unfitting for emotional and affective work, a task typically assigned to women at home, particularly when raising children. The notion of "quality time" illustrates these contradictory demands well. During quality time, children are supposed to receive all the attention they deserve, but this is rationed out within a bounded temporal lapse. As every parent knows, timing at home never works this way. Most of the workers found themselves trapped trying to do parenting in residual times of an already overcrowded daytime agenda. There exists then a "third shift" to be added to the first and second ones: the emotional work necessary to make a home worthy of such a name. Borrowing from Batesonian jargon, Hochschild argues that this kind of double bind with time was the hidden scenario underlying the decisions made by the employees regarding the flex-time offer. The analysis is memorably personified in one of the main characters in the monograph, a senior line worker. This strong woman, who lived in a trailer in a working-class neighborhood, was good at providing care and support for others. So good, in fact, that she tended to unwittingly invite the many problems of her kin, neighbors, and even abandoned pets in the vicinity into her open home. It was not such a mystery why she was progressively choosing to put in more hours at her job, where she felt recognized and appreciated, while reducing her presence in such a troubled home (Hochschild 1997, 163).

It is remarkable how Arlie Hochschild's work has followed the historical movement of her object of study throughout the years, as a kind of allegory. It begins with the moment of incorporation of women into the workforce (in *The Managed Heart*); it continues with its hidden impacts at home (in *The Second Shift*); it then highlights the reciprocal influences of home and workplace under the corporate economy (in *The Time Bind*). In *Global Woman* (2004), Hochschild faces—with Barbara Ehrenreich and other authors—the invisibility of nannies and migrant working women. Unlike her other books, *The Commercialization of Intimate Life* (2003) is not a monograph but a compilation of articles. It conceptualizes this evolution as a process of "commercialization," underlining the pressures of the market over domestic life. Finally, in *The Outsourced Self* (2012), we find a radicalization of this idea. The metaphor of "outsourcing," taken from the world of advanced corporate services, is transferred to the personal sphere in order to shed light on a plethora of new emerging professions devoted to providing market-oriented services in areas formerly covered exclusively by a domestic economy.

I want to extract two lessons from this extended trajectory. First, a methodological one: to make sense of intimacy, we need to approach both what happens in the intimate realm and what happens outside of it. This is the case regarding the corporate-home connection. We can learn more by linking these two realms than by dissociating them.

The second lesson has to do with the meaning of family work. Work is a central category of primary social importance, coined in the public sphere to refer to all kinds of activities related to the production and distribution of goods and services. It has been less naturally used to refer to the activities of consumption, reproduction, and care that are at the center of home activity. The revolution that happened in the last decades consisted, among other things, of our ability to look at these tasks and chores as the work that they are, to name them, to give them the recognition they deserve as a precious source of value. And, of course, in reckoning the historical protagonism of women within it. Still, there is the danger of mechanically importing from the public space a category of work that is reductionist and economicist. Can work in the intimate realm be deprived of the affective, aesthetic, and moral values attached to it? What I appreciate in Hochschild's way of handling this problem is her nuanced understanding of the economic process: not as a raw balance between inputs and outputs but as a moral flow of collective creation, circulation of gifts, and affective exchange. The productivity of family work is never just "the task done" (the energy invested versus the results obtained). It is always subject to another economy, an economy of "the gift" or surplus that extends generosity in time among the members of the group and beyond. Today we could call it a "moral economy" (following Thompson's famous critique of the economy of time under manufacturing production, 1967). This surplus that family work renders is inextricably material, affective, and moral. It is the kitchen where the stew of bonds, shared values, and individual recognition is cooked. The final outputs of such an economy are the very relations, the persons themselves, and the ultimate meanings necessary for living together. We owe a debt to Arlie Hochschild for having opened this social factory, highlighting its importance for individuals and society alike.

EVERYDAY ENTANGLEMENTS

Our next source of inspiration is the work by Orvar Löfgren, a Swedish ethnologist and coauthor of *Culture Builders: A Historical Anthropology of Middle-Class Life* (with Jonas Frykman, 1989), *On Holiday: A History of Vacationing* (2002), and *The Secret World of Doing Nothing* (with Billy Ehn, 2010). Löfgren has influenced the development of cultural, ethnographic, and historical analysis in the Scandinavian countries and central Europe. The first of these books recounts how Swedish urban bourgeoisies hegemonized the national culture at the end of the nineteenth century around notions like the high value of nature, a professional career, and practices of hygiene—things that today we embrace and take for granted. Through a mix of ethnographic and historical sources and in collaboration with other colleagues, Löfgren addresses a rich range of topics, including emotional economies, the informalization of everyday life (2013), how families cope with material overflow (2007; Czarniawska and Löfgren 2012), daily micromoves (2019a), everyday routines (2019c), material culture (2012), and the home as a moral economy (2019b).

We have seen how Giddens frames his object of inquiry as "intimacy": a terrain for the deployment of individual subjectivity. Hochschild frames it predominantly in terms of "home" and "domestic life," a site of conjugal arrangements of roles and tasks; the contraposition of the worlds of home and work sets the scene. In Löfgren's research, instead, the preferred concept is everyday life. While the home/work couplet asks for a spatial representation, and the idea of intimacy evokes subjective feelings and relationships, "everyday life" puts time first. The world of the everyday is one of routines, repetition, and taken-for-grantedness. What happens and recurs day after day forges a regular, predictable frame for human living. Habits and routines, Löfgren says, are both invisible and powerful: they are "activities and choices that turn into an invisible pattern, but at the same time their apparent insignificance may cloak larger issues; they carry a hidden power," (2019c, 1). These two traits (invisibility and power) go hand-in-hand. Very much in the vein of Perec's infra-ordinary, the realm of everyday life is "about economizing, tacit agreements, indirect negotiations, cutting corners. It is about the half-said, the shrug, the nod. Social and emotional messages go back and forth, often without being put into words," (2019c, 2). Like previous writers on everyday life (Lefebvre 2004a; De Certeau 1990; Hall 1969), Löfgren emphasizes routines, rhythms, little rituals, and multitasking—more what people do than what they say. Also the importance of apparently minor activities currently considered nonevents because, due to their nonpurposive nature, they tend to go unnoticed, such as waiting and daydreaming (Ehn and Löfgren 2010, 4).

The notion of the everyday is a holistic and fuzzy one. For that reason, it has to be grasped by concrete, well-analyzed examples, as Löfgren does when he observes the many ways of packing luggage, the "junk technology" abandoned in an attic, or the microrituals announcing bedtime. He also offers analogies like a "black box" (2014), an "undercurrent" (2019c), "non-events" (and Ehn 2010), and "emotional landscapes" (2013) that convey the inherent difficulty of capturing the everyday—notwithstanding its omnipresence and power.

The concept of everyday life is grounded in the curiosity about the lives of others. In a beautiful short video, *Orvar Löfgren's Ethnological Sensation*, Löfgren (2015b) confides how this kind of curiosity lies at the heart of his quests:

> When I started out as an ethnologist, right there in the train . . . I had this idea when passing this one house, someone is living there. I could get off the train, knock on the door, and say: 'Hello, I am an ethnologist, I would like to know what life is like here.' And still, I have this idea, when sitting in the subway or on a bus across from a person, I start fantasizing about what kind of life that is.

What is life like here? In its calculated naivete, this way of expressing interest in the everyday sheds light on both the nature of the question and its potential answers. First, inquiring about others' lives is reflexive in essence. The question only arises against the background of one's own forms of living, when we identify a puzzling cultural difference that begs to be accounted for. Second: What could possibly be an appropriate answer to such a question? A simple way to state "What is life like here?" does not exist. Whatever form a particular answer may take, it will always be anthropologically complex. It will entail, for example, following the meanders of specific practices, events, and routines. To describe unique places, rooms, and corners. To name singular persons, characters, relationships, and temperaments. To enumerate objects, their uses, and dispositions. To panoramically depict, beyond detail, overall atmospheres, fragrances, flavors, textures, and soundscapes. To evoke origins, past events, memories, and oblivion, as well as prospects for the future, projects, and dreams. To wonder about styles, ways of acting, knowledge and discourse, the said and the unsaid. To name forms of emotional tone and feeling. All this materializes in a variety of rhythms, routines, encounters, conversations, economies, and affects.

How to cope with such proliferation? In "The Black Box of Everyday Life: Entanglements of Stuff, Affects and Activities" (2014), Löfgren proposes to look at this complex set as an entanglement of persons, actions, objects, and affects in a space. *Entanglement* is the key word here. It indicates that these heterogeneous elements interact when they are mixed together. The notion of entanglement refers not only to the intangible dimensions involved—cognitive, symbolic, and cultural—but also and foremost to the very materiality of stuff. Following Massey (2005), Thrift (2008), Ingold (2010), Bennett (2011), and Hodder (2012), Löfgren (2016, 127) defines entanglement as "the ways in which humans and things, as well as sets of things, become co-dependent." The idea of entanglement dialogues with recent theoretical turns like non-representational, actor-network, and affect theories (consequently, with notions of assemblage, intensity, and shared agency akin to these modes of theorizing).

I envisioned the ethnographic potential of this concept while listening to Löfgren's keynote address at the opening session of the Twelfth International Society for Ethnology and Folklore conference in Zagreb, Croatia. It was titled "Living in the Past, the Present and the Future: Synchronizing Everyday Life" (2015a). Actually, the topic of the talk was far more mundane. It addressed the many different ways of packing a suitcase. With real virtuosity, this talk (which the curious reader can access online) evoked suitcases from Hollywood films, women and men, bourgeois travelers and forced refugees, Auschwitz prisoners, and mental asylum patients. The focus was not on the content of the luggage but on the practice of packing as such. For, as Löfgren explained, "suitcases can do many things besides carrying belongings." They are not only "a container for stuff, but also for affects, for dreams, anxieties, and ideals." The suitcase is an object into which "affects and materialities are crammed and intertwined in interesting ways." Following Massey's image of "thrown-togetherness" (the way in which diverse elements come to cohabit in a given setting, often as unexpected neighbors), he disentangled how a suitcase may become "a condensation of the future, an icon of mobility, a last resort, a comforting or threatening object, a defense against a hostile world" (2016, 126). Not by accident, the title refers to the temporal dimension. Because it is not only souvenirs, clothes, and other personal items that become entangled through the act of packing: the very past, present, and future are in this way tied together. A sort of time-binding is reached by both an anticipation of needs and events to come and by an evaluation of what legacies of the past will be essential to keep. "With the Gestapo waiting"— Löfgren (2015a) quotes—"it is what you put in your pockets that comes to remain your home."

BOUNDARY-WORK

The public/private couplet stands out among the concepts naturalized in everyday life. By its naturalization, two sets of norms for social behavior are given a legal, compulsory character. Publicity and privacy regulate what can—and cannot—be done, said, or shown on each side of the divide. Both the idea of public space and its private correlate have a long genealogy in modern societies, involving many institutional actors and frames. To tackle them in depth is beyond our scope.

However, we must consider publicity and privacy not as raw facts but rather as ideas. A clear-cut wall separating things public from things private does not exist. Or, to be more accurate, wherever such walls exist, they are constructed space, the result of a prior conception (Lefebvre 1991). Certainly, actual architectures are filled with boundary markers in order to segregate the two settings. Formalized rules are prescribed to keep things distinct. But this is so precisely because such divides tend to blur easily. Consequently, boundary-making has to be performed on a daily basis, ceaselessly, on a variety of levels. Public/private is not a natural thing. It is the product of an immense social construction, for which all kinds of actors, both human and nonhuman, have to be put to work.

Christena Nippert-Eng used the term *boundary-work* to describe the ways people actively engage in the making of this divide. She used the concept in her monograph *Home and Work: Negotiating Boundaries in Everyday Life* (1995) and more recently in a second one, *Islands of Privacy* (2010). The latter was written after the revolution of computers, cellphones, and the Internet, which has subverted the former boundaries of privacy in unprecedented ways. Yet, the conceptual seed is the same in both texts: privacy is not a fixed thing, a taken-for-granted given that people enact in uniform ways and do not question. Rather, it is an actively sculpted space whose management by individuals, groups, and organizations experiences broad differences in conception and practice.

Nippert-Eng is a cognitive sociologist. This trend of analysis owes much to Eviatar Zerubavel's (1991, 1996) research on the way people draw lines on the continuities of experience, lumping together and splitting apart different clusters of external realities to build a sound order of the world. This is a familiar style of thought traceable in classical authors like Mary Douglas (1966, 1985), Edmund Leach (1961), and Erving Goffman (1959, 1967, 1981). In *Home and Work*, Nippert-Eng begins by noting how the frontier between home and work is not only physical but also behavioral and conceptual. The border has to be drawn. Boundary-work is defined as "the practices that concretize and give meaning to mental frameworks by placing, maintaining, and challenging cultural categories" (1995, 7). A variety of quotidian things are put into play to enact this red line: from keychains to calendars, from wallets to purses, from furniture to cars, from ways of dressing to topics of conversation, from schedules to hellos and goodbyes. A daily alchemy erects and repairs the border. She also discovered an ample range of variations in coping with such a task, adapted to a plethora of personal and structural situations. Some people's cognitive style is highly "segmenting": they prefer to keep things separated as much as possible. "Integrationists" are more relaxed: they do not mind sharing details about their private identity and domestic life, or even talking about sex during work hours. They keep the line flexible, even ambiguous. Nippert-Eng also shows how this boundary-work is not just about building fences but also about keeping them open enough. Rituals and routines (like dressing and undressing, or preparing the departure and arrival to and from commuting) are put in place in order to transcend these limits. Having differentiated areas of social experience is essential, but allowing ourselves to go in and out of each one is equally important. Boundaries have to be porous. You need to trespass them and blaze the trail for others to do the same.

Islands of Privacy further explores this idea. By making the limits of privacy more malleable and contested, the Internet and cellphones have raised public concern. This second monograph faces the ever-growing predicament of the public/private divide, the high value given to privacy by the interviewees, and the creativity and agency displayed by people in providing themselves with the degree and kind of privacy that suits their needs. She implemented an extended survey with middle-and upper-middle-class Americans to explore through long interviews their ideas on privacy as well as the actual ways in which these persons enact them. Privacy is understood as the degree to which an individual feels in control over the accessibility of whatever she or he feels is "private" (Nippert-Eng 2010, 4, 22). As we can see, this definition is apparently recursive: what is or is not to be considered private depends on the perspective of the subject and where they draw the line. To get it, they pursue the principle of "selective disclosure and concealment."

The research protocol was riveting. Nippert-Eng asked the interviewees to make two piles with the personal objects in their purses and wallets: one with the more private ones, the other with the more public. This material approach to the topic led to an animated exchange. People wanted to keep talking, demonstrating that one's own private life is always something fascinating to share. The monograph presents ideas and practices on privacy in a number of selected arenas. The management of personal data in digital devices is the most obvious, and this has become an urgent issue in the public agenda concerning data protection. Other chapters are more in continuity with traditional ethnographies of everyday life, like a funny one devoted to the different ways in which people react when the doorbell rings (Nippert-Eng 2010, 211).

The concept of boundary-work is a useful tool for cultural analysis. First, it denaturalizes the public/private normative concept, showing it as the product of concrete gestures and behaviors. It is an order that we purposely enact, a structure to be creatively adapted to particular circumstances. Therefore, Nippert-Eng (2003, 2007) has been able to apply this idea to the line-drawing between public and private in organizations and design.

Second, privacy entails a particular kind of control: the selective capacity to have "the kind of relationship that you want to have with different kinds of persons" (Nippert-Eng 2011). To stick to a defensive, negative view of privacy, conceiving it as the mere protection of secret information would miss the point by which privacy is mostly appreciated: the ability to share what we value most and to have full agency over such a selective sharing of ourselves.

Privacy is about relationships, about what we can or cannot share and with whom. As Nippert-Eng (2011) explains,

> Privacy is not just integral to managing relationships with others. It is also important for managing your relationship with yourself, who you are, and who you want to be, and what you can think about. . . . And how creativity for many people can come when you are collaborating with others, and there is this wonderful give and take coming. But creativity often also involves alone time, when you can think things through, and you can be piecing them together.

The idea of privacy deals with the ways we manage our relationships with others and with ourselves. It has proven to be an indispensable tool for our inquiry.

DOMESTICITY IN ACTION

The French sociologist Jean-Claude Kaufmann has devoted a great number of inspiring monographs to everyday and domestic life. One of the earliest is *Le coeur a l'ouvrage. Théorie de l'action ménagère* (The Heart at Work: A Theory of Household Action; 1997). I love the nod to action theory in the subtitle. Action has traditionally been the core of sociological thought, discussing goals, decision-making, maximization behavior, and means/ends relations in fields like economic choice, political strategy, warfare, institutional planning, public opinion, and urban protest. This is what has been considered "action" to the full extent of the concept. Serious things. What about sweeping, tidying up, cooking, sleeping? Why should these activities not receive the status of "action" too? They certainly do deserve it. As Kaufmann (1997, 19) states in the introduction, "probably nothing is more important than the minutiae we engage with everyday minor chores." Brooms matter.

> Every morning, by putting his dirty bowl in the sink, by putting on his underwear before the rest of his clothing, by raising his arm in a complex movement that allows, through the use of a tool called comb, to give his hair a convenient form, by clearing breakfast crumbs from the surface of the table, by sweeping up the ones that have fallen to the floor, by putting them in a dustpan, by emptying it in a trash can, by pouring the latter into a bigger one (which will be emptied by the town's sanitation service, in case of being placed in a specific place at a specific time), every morning, by these gestures and a thousand more, the ordinary man reconstitutes the basis of a system of amazing complexity. A system of order and classification that defines the place of each thing in a set of arrangements that, despite its apparent modesty, creates the foundations of all civilization. (Kaufmann 1997, 19)

Kaufmann lyrically describes this modality of action as a dance of sorts: "dancing with things." The logic of such choreography is inscribed in gestures: forms of body memory, inherited from the evolution of the species and able to incorporate—new ones on top of the oldest—modern acquisitions like rationalized forms of practice. By splitting what is yours from what is alien, the clean from the dirty, the perennial from the disposable, remnants of what is more archaic in human beings are condensed and actualized: "the addition of new territories does not suppress the ancient ones, just reframes them" (Kaufmann 1997, 23). In the practices of cleaning, tidying up, and resting, vestiges of a "cooking animal" and the "ancient regime of gestures" can still be found. Today, though, this gestural memory bears the brand of more recent mediators: school, medical hygienics, family, the media, and the individual. Yet, household action is essentially conservative. Reiterative movements in the flow with things respond to a sense of automatization and economy, a "functioning intelligence" that helps to reduce complexity. For the home is an extraordinarily complex system: "thousands of little objects circulate simultaneously, following the most tortuous and uncertain trajectories" (Kaufmann 1997, 20). This kind of action is a serious matter where the heart is always at work. "Decor makes us what we are. A family is something to be built with our bare hands. The household is an existential work" (Kaufmann 1997, 9).

The first part of the book, "dancing with things," discusses a number of issues that are crucial for the understanding of this existential task: gesture, the system of objects, the dwelling subject (family, individual, and household), and their relation to time (mainly the family cycle, as well as other patterns of alternance and rhythm in which such a system is immersed). A second part is devoted to the hiring of housekeepers by the families, an ambivalent topic skipped over in many approaches to privacy. A third part theorizes on the work of sensations felt during housekeeping, focusing on particular dynamics ("an economy of sensations") between duties and habits, pains and pleasures. The final part wonders about the place of reflexivity and rationality in all this. The reader would have a hard time following the abstract conceptualizations of such practicalities if they were not accompanied by an abundance of rich ethnographic detail: from the weariness of a bachelor unable to confront the mountain of dishes that has been waiting for him in the sink for days to the nuanced comments by traditional housewives on their tricks for ironing an enormous pile of clothes properly and the confidences of annoyance and dismay by the many who wholeheartedly detest it. There is a remarkable emotional and temporal sensibility throughout the chapters, like that revealed by a housewife who reflects on the best moment in her day, once everyone has rushed to the street after breakfast and she finds herself finally alone, enjoying the last sip of coffee, and wondering how to begin her work day. A work day that, paradoxically, feels more her own the more it is devoted to others (Kaufmann 1997).

This observation invites me to indulge in a few considerations on the agent of dwelling, generally speaking. Sure, there is *"action ménagère."* But who does it? Throughout Kaufmann's book, the agent of dwelling is neutrally referred to as a collective group: *"le group ménagère." "Ménagères"* are also the individual interviewees of various genders, ages, and social statuses listed in the appendix, introduced as characters by way of a profile and a short quotation. Out of twenty-seven, two-thirds are women.

Kaufmann's account is narrated, then, from a fluctuating place. On the one hand, a rhetorical and abstract "ordinary man" casts a shockingly masculine point of view starring householder action. On the other hand, the book is specifically dedicated, in the feminine, *"à toutes les ménagères malgré elles ou ménagères fières de l'être"* ("to all housewives, be they so against their wishes or proud of it"). This book about the work of many women is then clearly written by a man. This asymmetry is, in my view, mastered with honesty but never fully addressed as it should be. The vacillation in the pronouns is indicative of something important. It announces a gap between the language of action, historically masculine, and the reality of homemaking, conjugated and lived in the feminine.

The issue of gender invites us to address other ambiguities regarding the subject who does the dwelling. *Ménage* and *ménagère* have interesting nuances in French that are difficult to translate. *Ménage* denotes a couple, with or without kids—also, the people living together under the same roof and the daily work of maintaining and cleaning a home. (For the sake of brevity, I leave aside other derived meanings, like economizing and preserving.) The uses of the word condense fascinating overlaps among place, people, and action. The etymology of the term indicates the same slippage, as *ménage* comes from the old *maisnie* (family), from the Latin *mansio* (house). Social group, dwelling, and house become entangled in a single unity. This metonymy resounds in different languages, as in the English home and household, the French *foyer*, and the Spanish *hogar*, *lar*, and *casa*. *Foyer* and *hogar* (home), from the Latin *focus*, synecdochically add to the above meanings the physical image of a fire, around which the family gather, find shelter, eat, and worship.

These ambiguities come to the fore when referring to the subjects who are doing the dwelling today. The social changes in home organization have turned the terminology around this domain into a metaphorical minefield, where things easily tend to sound slippery and go awry. Just consider how often political correctness forces us to choose carefully between housekeeping and householding, between housewife and homemaker, between house and home. In Spanish, the predicament of translating *ménage* is acute, since we do lack a collective name to refer to people doing the housekeeping together, but not necessarily coupled, or married, or family related.

Kaufmann's choice is to collectively name this subject "*group ménager.*" The sociological neologism is a dignified escape from the nominal trap. The family, the couple, singles, and the domestic community may emerge as episodic protagonists in different chapters of his book. And the sociological jargon of action *ménagere* helps to neutralize the semantic burden of inherited home terminologies, bringing action to the fore as the ultimate foundation for any dwelling ensemble. To sweep or not to sweep: that is the question. By doing the housekeeping together, a household exists. This idea is a jewel of postmodern wisdom. Today you don't need to marry, you don't need to be related, and you don't need to own a house in order to belong—although all these possibilities are to be expected. All you need is a shared laundry. A *group ménager* exists at the very moment when someone must decide whether or not to wash someone else's clothes and linen (Kaufmann 1998).

Jean-Claude Kaufmann has produced a long list of books on everyday life, many of them translated into English. The analysis of the couple through their laundry (1998), romantic narratives about the meant to be (2008), the first morning of love (2002), the content and uses of handbags (2011), annoyance within marriage (2009), cooking (2010b), new emerging patterns for online dating (2010a), and the hiring of help by families (2015) are among the many topics he has cleverly addressed. In all these works, the reader will find a combination of detailed observation and constructivist theorizing. In my research, I have made good use of *L'invention de soi* (The Invention of the Self, 2004), in which he unfolds a theory of identity much in line with the reflexive modernization theories mentioned apropos Anthony Giddens. His views on the dialectics between reflexivity and identity—between opening and closure—provide guidance for our exploration of the poetics of intimacy in chapter 5.

PASSIONAL AESTHETICS

We do not expect beauty all the time. But we do expect some beauty in our lives, at least sometimes. Whatever our expectations may be, beauty finally occurs. Ordinary life is—among many other things—about the revelation of beauty.

Ben Highmore has approached the issue of aesthetics in everyday life from a cultural studies perspective. In *Ordinary Lives* (2010, xii–xiii), he matches aesthetics with the concept of the ordinary:

It would simply be mean-spirited to permanently delete beauty from the realm of the daily. While few could claim that their daily life was suffused with beauty, many would, I hope, have some sense of beauty punctuating their daily life. Beauty might be a value that is routinely set against the sometimes-bland consistency of everyday life: a lovely meal, a wonderful sunset, a dog running in the park, a football match played exquisitely. Beauty can animate the daily and structure our experiences of it through its relative rarity. Beauty can initiate a sudden effervescence that casts a light which illuminates some things while casting shadows over others.

As Highmore warns, a productive view of this problem requires the deprioritization of beauty as constructed by traditional art theory with a focus on learned and exclusive objects of contemplation. He instead proposes looking at the cultural world as "an ecology of optimism and pessimism, of pleasure and pain," concerned with "the communal circulation of affects and passions," (Highmore 2010, 10). Because the object of aesthetics is passion, not beauty. During the Enlightenment, aesthetics was considered a science of passions, including what we routinely call emotions, feelings, and affects, but also phenomena of imitation, generativity, and identification (labeled as aesthetic dispositions from the times of Aristotle). Classical philosophy was confronted with the intersection of passions, tastes, sentiments, and morality. Aesthetics would then deal with "our lively sensitivity to stimulus from without and within; our sensate connectivity to a world of things and other people; our responsiveness to a world of feelings," (Highmore 2020, 11). Such a world cannot be disentangled from ethical ideas of virtue and good life, nor from the values through which ordinary life is lived. "Aesthetics, once it has cut its ties with the automatic privileging of 'beauty,' might be able to find new forms of beauty in what had previously been passed off as dowdy and dull, ugly and uninteresting, routine and irregular. It might involve learning to appreciate new forms of beauty that could be more sustainable, more precarious and more world-enlarging" (Highmore 2010, xiii).

The kind of aesthetics we are talking about is, then, not about a contemplative experience of noble objects but rather about the productivity of "sensual orchestrations" and "material ecologies" that punctuate everyday life. For Highmore, aesthetic thinking has four qualities. First, it shows the link of subjective experience with the social world, for "emotions come from without, not from within," (Highmore 2010, 9). They are the product not of isolated subjectivities but of a dynamic exchange with the public realm. Second, it depicts passions not as passive states of being but as modes of orientation. As "prequels to action," they attune us to the world; they propel us toward and away from objects of attraction, detraction, and indifference. Passions build a bridge between the feeling and the doing. Third, aesthetic thinking faces

the complexity of human creaturely life. The ways we are attuned to sensations, senses, perceptions, and sentiments are inextricably physiological,
psychological, and ethical. Aesthetics is about a "knowing from below" that
is always embodied. Fourth, this thinking takes style seriously. As an object
of analysis, style has often either been reduced to commercial forces or deni-
grated as superficial and banal, but it is a key aspect of our daily involvement
with material culture (Highmore 2010, 10).

There are three aspects of Highmore's argument that have been useful for
the present work. One is the idea of aesthetics. If understood as an art of living, this idea was at the center of the stories of the people who participated
in this research. For them, beauty really mattered. Not only had their indoor
ambiences been meticulously worked on and cared for but the very storytelling around them was as well. In this sense, Highmore's "aesthetic orchestrations" and "sensual ecologies" run parallel to poetic searches for atmosphere,
closure, and poetic justice in verbal style. Second, Highmore has supported
this view in a thorough retrospective reading of a long tradition of cultural
analysis on everyday life that covers some of the field's classic writers, such
as Simmel, Benjamin, Lefebvre, the surrealists, and de Certeau (2001, 2006).
Notwithstanding a few absences that one could want to remedy (Goffman,
Schultz, Elias), it is a truly solid and inspiring source. Third, the idea of
the ordinary deserves attention. It complements other concepts, such as the
everyday, common, and normal. Other authors have pointed in the same
direction (e.g., *Ordinary Affects* by Kathleen Steward, 2007), and some offer
critiques of the potential use of the category of the ordinary as a normative
model opposed to "deviant" ways of life (e.g., Hellesund et al. 2019). While
the idea of normality conflates the two different notions of the norm and the
statistic mode, *ordinary* simultaneously refers to the common (in the sense of
undifferentiated), the vernacular (in the sense of local), and the vulgar (in the
sense of low and uncultivated). Therefore, the ordinary reveals itself to be a
terrain as elusive and fuzzy as those of *intimacy* and *everyday life*.

THE ART OF NARRATING LIFE

Narrative is not a literary genre; it is an epistemic category. Through narrative
we understand the world, build ourselves, and connect with others. The power
of narrative goes beyond the cognitive dimension; it also involves ethical and
ontological ones (McIntire 1981, 190; Ricoeur 1983; Ochs and Capps 1996).
Telling a story is never innocent. Stories have consequences.

This strong stance would apparently be at odds with the contemporary
absence of a unified and credible global narrative. Modernity is lacking a
tale. This scarcity or state of "amythia" and "homelessness" has long been

predicated on modernity, both early and late, by thinkers from both the right and left sides of the political spectrum, from Lukacs and Benjamin to Ricoeur, Rue, McAllister, and Lyotard. Once faith in progress and Enlightenment became eroded, we seem to have gotten accustomed to living in the aftermath. The grand political ideologies of the twentieth century are good examples of such a state, considering the successive sinking of nationalist, fascist, communist, and liberal credos as comprehensive secular stories that provided individuals with a defined place in the evolution of history as a whole (Harari 2018). It could be argued that both traditional religions and modern science strive to occupy this void. Yet their suitability for totalizing the modern world, and for fixing our collective and individual place within it, remains unproven. As a means of storytelling, modern science falls short. It is an ever-changing and fragmented tale. Even in terms of time-space, it fails to render our existence comprehensible. For example, what is called "deep time" among scientists (the complicated calculations and periodization of universe, earth, and life) is not yet fully integrated but rather compartmentalized in the cosmological, geological, and biological accounts, respectively (Shoshitaishvili 2020). Beyond theories, experiments, manipulations, and calculations, scientific discourse takes a step back precisely at the edge where existential questions about meaning, value, and the fate of human presence begin to arise (Bellah 2011, 47). One could optimistically think that this is what social sciences and humanities are called on to provide. For a variety of reasons—their own historical record to begin with—my skepticism about such a possibility is justifiable.

However, this apparent state of narrative failure in the modern world is in sharp contrast to the fact that robust narrative approaches and strategies of inquiry have been thriving over the past two decades, becoming pervasive in the disciplines of anthropology, history, communication, folklore, linguistics, literature, and cultural studies (cf. Chase 2005; Ochs and Capps 2001; Bendix 2019; Abrahams 2005; Bauman 2004). They even gave form to the expression *narrative turn* at the end of the century—a turn to be put among the various other theoretical ones (topological, chronotopic, material, ontological) we have been experiencing since then in the social sciences. A temporal landmark would be the 1997 reprint by the *Journal of Narrative and Life History* of the seminal paper "Narrative Analysis: Oral Versions of Personal Experience" by the sociolinguists William Labov and Joshua Waletzky (1967), with then-current assessments by forty-five highly relevant scholars in this field, such as Bruner and Schegloff (1997, 61–68, 97–106; Chase 2011, 656). Even in supposedly nonnarrative arts like music or architecture, you will nowadays find inspired examples of a narratological approach. This kind of inquiry makes incursions in neurosciences, law, ecology, and cognitive science as well (Bruner 2002; Herman 2005; Bernaerts et al. 2013). Narratology goes beyond the sociological, literary, interactional, and linguistic realms from whose seeds it has grown, encompassing new practices and subfields. In the form of storytelling activities, it fosters the mundane tricks of the trade of business, media, and organizational life. You also discern it in the guise of an interpretive undercurrent in serious works of sociocultural analysis nurtured by totally different traditions.

Three notorious examples of this recently came to my attention. The first is the overtly narratological approach of three successful best-sellers by Israeli historian Noel Yubal Harari, particularly his last essay on contemporary global concerns, *21 Lessons for the 21st Century* (2018). A second example is *La sociedad sin relato* by the Mexican Argentinian anthropologist Néstor García Canclini (2010b), where the diagnosis of a "society without a narrative" provides an overarching umbrella for a rich palette of interpretations on contemporary Latin American urban life, politics, art, and literature. Finally, Arlie Hochschild's *Strangers in Their Own Land* (2016), a monograph on the Tea Party in Louisiana and the rising support for the right in the so-called red states, surprised me for one reason: as the reading progresses, the narrative approach becomes more and more essential to the argument. At first, the rationale of impoverished, sickened, and disappointed voters in an ecologically devastated polity grows enigmatic, opaque to mainstream political reasoning. As Hochschild explains, her informants' ideological contradictions were hard to deal with until she was able to envision a "deep story"—story as it is felt—good enough to condense their perspective in a single blow.

> I begin to realize that the way values express themselves is by making a story feel true. And the way circumstances really imprint themselves is again the way it makes people believe a story to be true. What is a deep story? Deep story is a story that feels true. It is described by the objective correlatives of feelings, that is, it's what all the details you believe to be true, that account for why you feel what you feel. . . . By the way, all of us, underneath our political beliefs, have a deep story. (Hochschild 2017)

The American dream, transmuted in an imaginary queue, is the story line she came up with to organize the bulk of the account, rendering facts and attitudes intelligible (Hochschild 2016, 135). (Intelligibility is, finally, one of the virtues of narrative thinking.) This sociological use of narrative shows a certain evolution regarding the status Hochschild used to give the interviewees' discourse. In *The Second Shift* (Hochschild and Machung 1989), for example, the label "myth" was systematically applied to refer to how couples negotiate a shared narrative about themselves: a story cementing complicity between spouses but not necessarily matching the objective situation. There is a long way from a "myth" to a "deep story."

It is worth noting that the narrative turn of the 1990s is coeval with a breakdown of the grand narratives that guided us along the twentieth century. This triumph of narrative understandings comes, then, paradoxically, in times of narrative failure. I do not deem these two horizons to be incompatible; in fact, they both define the perspective of this book. On the one hand, I have relied on the power of minimal narratives in daily life. On the other, maybe it is precisely the bankruptcy of overarching, grand narratives that makes these minimal ones even more relevant in their dispersed proliferation. We need stories to live by. If the glory of the nation, the making of progress, or the advent of revolution does not suffice, stories about your cat, your garden, or your personal adventures may help fill the gap.

Regarding the present research, two books have been particularly influential. One is Ruth Finnegan's *Tales of the City: A Study of Narrative and Urban Life* (1998). The second is Jose Luis Pardo's *La intimidad* (Intimacy, 1996). The British anthropologist Ruth Finnegan is well known for her long-standing work on literacy, oral poetry, and amateur music (1977, 1988, 1989, 2013, 2014, 2015). Before becoming an anthropologist, she studied classical languages. Her trajectory took her from Limba oral poetry in Sierra Leone to music-making in the town of Milton Keynes, where she uncovered with ethnographic detail how the bustling but invisible activity of amateur groups in different styles (from rock and pop to church choirs and brass bands) provided "paths in urban living" for those hidden musicians, their families, and local audiences, turning the anonymous space of the city into a familiar, owned landscape. *The Hidden Musicians* (1989) became a must-read for ethnomusicologists and urban anthropologists alike. In a second monograph about this same town, she continued her search for how urban space becomes meaningful—livable and lovable. This time she applied a narratological perspective to a variety of discourses on the city, including urban theory ("the crystallized and abstract tales told by the scholars"); the bird's-eye views of planners, promoters, and authorities; the local chronicle; and personal everyday speech (Finnegan 1998, 3). Her methodological approach is of practical use. First, she defines *story* in a flexible and nonrestrictive way as "a presentation of events or experiences which is told, typically through written or spoken words" (Finnegan 1998, 9). Far from formalist stiffness, under the heading "What's in a 'story'?," she summarizes four elements of analysis: (1) a temporal or sequential framework, (2) some component of explanation or coherence, (3) some potential for generalizability—the universal in the particular, and (4) a set of recognized generic conventions related to the expected framework, protagonists, and modes of performance and circulation.

This scheme considers different kinds of elements. First, narrative structure. The existence of a temporal framework is what we normally expect from "a story." This implies a sequence of events and actions, typically depicted in a series of verbal past tenses (in contrast, for example, to a synchronic description, a request, or a question). Yet, this temporal ordering admits a wide range of possibilities. Beyond chronological and linear sequences, there are many different byways, diversions, and circularities (Finnegan 1998, 10). The time scheme may be minimal or understated, but it is what makes a story recognizable as a story, guiding the expectations of both the teller and the listener. Second, in a story, we expect some degree of coherence in the form of "an intelligible plot." Intelligibility is of the essence. The plot might be formally patterned, as in the widely recognized genres identified by folklorists and literary analysts, at the level of elements like the characters, their goals and motives, their action, the obstacles they overcome, and the resources they can count on. This formal content is bound to the temporal scheme mentioned above, as the timeline of the action implies patterns regarding beginnings, complications, and endings (the presentation of the plot, its node, climax, and resolution). Less evident is another source of coherence: the one provided by evaluations and presuppositions subjacent to the story. They are nested in a moral order, presumably shared by the participants. This is an important point that I will retake in chapter 3: storytelling implies evaluation. Value is the glue holding the plot together. This tacit condition makes it both invisible and important, as it is what allows the exercise of interpretation itself to be interesting—not only to the analyst but also to the participants themselves. Stories are "good to think." The underlying evaluative theme may be more or less explicit or subterranean and may take many forms. To work this out, we don't need to go looking for "hidden" or "ideological messages" (as poor semiotics is inclined to do) but rather to track and help emerge the shared world that every story purports to build. Third, in close connection with this causal and moral level of coherence, there is an inherent element of generalizability. Such an element is rarely explicit. It responds to the question, What's the point of all this? Every story appears as a performance of a genre, a case of a type of event, or an example of a more general universe. The themes that resonate in the story help build (or reinforce, or contest) the common understandings that make it intelligible. Fourth, generic conventions regulate form, content, and delivery. Ways of recounting, listening, and participating do not always exclusively pertain to a closed community. Nowadays, they are difficult to bind under strict stylistic limits, as generic conventions are increasingly expected to be hybrid, mobile, and intermixed: emerging rather than fixed (Finnegan 1998, 11). As I will show in chapter 3, we can still find style and form in them, but they address open constituencies and respond to a polyphony of genres of speech. Finnegan's ideas on the subtle relationship between narrative form and its moral coherence have guided the analysis of the stories presented here.

La intimidad (Intimacy, 1996) is an essay by the Spanish philosopher Jose Luis Pardo, published practically at the same time as *Tales of the City*. Pardo makes an appraisal of the idea of intimacy based on a strong critique of its confusion with privacy. Sociological and psychological analyses, as carriers of the modern common sense of an information society, would have tended to conflate them, focusing on private matters understood as a right to ownership and secrecy—a legal limit to the public rule. Intimacy, Pardo argues, lies somewhere else. It is not about the right to privacy, about secrets and confidences, much less about racy issues that one would be ashamed to confess. It is not, either, "a deep or ineffable essence," "an interiority of the self," "the deepest layers of human nature," "a sacred zone" accessible only in solitude (1996, 12). Intimacy, for Pardo, is an effect of the use of language. It is a constitutive dimension of speech rooted in its double-sidedness, its "folded" nature. The ability to speak depends on the existence of public codes and conventions but also on the particulars of enunciation. Every utterance contains an opaque, singular, and personal dimension of meaning, inaccessible to anyone "except for the one who speaks from inside."

> In order to access language, we have to speak one in particular (the mother tongue, or tongues, to begin with), and we have to speak it from the inside, with our own voice (expressing our pains and pleasures with it), and with our own tongue. Hence words leave their remains on the tip of our tongue, a distinct flavor in the mouth (sweet or bitter, good or bad). Such words' remains are what let us know (what gives us a taste) of ourselves, something that no one else may know. Because no one can taste them with our tongue and mouth, they can sound to nobody as they sound to us. (Pardo 1996, 52)

The notion of this interiority or "foldedness" leads Pardo to, first, characterize the idea of intimacy in a very original way and, second, display a severe critique of semiotic and informationist theories, those that flatten and vacate this intimate dimension by reducing the richness and density of connotative life to mere denotative or informative content. No clear-cut definition of intimacy is given. This elusive side of language is approached tangentially, by means of examples and metaphors. Intimacy has to do with the presence of the speaker in their voice, "the way you sound in your words" (a resonance), "the flavor words left on your tongue" (an aftertaste). It has, then, a sensory character. Also, an affective one, as it has to do with desire before or beyond the words themselves: a "wish or willingness to say," an "inclination" to be bent toward likes and dislikes in life, those that constitute who you are. Intimacy is also about "having yourself," although Pardo carefully warns against the notion of a fixed "identity." Instead, what is revealed in the intimacy of language is an implicit recognition: that of "being nothing," "nobody." Vulnerability and nakedness are the basic conditions for experiencing intimacy. This "being nothing" entails an affirmation of presence and veracity, for the intimate side of language is "the truth about oneself," "the way they [the characters in great novels] feel themselves" (Pardo 1996, 14, 28). Other metaphors depict intimacy as an extra, an excess, a leftover, a waste, a reminder, a limit, a crack, an unbalance, a dark face, a border, a shade, a murmur, a thickness, a density, a void. Something in our words that resists analysis, incalculable, unpredictable, suggested, pointed at, indirect, tangential, tacit, implicit, and complicit. Intimacy is the source of words, the place from which the desire to talk and listen springs, the drive that keeps conversation alive (Pardo 1996).

Amid the Bakhtinian 1990s, it surprises me that Pardo spares the dialogical concept of voice, which is, after all, what all this metaphorizing seems to be pointing to. Certainly, there is something singular, intractable, in the very notion of voice. In the end, the Bahktinian voice is a literary trope, trying to condense what is unique, and remains unanalyzed in the locutionary source. The voice is a moral image borrowed from a bodily organ and the physical sound it produces. Even if we think of voice as a connection between "what, how, and where" something is said (Chase 2005, 657), still a singularity irreducible to analysis remains, which a dialogical sensibility aims to respect. Roland Barthes, intrigued by this mystery, believed he found an answer in the physical quality of the timbre that opera singers call "the grain of the voice," something he enigmatically defined as "a friction between the music and a particular language" (1977, 185).

Pardo grounds his suggestive but roundabout characterization of intimacy in a more concrete critique of what he calls "the fallacies of intimacy" and the negative impacts of information society as a whole. The critique extends to the flaws of positivist approaches to language, which would have neglected the connotational aspects by treating them as remnants. From Frege and Quine to speech act theory and information analysis, the reduction of meaning to its public and coded dimension flattens whatever is not abstract, ideal type, and logical/propositional in speech. Distinctions between meaning and sense, use and mention, or denotation and connotation are part of this long history, guided by the presumption that all meaning can (and should) be made explicit. "Therefore, it is clear that in order to make possible this semiologic ideal of 'expliciting the implicit,' or exhausting the sense of language by turning it into meaning, it would be necessary to abolish the intimacy of language (deprive it of resonance, flavor, and touch). And this would only be possible by setting the voice (or the letter, that is, the hand) who touches the words aside" (Pardo 1996, 86).

This critique results in a pessimist foresight of irremediable loss or decay of intimacy, opposed to the sociological announcement of its rise in an individual-driven society. For Pardo, the linguistic derision of the connoted life of words goes hand-in-hand with the degradation and banalization of intimate life, its downgrade into "mere privacy." Privacy is just "intimacy spoiled": privatized, commercialized, trafficked. The scientific dogma that "everything can be made explicit" becomes, under the information society, a moral dogma: everything must be made explicit, becoming freely accessible in the guise of "information" (Pardo 1996, 100).

It is easy to connect this theory with narrative, as intimacy can be understood as "the art of narrating life":

> Those who listen [to a story] experience a direct contact with the intimacy of that which is recounted. They even feel somehow "in intimacy," with the sharing of a story. Both observations break two extended prejudices down: first, that intimacy is something ineffable and non-communicable, unrelated to language; second, that it is only authentically or quintessentially experienced in loneliness, when all kinds of relation with others is excluded. . . . What literature displays through the talent of the narrator, what novels make perceptible to the reader, is the same thing that weaves peoples' intimate relationships. Intimacy is linked to the art of recounting life. . . . The narrator isn't able to create intimacy by saying about his characters things like: "He was frightened," or "that made him sad," this is only achieved when he/she makes dread or sadness tangible without naming them directly. And this is what creates intimacy among human beings; not confessing filth, nor secretly carrying its burden on one's consciousness. Because the art of recounting life (of realizing it, of taking it into account) is none other than the art of living. To live artfully is to live recounting life, singing it, savoring its flavors and woes. And, of course, you can live unartfully, recounting nothing, not being taken into account by anyone or anything, and without counting on anyone or anything. And not taking anyone into account either. You can live without intimacy . . . because intimacy is not indispensable for living. It is only indispensable for the enjoyment of living. (Pardo 1996, 28–30)

A FUZZY, MESSY, AND SLIPPERY DEFINITION

How does narrativity get along with the other components reviewed in this toolbox: self-identity, conjugal roles, domestic work, materiality, entanglements, privacy, cognition, householding, moral economy, aesthetics? Although narrativity does not match up with any of these things entirely, it is an essential complement to all of them. In Giddens's theory, this connection is manifest since the development of a coherent narrative of the self is a key dimension in the historical process of the rise of intimacy. In Hochschild's work, as I pointed out, the narrative thread comes about subtly, swinging from "myth" to "deep story." What about the relations between materiality and narrativity? Recent material and ontological turns in anthropology may eventually be presented as "nonrepresentational," implying a bold opposition to the symbolic and discursive realms. Instead, I see the materiality of space and objects as congenial, not opposed, to narrativity. As Doreen Massey (2013) put it, space is not "a dead flat surface that we cross" but rather "a pincushion of a million stories." And it is partly through stories that we gain access to the animated life of things in space (Cruces 2021). Löfgren's writings offer a prominent example of this. While warning novel researchers against an exclusive focus on what people say—instead of what they do—his analyses disentangle the embeddedness of the narrative in the material and vice versa. It is also clear that a cognitive gaze on boundary-work, and a reflexive and aesthetic one on ordinary stuff, are in tune with this book's poetic approach, to the extent that they bring processes of cultural *poiesis* to the fore. Of course, other research strategies and sources of data could be legitimately followed. Narrating intimacy is, nonetheless, the specific challenge I take on from the set of readings presented above.

As the ancients wrote, we stand on the shoulders of giants. We owe the scope of our view to the stature of those who came before. These authors notably belong to different areas and traditions. Taken together, they do not provide a tight theoretical framework, but their work suggests creative guidelines for the study of intimacy. Borrowing from them, in the following sections, I will sketch out my own definitional discussion of our object of study and a bird's-eye view of the deep changes it is experiencing.

In its common uses, the term *intimacy* refers to close and personal relationships as well as to states and feelings of familiarity and closeness. It can be applied, by extension, to concrete places or atmospheres marked as "intimate." In a displaced sense, intimacy also denotes "a close association, detailed knowledge, or deep understanding of something," as well as sexual intercourse (Longman 1993 , 690; Merriam-Webster 1992, 529). Relationality, spatiality, and affect are thus essential components of the definition. We think of intimacy in terms of intense social relations, held with affective involvement in spatial proximity. Of course, these components can occur separately: we can find ourselves crammed in a subway train with zero intimacy, forced to share our space with strangers, or passionately involved with someone at a distance. Yet, "to have intimacy" implies some form of entanglement among these three things: relation, space, and affection. The very meaning of the word encodes this idea through a number of interesting semantic contaminations. We represent social, personal, and spiritual "closeness" by means of a mental and linguistic association with a spatial experience in the physical world. Similarly, "familiarity" is conceived by analogy as belonging to a family group. Without having had a family and dwelled in a place, one could hardly know what intimacy looks like.

Following these ordinary uses, I define *intimacy* as a sphere of experiences of familiarity and closeness linked to a sense of self-identity. The reference to the self is made explicit by individualization and reflexive modernization theories (Giddens 1990, 1991; Beck, Giddens, and Lash 1997; Beck and Beck-Gernsheim 2001; Kaufmann 2001; Bauman 2001; Bourdin 2005; Lahire 2006; Corcuff, Le Bart, and De Singly 2015; De Singly 2016). Familiarity and closeness are inextricably bound to the reflexive self, given that they inform a singular point of view. This unity and singularity find a diversity of modes of expression. Spatially, by drawing a personal territory; discursively, by founding an "I," an enunciative center from which to speak; interactionally, by establishing recurrent patterns for relating with others, what Goffman called "character" (1967); and narratively, by getting a voice. The self is neither a permanent "essence" nor a stabilized "thing" but rather a psychosocial dynamic process of coming into being and into consciousness, involving all these different levels of communication. Having intimacy is a crucial part of such a process, both as cause and effect. Early in life, intimate experiences are the essential source for becoming a person. Later, intimate life will result from a web of subjectivation processes that engage the relationships of the self with significant others, social institutions, and the world at large. Intimacy and subjectivity, not being exactly the same, are tightly bound. Only subjects have intimacy.

This definition is still rather fuzzy. It may apply to what the self is entitled to do: almost everything, everywhere. The previously presented perspectives narrow down such a broad scope by adding qualifications of space, time, group, and setting. (1) The geographical concept of "domestic space" involves a delimited built area where a set of activities related to the biological and social reproduction of the group takes place. Here, space goes first. Dwelling and care activities, conjugal roles, and sexual as well as age divisions are at the center. (2) The anthropological concept of "home" underscores the sheltering function, the density of primary and affective relations, and the social belonging to a group (a family, relatives, a tradition). This collective and relational dimension is at its best in the management of commons: a budget, a moral economy, and the work needed to fix this particular "organization of space over time" (Douglas 1991, 294). (3) Sociological "privacy" resounds, instead, with modern political, economic, and legal overtones, drawing a juridical line that establishes rights of ownership, use, and control over space, actions, objects, and—this is crucial nowadays—the flow of information within the private sphere. Whereas "home" and "domestic space" bear an ancient communal flavor, the idea of private space brings with it a modern horizon where the individual emerges as the holder of rights over a personal sphere, about which they maintain a legitimate expectation of control. (4)

"Everyday life" and "ordinary life" frame the scene within temporal and cultural lines (rather than spatial ones), focusing on routine and habits, the recurrence of events, their materiality, and the cognitive, affective, aesthetic, and moral qualities of the experiences produced in such realms. The notion of "everyday life," well-trodden in classical sociology from interactionist, situationists, and Marxian traditions, also has currency in ethnology, folklore, and cultural studies. (5) Phenomenology has conceptualized these domains in terms of "worlds" and "regions" of experience, differentiating, for example, "the world of life" from "the social system." In the world of life, things are taken uncritically, in a "natural attitude." The intimate world is a naturalized one, internalized as unproblematic (Schutz and Luckmann 1973). (6) Under the ecological label of "habitat," architects, archaeologists, and biologists put dwelling activity—both human and animal—at the center of their consideration of buildings as enclosures: material products of the dweller's forms of agency (Ingold 2000; Eleb and Debarre 1995).

Should these various definitions be part of an ethnographic approach to the intimate space? Or should they rather be considered as differentiated—although partially overlapping—realities? On the one hand, any definition of intimacy that fails to take them into account will be missing essential elements. Home-cooked meals, birthday celebrations, conjugal quarrels, personal secrets, getting up early, going to bed late, fulfilled and unfulfilled sexual desires, tricks for ironing properly, strategies for coping with loneliness, escaping boredom, or feeding the kids: these kinds of very different things—and a thousand others—are enmeshed in the depictions that people give of their intimate world. To limit the understanding of intimacy to exclusively one among all these spatial enclosures (domestic, familial, private, ordinary, and everyday habitats) would seem, then, artificially restrictive. On the other hand, any effort to reconcile these divergent definitions will instead probably sound too fuzzy and too messy. "This is not intimacy!": this was the reaction of a friend of mine, a geographer and urbanist, the first time I explained what I was working on. Pardo's (1996, 22) philosophical rejection of conflating intimacy with privacy—what he sees as a typically sociological confusion, when not a malicious obfuscation on the part of psychologists—contains a similar intransigency for the sake of clarity.

I have not found a clear-cut solution to this definitional dilemma. It probably does not exist. Of course, we could always resort to an "ideal type" stratagem: theoretically differentiating several kinds of spaces in abstract contrast to the notion of public space as the dominant pole in the categorization. This nonpublic realm could be alternatively conceived of as "domestic" (having to do with reproduction), as "private" (having to do with exclusive rights), or as "intimate" (having to do with the formation of subjectivity). What these definitions share is that they are figurations of the subordinated pole of the dichotomy. The public space is foundational to them. (This is why, paradoxically, any exploration of intimacy begins and ends in the public space.)

But this would be a categorical fiction, valid on paper only. Domestic, private, and intimate things empirically overlap. They take place in the same physical space, enacted by the same agents. The ideal type solution is as elegant as it is phantasmagorical. In their practices and discourses, people mess up all these categories. As Nippert-Eng (1995) has highlighted à propos of the home/work divide, it is the result of "boundary-work." The boundary cannot be traced beforehand. It is, instead, the very problem to be explored.

We could not, then, build the habitat, the house, the home, the domestic space, and the private space as separate ideal types simply because in practice, people build their intimate life from a complex and varying overlap of all these forms of spatialization. The figuring of intimacy as "a sphere" underlines that it results from practices of spatialization: intimacy is always inextricably bound to "one's own space," wherever it may be. But an "intimate space" does not exist on its own. It is a mix resulting from each person's experience and cultural practice. Consequently, there is no way to establish what "intimacy" means to someone beforehand. We need to explore their particular ways of building intimacy, through boundary-work, on all the different dimensions mentioned above.

What is needed, then, is to recognize the locally constructed nature of our object of study. This constructivist hypothesis can be formulated as follows: intimacy is not a universal given, with fixed boundaries that should be taken for granted. It is, instead, a relational frame, built locally by dwellers of a certain habitat, through a continuous activity of boundary-work. Such activity is inextricably material, practical, cognitive, affective, and discursive. It is individual and collective, productive and reproductive. Lacking preestablished boundaries, the intimate sphere has to be continuously grasped as a work of imagination: by means of tropes, narratives, and images. Its mode is naturally that of a synesthetic, synkinetic, multimodal, and poietic experience. Hence, it has to be figured (imagined, represented, and enacted) both by the internal agents and the external observer. It cannot be just defined; it has to be ethnographically documented. The importance of this boundary-work on intimacy cannot be overestimated. It constitutes the very core of the human making of habitat.

Although the problem of defining intimacy may seem a purely conceptual matter, it is not so. Socially, it has become not only a fuzzy and messy task but also a slippery one. The difficulties we face in drawing its limits do not come simply from a discrepancy in the conventional approaches among disciplines (with differing priorities and epistemological emphasis) nor from indolence or intellectual inertia. Since the public space has dramatically changed, the frontiers of what we used to consider public and private, productive and reproductive, work and home, professional and amateur, masculine and feminine, have shifted. Changes in these borderlines reveal an erosion of couplets that were once foundational to first modernity and to the sense of urbanity that came with it. They used to put each thing in the place where it was deemed to belong. This is why the feminist motto "personal is political" was once, and still remains, so appealing. Today, these borders have been drastically displaced, and nobody has a monologic authority about where to draw the lines. It is a matter in dispute. Not an innocent issue, the definition of intimacy is today the locus of multiple personal choices and also of cultural wars and political controversies. Visibility, politicization, and contestation are current metamorphoses of intimacy. They have turned any definition into a potentially contentious thing.

MUTATIONS OF AN EMERGING DOMAIN

The argument presented here focuses on the transformations affecting the intimate sphere during the last forty years, a period when its visibility, politization, and universalization came to the fore. Certainly, the emergence of the intimate sphere is the result of a much longer evolution. In Western societies, it goes as far back as to the slow emergence of modern individualism since the late Middle Ages (cf. Ariès and Duby 1985; Dumont 1985; Elias 2000). According to Simonet-Tenant (2009, 43), a key moment in this process took place among the enlightened elites of the European eighteenth century, with the interrelated adoptions in everyday life of the lock, the mirror, mail correspondence, the right to privacy, and the personal diary. A second series of important developments occurred in the urban milieus of the late nineteenth century, with a generalized urbanist intervention on transport and housing, hygienists' discoveries on sanitation and public health, and the spread of a Victorian code of manners around the liberal figures of the modern individual and his nuclear family. Nevertheless, the temporal scope of the argument posited here is much closer to the present. It takes as a point of reference the formalization of "urbanism as a way of life" brought about during the first half of the twentieth century by the sociological German and Chicago schools (Sennet 1969; Hannerz 2012; Cruces 2007). They modeled what it meant to be urban. Their definitions of the city and associated dispositions— "urbaness," "urbanism," and "urbanity"[2]—focused on the predominance of the public sphere, productive life, political and economic structures, and secondary social bonds. These ideas would be eroded during the second half of the twentieth century by a conflictive, reflexive, and contradictory radicalization of modernity. Processes like the globalization of productive chains beyond national scale, the incorporation of women to the labor market, the legal reform of reproductive and sexual laws, demands having to do with gender identity and sexual preference, a generational gap born of the irruption of youth culture and countercultural trends, the informalization of private and public mores, and a technologically run revolution (brought first by computing and afterward by the Internet, cellphones, and social media) that allow interaction at a distance—all these phenomena have deeply reconfigured the intimate realm at a global scale during the last four decades. They· set the stage for the ethnography presented here.

From a philological perspective, Anne Coudreuse and Françoise Simonet-Tenant (2009) have followed the history of the semantics of intimacy in French literary genres, particularly the letter, the novel, and the diary, tracking variations of the concept in its modern evolution. The early notion of a selected friendship, inherent to the Renaissance ("intimate friend"), will arrive in the nineteenth century transformed into a romantic centering in the self and one's deep feelings. After its normalization throughout the twentieth century, in the last decades we have witnessed new mutations of the concept, with the paradoxical character of an "extimacy" increasingly displayed and enacted for others on the Internet, social media, and political show business (Coudreuse and Simonet-Tenant 2009, 10, 21, 39; see also Lejeune 2009a, 2009b).

The massive incorporation of women into the labor force has no doubt been a fundamental factor in the current transformations of intimacy. Social and spatial visibility of women has simultaneously transformed the working, street, and home environments. This process, described by most participants in our project as "an exit" of women from the confinement of the home, was accompanied by a correlative "entrance" of men to home responsibilities, although in a more limited and reluctant way.

We have also seen a diversification of the forms of living together. The acknowledgment of sexual preferences, the prolonging of the human life span, and the variety of life choices and styles are important factors that account for a radical but silent change of the indoor landscape of the city. Let us think of phenomena as the extension of the period we call today "youth"; the family delays in child-rearing; the growing number of elderly people living alone; the couples who explicitly choose not to have children (sometimes called "dinks": double income, no kids); the acceptance of adoption and assisted reproduction; the trials in experimental or transitory communal bonds by students, activists, urban squatters, or professionals who share the same living space; cooperative residential initiatives like cohousing, ecovillages, and gated communities for retirees, and so on.

These structural changes have a direct expression in the indoor distribution of houses as well as in the practices and values of their dwellers, linked to a myriad of lifestyles. The global city was initially characterized by its strong centralization of corporate functions and advanced services (Sassen 2000). Today the symptoms of metropolization can also be traced to the personal services, leisure activities, and remote jobs boom. Contemporary cities are also a lab for countertendencies of a communal, countercultural, and experimental character. The defense of intimate space is placed at the center of demands by different social movements: LGBTQ, feminists, urban settlers, ecologists, and social economy cooperativists. Fights against evictions, demands for daycare services, exploration of polyamory bonds, cobreeding, producer and consumer cooperatives, and different forms of coresidence incarnate a philosophy oriented to deinstitutionalize sexuality and cultivate alternative forms of intimate bonding, parenthood, and neighborhood. Intercultural, anticapitalist, and antipatriarchal ideologies open up practices re-creating alternative ways for living together, as well as expressive experiments, where lullabies may become as important as money and affect as important as strategy.

If the burgeoning offer of domestic services has the effect of transforming them into commodities, activist politicization publicizes them as common goods: services and resources that can be accessed freely in a circuit imagined in terms of community. Both the commoditization and the mobilization of intimacy can be comprehended as modalities of the same process of late modern individualization. Both phenomena have in common the fact that they erode an acritical, unproblematic view of the home that was once implicitly contained in the public/private opposition. Following its assumptions, the subject was rooted or embedded in a group to which they belonged by kin, class, religious, and/or cultural origin. In modern times this metaphor of the blood origin has been much put into question, ever since the days of Romeo and Juliet. What we modern people do take seriously is the underlying narrative of emancipation: the lived drama of the subject torn in the task of becoming themselves, beyond the determinations of any inherited identity. This emancipation from the past may equally arrive embodied in the invisible hand of the market (as free choice) or through utopia (in the form of a shared invention of unprecedented forms of interdependence).

Contemporary domestic space is nowadays reconfigured beyond the civilizatory conception that was contained in the idea of home as hygienist locus for the reproduction of the family group (with the basic functions of shelter, protection, rest, personal hygiene, nurturing, cleaning, sociability, and child-rearing). This reconfiguration pushes in three directions:

1) Personalization and individualization of space, following principles of personal autonomy and right to privacy. Paraphrasing Virginia Woolf, Remedios Zafra (2010) reclaims young women's ways of dwelling as having "a connected room of your own." And regarding family meals, François Ascher (2005) analyzes the functionality of the microwave oven as a technology that, along with

the freezing of food, makes the fast preparation of food with a differentiated attention to every dinner guest possible.

2) A growing influence of issues of leisure, taste, and choice. They allow the expression of a unique way of life, publicly uprooted from any bound of class, origin, or profession. What was once secondary now becomes central. Some of my informants do not welcome visitors in their living rooms anymore. They now often do it in the kitchen, while leisurely gathered around a designer stove. Bikes can be wherever—in corridors, at the entrance, even hanging from the ceiling. Gyms, bars, and treadmills occupy places once assigned to the couch and the TV cabinet. One of our interviewees, a bachelor who's an engineer, had set up his living room with three big screens and a freezer. Someone else had five big armchairs—one for every inhabitant of the house. Others save the spotlight for antiques repaired by themselves, musical instruments, or cult movie posters. You find houses with no doors and beds the size of whole rooms.

3) Wiring and connection. New forms of work, particularly those of the creative industries, entail an increasing taking up of space by file cabinets, desks, and computers. Home times and routines also become fuzzy and have to be rearranged due to a 24/7 work activity. In collective research on New Economy companies in Spain (Valenzuela, Reygadas, and Cruces 2015), we found how the workplace tends to absorb the life of the worker, blurring the boundaries between the outside and the inside. Of course, this has a technological expression in household appliances and wiring but also a subjective and moral one. While the workplace aims to become homely and hospitable, the home gets reformed in accordance to the work demands. Times and tasks become increasingly taylorized (Hochschild 1997). New wireless technologies interact with former mediations like telephone, television, and radio, reconfiguring the sensorium.

As I will present in chapter 3, some of the participants in our workshops mentioned how television has fallen out of favor regarding the ascent of digital media consumption and the glamour of futuristic objects like electronic food processors.

Digitalization is, then, the last wave of a longer technological process linking the home with the outside. Every new wave gets added to the former. As the telephone was not displaced by the radio, nor the radio by the TV set, the most recent acquisitions have not substituted older technologies but rather overlap and reconfigure them. In a remarkably short lapse of time, we have seen the successive incorporations of the computer, the cellphone, the Internet, social media, the tablet, and household robots and appliances. The indoor impacts of the digital are manifold, and it would be a mistake to reduce them to nuts and bolts. The mutations at play involve the subjectivity of the users: their identity, sociability, and sensorium. The mutations in the practice of reading are a good example. Texts on screen have not discarded the use of paper but have deeply modified the writing, reading, and working ecologies (Cruces et al. 2017a). The same applies to the ways we buy, chat, watch movies, travel, walk, and keep in touch with our dear ones. This technological turn demonstrates to what degree we are made by the objects we use. Connectivity. Multitasking. Digital identity. Dispersed attention. Trending topics. Netiquette. Data mining. Likes and dislikes. Hashtags. Parental control. It would take a whole treaty to address the extension and depth of the impact of these realities. Let's only state that although technology has profoundly transformed intimacy, the opposite is equally true (Löfgren 2014). The boom of social media and the use of mobile technologies evidence the power of everyday life. The success of digital services, products, and activities is nourished from the wish to access, keep, and share human contact, personal confidences, daily routines, and common affects.

These mutations in relationships, spaces, markets, and practices match others at the less visible level of attitudes and dispositions. What we have called here the rise of intimacy is a long-term process that informs subjectivity as a whole: the spread of individualized lifestyles; the generalization of an ethos that takes life as an art and cultivates gestures once reserved for elites and the so-called leisure class (the selfie would be a good example of this; see Lasén 2012); the notion of "life project," which pushes the subject to achieve coherence in the telling of a life oriented toward conquering the future; the cultivation of a language of feelings and passions; the informalization of life, by giving value to spontaneity in all contexts, including those—as the school and the workplace—typically considered formal; the adoption of a transgressive expressivity, American style (the "cool"), understood as the display of a personal distance from any binding grammar (cf. Thomas 1997); in short, the uprooting of social identities of reflexive modernity.

These transformations show a greater visibility regarding the process that shielded the inner core of the home and its silent work. They also speak about its growing politicization, with the apparition of alternative possibilities, demands for empowerment, contestation, and controversies (Mossuz-Lavau 1991; Berlant 2000; Murillo 2006; Roseneil et al. 2020). In the end, what is at stake in this "life politics" is the right to be oneself and how this right should be valued and secured.

Intimacy is a glamorous word today. You can sense it by seeing how any initiative that makes it possible for people to name and share their day-to-day gets a good response. This has been the case with our research project.

NOTES

1. Taylorism is a system of rationalization of work, based on a detailed division of tasks, their specialization, and a tight control of all the elements in the production chain. To enhance productivity, the tayloristic organization model typically sacrifices the temporal autonomy of workers by fragmenting, standardizing, and measuring tasks and performances. Inspired in the works by Frederick W. Taylor in the nineteenth century, it was later refined during the twenthieth century by systems like Fordism and Toyotism. In Hochschild's theorizing, the idea of a "taylorization" of domestic work refers metaphorically to the ways in which this kind of discipline, based on fragmentation of tasks, compartmentalization of competences, and measurement of performance, tends to be mechanically transferred to the domestic setting, a context in which household chores were traditionally done in a much more holistic, personalized, and on-demand manner.

2. *Urbanity, urbanism*, and *urbanness* entail in English a whole range of different connotations, from "belonging to the city," to "being an urbanite," to "behaving in an urbanized, civilized manner." In Spanish, *urbanidad* covers the three meanings in a single word. In what follows, I use *urbanity* in a general sense to refer broadly to the dispositions necessary for living in a city.

Chapter 2

Exploring Intimacy

LET'S TALK BABY BOTTLES

I did not begin this study solely out of intellectual curiosity. Raising two kids had a Copernican effect on me.

When my first child was born, I spent quite a lot of time with him at home. And at the park, where other moms stared at me with curiosity while I played guitar beside the baby trolley. Hours seemed to last forever. I had never imagined myself to be proficient in baby bottles or skilled in the bathing of a baby. As with everything to do with care, these tasks cannot be reduced to mere practical considerations. They stand on a firm ground of essential forms of relation to and knowledge about life, of which I was mostly unaware. It is not just that I ignored how to alleviate a colicky baby; I did not even suspect that human beings needed to be taught how to go to sleep. My wife and I wondered, What was the proper age for the baby to sleep in his own room?

The new situation brought two kinds of disarray into my life. First, I began to live depending on others. For a middle-aged man devoted to his career, such novelty has a bittersweet flavor. My elder friends made wise recommendations to me: to regard it not as a sacrifice but as a privilege. For many Spaniards from earlier generations, participation in the household was more limited: gender-segregated when not rhetorical, inexistent, or impossible.

The second disarray was less clear. I wanted to talk about what I was experiencing. Birth labor, first words, nutritional issues, and sleeping arrangements seemed genuinely interesting. Middle-class moms and dads are used to talking about these things, ceaselessly. Upon my return to the ordinary, I stumbled across the sociolinguistic law by which each topic must be discussed within the context it belongs to. At the university café, talk revolves around exams, academic posts, and politics. Among friends, about cinema, work, and travel. As a newcomer to the world of carers, I tended to exhibit shameless baby-talk in those circles, speaking about intimate experiences in the wrong settings. Conversely, on more than one occasion, I had to improvise an alibi at the workplace that could be better accepted than the care of my kids.

Why don't we talk about baby bottles in public? (Here some female readers will rightfully protest: we do; tell me something I don't know.) We speak of these things with a noticeable freedom now when compared to a few decades ago. But still, we cannot overlook distinctions among contexts (public/private), genders (masculine/feminine), and cultural hierarchies (serious things/baby bottles) that underpin our cultural assumptions. My Copernican turn was, then, a distancing experience: an eventual estrangement with respect to fences that, in this and many other cases, have become increasingly blurred or weakened in response to the demands of current living. My hesitations responded to a cultural atmosphere: the problematic and visible condition of processes belonging to a sphere of experiences with claims for public legitimacy. We can think of this change as an emergence (in the sense of something welling up to the surface) or, in Foucauldian terminology, a "coming into representation" of actions, needs, and agents formerly kept to the backstage with respect to the preeminence of the public space.

THE PREDICAMENT OF INTIMATE ETHNOGRAPHY

My professional practice as an ethnographer of urban life pushed in the same direction. Three decades of ethnography in and of the city illustrate the predicament of the ethnographic method in the face of this emergence.

Doing fieldwork in your own society is always a tricky task. First, you must combine your daily life with a research agenda. Then, the people you must follow have, in turn, agendas of their own. Methodologically, this entails the need to imagine ways to locate yourself, as Goffman (1967, 186) put it, "where the action is." But where is the action? In the never-ending metropolis, the sites of action are, by definition, countless.

Therefore, most urban ethnographers choose to document collective events that take place in the public space. This was also my approach in the 1990s, doing fieldwork in Madrid, Mexico City, and Bogotá on urban festivals, political demonstrations, music consumption, and oral histories (Cruces 2007). Then I studied Madrilenian organizations (Cruces et al. 2002; Velasco et al. 2006), finding that specialist institutions based on a tight division of labor set strict limits on the role of intruder-observer. The researcher has to either look for formal entry into the organizational body or, more often, opt for a somewhat furtive access through the backdoor of bureaus, hospitals, airports, ministries, banks, schools, and companies. Again: where the action is.

This methodological predicament of urban ethnography increases exponentially in the study of intimacy. Everyone in the city becomes a locus of action. Every woman, man, child, youth, or retiree has a life of their own, an intimacy to build, tasks to do, an engagement in the work of self-making, purposefully, endlessly. How to cope with such Certeaunian proliferation?

This may seem a quantitative consideration, but it goes far deeper. The first question to tackle is singularity. Often, what one finds in others' intimacy is what they deem unique and unrepeatable. Far from the predictable reiteration of the same, in the encounters with urban dwellers you will be confronted with a series of serendipitous ups and downs. Of course, singular lives are informed by general patterns and categories that the analyst tries to discover and superimpose. But sooner or later you realize that one's gaze on the other is merely a poor reflection when compared to the richness and meaning of their practices, stories, and actions. To have intimacy is to inhabit a universe. Ethnography cannot be but a pale, graceless resemblance of it.

A second methodological predicament has to do with intrusion. As Juan, a young photographer in one of our workshops, put it, "When you portray someone in their intimacy, this has to be understood as an offering that this person is giving you." Juan contextualized the exchanges between the observer and observed as a moment in the chain of the gift. This is a chain that anthropological analysis has highlighted as a fundamental human institution (in the tradition of Marcel Mauss 1970). Each and every act of giving is just a point in a reciprocal circulation of gifts and countergifts—hence, of debts, borrowings, and returns. The give-and-take of social life is deeply embedded in this never-ending chain. Understanding intimacy in this frame of gift, debt, and reciprocity has serious implications. It points to the bond that emerges from such exchanges, which is precious, vulnerable, and somehow sacred, underscoring the obligations acquired by the one who asks the questions and takes the photos. There is no way to escape from such a sense of obligation, since the gift is based not on a simple duty to give, neither on the duty to give back, but on the duty to take on debt. It is about learning how to receive— there's no such thing as a free lunch.

To begin an ethnography on intimacy under metropolitan conditions, two different paths seemed to open. The canonical strategy has traditionally prescribed "to follow the people" (Marcus 1995, 106). To document practices in the intimate realm, I could have reasonably chosen four or five homes and tried to be there when meals were cooked, children were bathed, family gathered around the TV, and couples quarreled over the division of chores and errands. Gullestad's *Kitchen-Table Society* (1989) and Hochschild and Machung's *The Second Shift* (1989) are masterworks in this genre. A similar option would be the sociological path set by Jean-Claude Kaufmann (1997) with his lively exchange by correspondence and interviews with informants on the petty details of laundry, ironing, and housekeeping.

On the other hand, the emergence of the intimate sphere has recently been accompanied by an escalation of new modes of ethnography-making online, including participation in forums, blogs, personal sites, and a wide range of research formats. From the most diverse forms of privacy to your desk, there is only a click.[1]

Neither of these options seduced me. For reasons like the one argued by Juan, I wanted to avoid the conventional intrusion in someone else's life, in a role of theoretically neutral observer. The precious and vulnerable matter of people's lives—the death of a father, little allures, favorite objects, furtive confessions, and gripes between fiancé(e)s—offers you an unbearable amount of gift, much more than what you could ever hope to give back.

Certainly, any ethnographic process conducted with honesty opens opportunities for a fundamental restitution of sorts. I think of those moments in which you discover that the other really appreciates the simple fact of you being there, listening, and trying to understand. But this asymmetry, generally uncomfortable for the anthropologist in both the public and the organizational space, in this case seemed truly insurmountable.

How can we accomplish the well-intended wish to illuminate and value the processes of intimate life? Surely, not by taking what was carefully protected in someone's quotidian life and just mechanically throwing it into the public domain. We live in a time marked by a tendency that could be called "extimacy": a growing social pressure to disclose things intimate, to overexpose them to cameras, Internet, and other media (Coudreuse and Simonet-Tenant 2009, 9; Simonet-Tenant 2009, 11; Tisseron 2002, 2011; Lejeune 2009a, 14). To put it bluntly, I didn't want to become anyone's Big Brother. This was not merely an ethical stance but also a theoretical one. In the old times, a cordon sanitaire encapsulated the realm of the home, rendering its beauties and miseries invisible. What we face now is, on the contrary, the threat of its overrepresentation: the theatrical affectation of every social bond, the mediatic drive to render the whole world of life transparent to the public gaze.

This is why I decided to try a slightly different approach to gathering data.

COLLECTIVE EXPLORATION WORKSHOPS: THE CEWs EXPERIENCE

A few cultural institutions in Madrid were partners in our research project *Cosmopolis. Emerging Practices and Metropolitan Processes* (Cruces et al. 2016). I proposed Medialab Prado, a city council-run media laboratory, jointly organize a series of workshops on the topic of intimacy, to be attended by volunteers. We called them collective exploration workshops (CEWs). The weekly sessions were advertised via the lab's website.[2] Participation was open to its wide, lively network of users, who were mainly students, young professionals, and entrepreneurs engaged in technological, artistic, or cultural initiatives. Some of them showed interest in this collaborative proposal for a variety of reasons. A few were running initiatives on architecture or urban planning. Others were activists in social movements. Still others were artists engaged in projects on photography, performance, or design in the private realm. Most participants shared a genuine curiosity about intimate life, a desire to catch a glimpse of others' internal life while revealing a little of their own.

I developed most of my initial fieldwork in this unconventional setting. Other, more classical sources of material have included a comparative online survey of a thousand young Internet users in Spain and Mexico (Guaderrama 2012), a series of in-depth interviews with young cultural producers (trend-setters) in their homes and studios (Cruces 2012, 144), and filming at some informants' homes (Moreno Andrés and Cruces 2018). In this last case, the inner space of the house and its system of objects added their voices to the choir of this indoor urban symphony.

The workshops were structured as follows. Normally, we would talk and interact for two or three hours around a topic or activity that I had suggested—things like bringing personal photos, preparing a meal, sketching a map of the appliances in our houses, compiling a music repertoire, dancing, storytelling, or drawing. We commented on beds, laptops, lullabies, and Tupperware. We invented nicknames, shared childhood memories, and confided about family quarrels, favorite songs, and bodily noises. Anything goes. The task at hand focuses the group's attention and confers a common goal that allows the group to constitute itself, thus prompting a more lively exchange of experiences, anecdotes, and confidences.

Given the coauthorial nature of the exploration, in this kind of setting the ethnographer becomes involved not only as producer of the event but also at a more intimate level, as simply another participant contributing with their own experiences. The collective focus smoothly swings from concrete details to abstract reflections—something that, from the onset, was stated as an explicit purpose of the meeting. The ethnographer is often requested to intervene as host and interpreter of the situation. This takes them away from any ideal, unintrusive role as detached observer. However, this loss in neutrality is compensated by a gain in proximity, trust, and dialogical possibilities. This kind of setting also makes it possible for the ethnographer to obtain more than mere discourse, as the group explores their diversity of *manières de faire.*

The leading principle is not to explore others but rather to explore *with* others. Although the call for the sessions was open, I made sure to guarantee a setting that was as protected as possible from any external gaze, to promote trust and spontaneity. Its periodic character allowed us to try out little exercises in performance, observation, and analysis that we could have in common throughout several weeks. We also tried to spatially open the experiment to the city, scheduling each of the sessions in a different Madrilenian venue: the council lab Medialab Prado, the La Tabacalera de Lavapiés self-managed social center, the Off-Limits art studio, and the Designit innovation company.

Our first call, made via the Web in 2010, focused on the idea of "prosumer"—a neologism introduced by New Economy circles as a figure of the productivity of the consumer in daily life. We intended to focus on those activities that our participants, who were mostly young, could possibly be prone to show in a spontaneous manner. Each session was coordinated by a member of the Cultura Urbana team and was devoted to a specific topic: the consumer's agency (Producing by Consumption), self-photography (Image-ing), text edition (Publishing the World), music (Musicking), walking (Itineraries), home stories (Housekeeping), cooking (Eateries), and art (Urbane@rt).[3] Our proposal presented it in this way:

> We want to show what we do by way of musical, visual, and plastic contents; domestic artifacts; personal and familial memories; exchanges with friends; forms of self-representation. And to reflect from it. We wish to inquire about these fertile fields of individual and collective creativity. At the same time, we will open a space where participants—in their capacity as *prosumers*—can show their best productions, exchange experiences, and reflect together about the logics of production/consumption that rule our habitat. For a noticeable blurring of the boundaries between the role of receiver/consumer—of messages, works, services, and cultural products—and the condition of emitter/producer is a sign of our times.

> We will focus on this frontier. The new technological culture implies it's blurring, intrinsically: to Photoshop images, to share tips and ideas, to articulate texts, to interconnect gadgets, to imagine unexpected uses for cellphones and their cameras, to generate new languages for the screen and keyboard. . . . All these things have become routine in a relationship to technology always conjugated in the active and subjunctive modes, by means of verbs like editing, browsing, surfing, interacting, sharing, exporting, uploading, downloading, cutting, pasting. . . . This speaks of a capacity for self-affirmation, by creating an environment of one's own. Also, of a desire to make it unique, singular, meaningful.

I had borrowed the notion of "prosumer" from Toby Miller (2004). He criticized this mystifying figure introduced by powerful creative industries to sublimate a supposed empowerment of the subjects via new communication technologies. At its dawn, Internet 2.0 was presented as the best example of that: given that the users were the ones who would produce the contents, products, and the very network of social media, the promise was that now anyone could become a "writer," "artist," "scientist," and "programmer." Among advocates and critics, my intention was not to discuss the political background of this figure—I did not want to go there. I wanted to appropriate it. It sounded terrific. What I found in the notion of prosumer was an alibi to bring everyday inventions and tricks to the surface. They resembled those that Michel de Certeau (1990) had called *manières de faire* and consuming productivity in *L'invention du quotidian*.[4] Toby's reaction was humorous. He celebrated the possibility that a concept arrived at by the hand of big industry could be recycled to spring forth other visions and experiences from the above.

This was precisely what happened in our Prosumers series. We obtained a rich stream of stories and reflections around most of the topics. In the session about text editing, someone confessed her painful but loving relationship with literature; in the session about selfies, some dared to reveal, beyond the trivia of the selfie, other stronger uses that involved erotic exchange, nudity, and self-image of the body; in the session about food, we prepared dishes meshed with gossip, recipes, regional origins, heirlooms, as well as dietary anxieties and quests.

"Things Are Not This Way Anymore"

The call for the session on housekeeping read:

> Welcome to Madrid-Ville, this is your home.
>
> Our home is made of stories. Little, funny, cruel, depressing, nasty, faithful, disconcerting, tidy, chaotic, calculated, improvised, desperate, dull, or hopeful.
>
> To tell stories. Why not? We always do it. A day at home is a day of recounting.
>
> Let's build a home together. Just for a couple of hours. By sharing stories.

We painted an imaginary domestic space on the floor (as in the staging of *Dog-Ville*, the movie by Lars von Trier). My colleague Karina Boggio and I dressed up as a traditional couple to represent a satire of daily life within this perimeter. We parodied a familial scene that included the cleaning and sweeping up of the place, the gender division of roles, and a little quarreling between husband and wife. Doña Pepi, shawl on her head, tidies the place up. She removes dirt, hums tangos and *coplas*, and complains bitterly about how

the men of the house never leave the toilet seat down. She chats noisily with
the neighbors through the window that opens onto the patio and yells at her
children, who are playing outside. Then the husband shows up in the scene,
exhausted from his workday. After a clumsy, unwelcome sexual advance on
his wife, he plops down on the couch and muddies the floor with his dirty
boots. Reprimand, couple quarrel, end of story. Following this, we prompted
the participants to enter the fake home and tell a story of their own from there.

> Your sketch has reminded me of something that I always yearned for as a little
> girl. Because we never had this kind of situation at home. At my house, every-
> thing was hyper-ordered, always. This was so, not just because my mother tidied
> up a lot but mostly because we had very few things. And there were so many
> rules at home! Especially whenever we visited relatives. Then, it was "Watch
> your mouth," "Please behave," "Mind the way you sit at the table." There were
> four pieces of cutlery on one side of the plate and four on the other; you never
> knew how to use them. Like in *Pretty Woman*. I lived this typical scene many
> times at my grandmother's house. I sense that things are not this way anymore.

With this comment, Manuela kicked off a crescendo of personal memories
and stories. Most of them revolved around what could be called the discovery
of one's own order: its pleasures, difficulties, and surprises. Manuela began
by evoking the rigidity of the family rules at her grandmother's place, from
which she was able to escape only by moving to Madrid. Don't talk at the
table, don't touch this and that. Then Noemí set these memories in sharp
contrast to her own: those of an incredibly rule-free childhood, with children
running wild among mountains of books owned by liberal (and librarian)
parents. Marga spoke of her experience of going to live alone in a centric
neighborhood, just to discover how compulsory, invasive, and binding the
relationships in any community of tenants can be. "I talk with Puri, my neighbor, right from the balcony. She is exactly like the character you played!"
Living is never living alone: it means having to live with others, within the
same building—whether you like it or not. Ramón got some laughs by tragi-
comically evoking the terminal dispute with his ex about the ownership of a
Thermomix (a beloved food processor). Julia confessed she felt uncomfortable with her partner's obsession with cleanliness and order. "I feel filthy."
Irene, a lover of the arts, confided how she looks for the hidden beauty that
lay underneath trifles like the linen in the dirty laundry basket, which she
photographs. "These are silly things, I know." After reading the poetic chant
to the infraordinary by George Perec out loud, she shared a series of those
photos. Then Alberto, a divorcé in his sixties, explained in a mysterious
and rather sad way how he lives in "a house haunted by me." As a modern
Sisyphus of refurbishing, he feels compelled to initiate works in the house

that, after having lost the initial drive, he never finishes. Vero, who had been silently listening to the rest, introduced us then to her old teenage bedroom, surrounded by an atypical, meticulously cultivated chaos: cigarette butts in the drawer, upside-down armchairs, clothes hanging from the lamps . . . The rest of the family just gave up. Her story ended with a confession. Now that she is living with a partner, she is worried about a noise growing from inside: the draw of this adolescent desire for disorder. To close the session, the convenors offered their little stories too. I chose one about a terrifying earthquake I experienced in Mexico City while cooking in my underwear on the eleventh story of a high-rise building.

This first-person account, in the form of a lived story of the self, is the main discursive genre in these workshops. The whole ethnography became a narrative corpus of this kind. As we will see, from a formal point of view, the will for style is their most interesting trait. These stories form a genre endowed with conventions of its own. Many have a dramatic structure that swirls around the task of ego: tales of self-discovery, little triumphs and defeats, projects and fulfillments, assertions, and resignations. As in the genres of oral tradition, obstructing and facilitating actants do their job by messing around with the ultimate goals of a protagonist character. These actants are things like the family of origin, the partner, the neighbors, the roommates, the landlord, the lack of money or a job, bad luck, personal flaws, health problems, loneliness, even the objects that surround us. The underlying moral presents the agonies of ego pushed to make itself. For the self is in permanent reinvention, projecting one to the future, overcoming the difficulties of the present as much as the burdens of the past. The tone is not necessarily heroic. You more often find dramatic and lyrical moods and parodic and humorous ones, for in the end, life is a Mardi Gras—and its paradoxes and contradictions a joyful thing to share. The hero—oneself—may even appear in the guise of an antihero, a loser, a rogue. The best among these stories are endowed with a deep sense of poetic justice. The tension created in the plot comes to an elegant resolution by means of a closure charged with moral sense, for example, when someone tries to deceive but is deceived instead; when sons or daughters unveil family issues jealously kept secret by their parents; when lost properties are returned to their legitimate owners or exert quasimagical powers of evocation and agency; when the expectations that someone had placed on someone else, or on life itself, are brutally contradicted and discarded; or conversely, when a suspicion is unexpectedly confirmed, a wish joyfully pursued, a fantasy fulfilled against all odds.

Nevertheless, the most noteworthy stylistic trait in this discursive formation is its openness to dialogue. From a formal point of view, these stories are unfinished. They are sketched outlines demanding to be completed. They work through the mediation of the listeners, who help to deploy the plot and find out its true meaning. The structure of this genre belongs to the order of conversation rather than that of storytelling properly speaking. These stories are part of a bargain, bridges in a collaborative effort to clarify the opaque evidence supplied by the everyday. Both their form and their content are shaped in the very act of enunciation, through the active participation of an audience.[5]

Doing Things Together

The activities in CEWs are not restricted to mere discourse. The success of a workshop depends on proposing very concrete tasks that can mobilize the group and transform the encounter into something more than just a dry exchange of opinions. In matters of intimacy, theoretical parlance is value-less. During our workshops these actions consisted of very diverse things: building a musical repertoire together; making lists of home appliances; visualizing the shelves where we keep our collection of records, cassettes, and CDs; commenting on family photo albums; retrieving memories of the bedrooms we had dwelled in; bringing in one of our favorite things. We held an anticontest for ugly people, a picnic in the classroom, a dance, a prom-enade. Relaxation sessions on the floor. A Tupperware party.

What is the benefit of proposing such activities? They allow for the group to enjoy, to own the situation, and to diversify the reflexive formats. First, by displacing the attention toward the task at hand, we activate unexpected possibilities in a sensory direction. What matters is to collectively produce an experience, not just to exchange words and ideas. People drop their guard, laugh and cry, so in the end they can celebrate the encounter as something personally enriching. Second, the requirements of the task make it so that emerging forms of leadership and bond appear. These give a momentary structure to the group. The convenor can then retreat to a more discrete, sec-ondary role in the background. Finally, the participants highly appreciate the condition of becoming both objects and subjects of reflection. Conversely, the convenor finds a certain freedom in the position of a participant like any other. And they can combine this kind of participation with a more demand-ing role as an expert who provides interpretations about what is going on.

The outcome of collaborative work does not rest, by definition, on the convenor's merits but rather on the collective capacities and understandings that arise from interaction. This does not make the convenor exempt from two important responsibilities. On the one hand, we must abstain from stirring delicate feelings and situations that we do not have the capacity to heal or repair. On the other hand, the convenor must propose norms of mutual care and respect so that nobody's trust is betrayed.

Given the good results of the first experience, I continued it in Medialab for two more years. The topic of intimacy was now made explicit in the very title, Metropolitan Intimacies: "This series of workshops proposes a shared trip to the Madrilenian indoors of our times: a collective effort to explore contemporary urban dwelling. Our city is undergoing major changes. What is changing in your ways of dwelling? Things deemed 'intimate,' 'private,' 'domestic,' what are they made of?"

The call proposed to (a) collectively document our personal spaces, (b) discuss their meaning, and (c) produce a negotiated representation of these domains. We focused on household appliances, strategies for feeling at home, relationships among people living together, the body, music and dance, photo albums, cleaning and tidiness, the distribution of chores, favorite objects, and the use of Tupperware.[6]

The number and composition of the groups resulting from this call was uneven. Sometimes I was able to gather up to twenty people, sometimes only three. This is an effect we can expect from our overwhelmed urban milieus, where public attention is extremely fought-over, and audiences follow quite tidal rhythms. In our city lab, the standard participant responded to the multicultural and technological profile of the environment: youth-not-so-young, a made-up category that accounts for the present spread of a lifestyle associated with youth that has extended to the ages of thirties and forties; cultural mediators and producers with high levels of formal education; self-taught techies with the do-it-yourself ethos typical of the Web 2.0 era; professionals and students with collaborative dispositions, endowed with both artistic and technological sensibilities, who feel at ease moving between disciplines.

A Transurban Voyage

Given that the experience in Madrid was fruitful, we decided to plan more workshops, this time in Montevideo and Mexico City. The choice was based on a rather opportunistic hunch about where it would be feasible for us to do the job. We were already familiar with these cities and could rely on both previous ground knowledge and trusted colleagues and institutions to help with logistics. Eventually we also held a few sporadic CEWs in small Spanish cities where I was invited to give courses or talks, like Palma de Mallorca, Torrelavega, Benicarló, Mérida, and Segovia.

There were also methodological reasons for this design. I looked for a transurban scheme. I did not want to get trapped within the confines of a single place, because ethnography as a technique contains a methodological inertia to be read as a "local sample" of a supposed encompassing territorial unit, be it the "city," the "country," or the "culture." In the metropolitan milieu, the cultural homogeneity of these units has always been a geographic fantasy. Under the contemporary flow of people, goods, money, technologies, ideas, and meanings, such representation becomes untenable (cf. García Canclini 2010a; Hannerz 2012). Our object of interest was not an encapsulated and essentialized difference among world cities but rather processes of movement and transformation that take place everywhere, in an open, fluid, global space. We understood the intimacies documented in each of the workshops not as samples of "national culture" but as observational units whose proper horizon of analysis is the global ecumene (Hannerz 2012). Somehow, this could be an urban update of the old motto by Clifford Geertz in which he described anthropology not as a study "*of* villages" but "*in* villages." I think I do not study "cities" but "*in* cities." Why should one assume that the young couple living in Madrid's city center must necessarily have more in common with the retired bachelor who lives by himself in the suburbs (just because of their spatial proximity) than with other couples of similar age, sexual preference, and professions in distant Montevideo? Any ethnography *in* or *of* the world system (Marcus 1995) faces this methodological dilemma, which is inherent to studying global processes in specific places. You certainly do not want to totally despatialize the object of study for, as we have stated, something in the very concept of intimacy has to do with proximity and closeness or, as Massey (1999) put it, with the coexistence of entities and identities. Nevertheless, I reject framing intimacies territorially, in the form of fictitiously homogeneous units, nested like Russian dolls. Our choice was then a multilocal design, guided by the rather globalist and individualist hypothesis that, in the metropolitan ecumene, strong similarities in the ways intimate habitats are made can be found across world cities. Such similarities have to do with complex clusters of variables such as income, class, status, profession, lifestyle, sexual preference, ideology, cultural level, age, residential pattern, family cycle, and household members. Some of these factors could indeed be observed in the workshops, although we did not have the capacity to filter or control them.

This transurban convergence results from the ubiquitous presence of global forces, processes, and agents. Expert systems such as the health, education, transport, and housing ones are prominent examples, just like the IKEA stores that we will visit in chapter 4. Insofar as they handle global operations, their ways of planning product design, marketing, and logistics reflect these same kinds of globalist/individualist assumptions. Instead of looking to reconstruct a fictionally homogeneous territory, we cartographically navigated similarities and differences between the intimacies of our many participants, imagined as belonging to an encompassing urban reality. Regardless of the limitations that this cartographic strategy may entail, its consequence was a marvelous freedom to experiment in three countries, moving back and forth between different cities.

Table 2.1. A sample of CEWs

Title	Place	Number of Participants	Theme
Giving Music a Body	UNED, Benicarló	25	Embodied listening
Producing while Consuming	Medialab Prado, Madrid	20	Activities of production and consumption
Housekeeping	CSA La Tabacalera, Madrid	15	Domestic stories
Naming the Everyday	Medialab Prado, Madrid	15	Personal definitions of intimacy
Make Yourself at Home	Centro Cultural de España, Montevideo	15	Experiences of feeling at home
Do You Recall?	Designit, Madrid	4	Looking at family photos together
You Are Making Me a Slave to the Home	Universidad de la República, Montevideo	10	The sharing of chores
Vulgar Objects for Very Special People	Medialab Prado, Madrid	20	Favorite objects that identify me
Eateries	UCM, Madrid	20	Ways of cooking
Tupperware Party	Medialab Prado, Madrid	25	The social life of Tupperware
Readers in the Circle of the Gift	UNED, Mallorca	15	The generous circulation of reading and books in daily life
Libraries of Babel	Medialab Prado, Madrid	15	Domestic and personal bookshelves
Imagined Objects	UAM-I, México	12	Fantasied stories about someone else's favorite object
Kitchenopolis	Universidad de la República, Montevideo	15	Who dwells in my kitchen?

Table 2.1 summarizes the cities and topics addressed in a sample of the CEWs. Over forty workshops were held, with the participation of more than four hundred people.[7] The topics do not encompass the whole domain of intimacy; however, they were not arbitrarily selected. Topics were chosen partly in function of occasion and place and partly to cover a variety of dimensions of intimate life. We also repeated sessions that had proven productive and

enjoyable. Music listening, housekeeping, feeling at home, relationships, equipment and appliances, cooking, kitchens, bookshelves, personal belongings, and family photos were our favorites.

Certain topics are obviously missing here, in particular romantic love; sexual behavior; pain, sickness, and resilience; conflict and violence; loneliness; loss, mourning, and death. When from time to time they would spontaneously appear, we integrated them as best we could. But we consciously set them aside as main lines of research. Of course, such issues have a place in everyday life. Most interpersonal crime, for example, is documented to happen indoors among relatives (Straus 1977). Conversely, the narrative and morals of romantic love are integral to our modern sense of intimacy (Giddens 1991; Beck and Beck-Gernsheim 1995; Kaufmann 2010a). Nevertheless, they are overprivileged themes, both in the mediatic versions of intimacy and in the academic accounts of it. For this reason, we consciously left them aside. They would have put the dynamics of the encounters at risk by stirring feelings and conflicts we could not expect to manage in the limited scope of our meetings. You do not invite strangers to share trauma, anguish, and regret, nor are you entitled to do so.

Moreover, a love-and-pain approach would have cannibalized the humble narratives about daily practices that we were after, giving them a dramatic tinge. If we wanted to summon petty details and personal treasures, it is because these apparently minor things are what imprint the everyday with their genuine texture and tonality, not because they obey the dominant and competing narratives of candid love versus bold violence, familial harmony versus rough domination, and passionate fulfillment versus unbearable alienation. A dichotomic picture of intimacy based on those grand metanarratives is totally misleading. The truth usually lies in between such extremes. Small is not only beautiful; it is also truer for most people, most of the time.

Although our initial series of workshops was focused on digital life, the overall design is balanced out with sessions devoted to both online and offline practices. After a few CEWs, we found that the participants did not make a clear divide between online and offline dimensions of their experience and that the drive that motivated their participation came from a broader range of everyday issues. It did not make sense to study the digital realm separately. In the beginning we tried to implement a double format for the workshops, with a wiki page where the exchange of posts, images, and experiences could continue online. It was a complete failure. The strong motivation for the participants was to gather face-to-face. Contributing online entailed an additional effort that almost nobody, not even the convenors, were willing to make. As the series progressed, the wiki faded, and for the next ones I simply dropped it. This does not mean, however, that the live CEWs did not render rich information about digital life, only that such dimensions became mixed with the offline ones, as can be appreciated in chapter 3.[8]

Regardless of methodological objections on the paper, our corpus was full of findings, stories, and surprises. There was, for example, an unforgettable workshop in Palma de Mallorca, Spain, in which participants provided an amazing spectrum on the familial use of books: from a mother of ten who used to retreat to a separate room to breastfeed while she read to the gift of a book with a pompous title passed on from father to daughter as a coming-of-age ritual (Cruces 2017a, 192). There were occasions when we reached heights of emotion and trust that surprised both me and the participants. One of the Mexico City sessions started with a young woman confiding the mourning of her recently deceased father. She exquisitely recounted how she had been taking care of the plants that he had on his rooftop terrace (terraces are, by the way, remarkable places at the historical core of Mexico City). As a veritable allegory, she was keeping the greenery alive. Beyond a testimony of love, what this practice performed was the continuity of life itself. At one point in the story, she broke down in tears. The group listened respectfully, helped her to recover, and moved on.

Of course, this collaborative ethos does not always rule. The conversation entails tensions and disagreements, and this undercurrent eventually leads to open discussion. The convenor can channel the consensual drive to render differences visible. This explicitation makes them a lot easier to handle. This was clear at a session in Montevideo about personal hygiene and makeup. The talk switched from daily personal hygiene routines to the controversial issue of how the masculine gaze—real or fantasized—impacts women's practices of dressing and putting on makeup. Some participants could not have been more opposed. A newlywed woman revealed how it pleased her to devote time and effort to appear relaxed and lovely for her husband in the evening. Another woman of the same age—pierced, tattooed, and proud of sculpting a look of countercultural autonomy—debunked this position as an acceptance of alienation and dependence. I intervened in my role as moderator, not to solve the disagreement but to reframe it in a way that helped to identify the existing variety of constructions of femininity, and reactions to the masculine gaze, among us.

The CEWs' dynamics also reveal significant lapses and denials. In Mexico City, a housewife who had recently moved in with her husband chose the single bed she was still keeping at her parents' home as her favorite object. She then noticed—not without embarrassment—how this choice suggested discomfort with, or at least resistance to, her new environment. In the same session, another woman resented her partner's insistence on keeping bedroom doors always open. She saw this as a disturbing sign within the relationship, one that she had not been aware of before. In Montevideo, in a workshop on kitchens, a woman introduced herself as someone who spent little time in this part of the house and felt very detached from it. Later, she would casually explain how the family took frequent trips to the market because they did not have a freezer. This shocked me. "Can you live today without a fridge?" "We do have a fridge," she clarified. "What we do not have is a freezer. We eat fresh food, buying groceries almost daily because my daughter is celiac. We have to do it this way. Actually, maybe I spend more time in the kitchen than I said before! But surely, it is more than I would like." This woman had been cooking for her daughter for over fifteen years, but this fact was somehow obscured in the discursive image she produced of herself, based on other markers of identity, as her professional achievements in the local police task force dealing with gender violence. Discursive dynamics nuances first impressions, provokes counterdiscourses, and inchoates revelations. As dialogue progresses, self-images adjust, statements are redressed or contradicted, and the collective power of reflection allows the selves to envision unsuspected truths in someone else's stories. Discourse is not a frozen object; it is thinking in movement. The concept of group dynamics refers to these maieutic virtues of interpellation to enlighten, contradict, and interrogate, as well as to the capacity of the subjects to move back and forth along different interpretations.

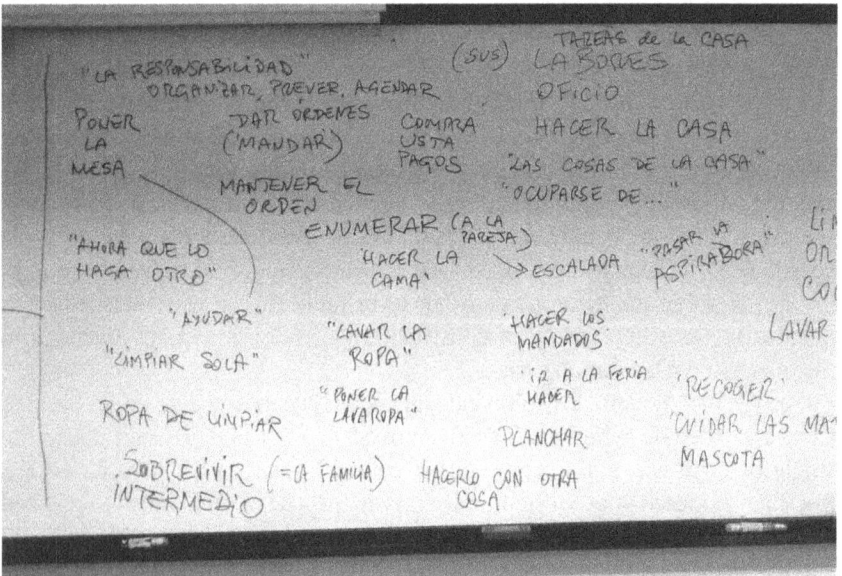

Figure 2.1. After the brainstorming on home chores. Montevideo, 2014 (courtesy of Jorge Moreno Andrés).

   This experience of CEWs in three world cities does not render a systematic set of differences but a series of common scenes and dilemmas. It draws sketches out of global objects: local variations of the same thing, tinged with a particular accent. The accent is very important here, though. Because when speaking about intimacy, it is the accent that counts. Intimacy is about accents, flavors, scents, lighting, feelings, atmospheres, memories—or as Pardo (1996, 53) has put it, about "how palatable things are to me." Traveling to other cities expanded this accentual quest, enhancing its poetic significance. The overall relevance of poetics is condensed in the stylistic beauty of personal ways of telling, which was in turn the factor that silently boosted the high involvement of people in the encounters. A good example of this was the participation of a teenager called Carlita in one of our workshops at Iztapalapa, Mexico. In a group with plenty of verbal virtuosity, she was outstandingly fresh and funny, animating the conversation with stories and comments. Everyone in the meeting seemed to be delighted with her anecdotes about how her little nephew had erupted into her life, filling it with fun-filled chaos. Once the workshop was over, I tried to interview her for our documentary. But, alas, Carlita had vanished without a trace. She did not formally register to participate. No one knew her. We were finally left without the thread of her beautifully told stories.
   This motivational force of the group dynamics was manifest in many of the workshops, for example in Eateries, a session with students from a master's program in communication in Madrid. The students' assignment was to bring something cooked by themselves in order to transform the classroom into a picnic. Christmas holidays were close, and exams were almost on top of us. It was not strange that some of the students found it difficult to find the time to cook mindfully. Yet, everyone tried. Nobody was indifferent. Some of them had combined cooking and writing in a way that was a source for clever reflections. "I have cooked my writing and written my cooking. I was following my grandmother's recipe. In the end, isn't a text also a kind of recipe somehow?" A student rushed to the street at night, looking for ingredients. Another student from China panicked and placed a long-distance SOS call to her grandma in Beijing: she could not remember the recipe for Peking duck. The act of offering food to others contains a compulsory force. Where does it come from? We concluded that the ritual powers of commensalism had been able to outshine even the strong bureaucratic strictures of the school institution.
   The comparative design affords occasions to put topics and formats to the test. In a CEW on favorite objects in Mexico, I changed the call I had previously employed in Madrid and Montevideo. Instead of asking the participants to select a cherished thing and tell its story, I asked them to make up a story about someone else's object. First, we wrote down all the names of the

objects on pieces of paper. Then we raffled them out among the people. The game was to try to imagine a story that would match the true one. The result of the experiment was amazing. Some of the guessed stories were shockingly close to the originals, illustrating the hidden cultural logic underneath. For example, one was about a serving platter that Adele had been using for years to bring her little son breakfast in bed. Mornings in Chiapas can be cold, and this devoted mother wanted to help her boy jump out of bed and go to school happy. To our astonishment, another participant had constructed a story from this object that, without being an exact double, contained the basic elements of its plot, like the little son, the breakfast, and the bed. In the opposite direction, some objects totally confused the narrator, evidencing eloquent forms of divergence between cultural expectations and individual choices. For example, a girl invented this story out of a revealing gown: the dress was something she was currently using at home while doing chores in solitude. Everyone in the group retorted with incredulity. Nobody would do chores that dressed up! This dress had been brought in by Samuel, a gay participant. He then gave us the original version of the story. The dress was a crazy gift from his best friend, a souvenir from nights of fun and adventure spent together on a trip to New York. This object, he confessed, incorporated his desire to dress in sexy, provocative drag.

FILMING AT MANY HOMES

At a certain point, I thought that the stories from the workshops were too good to be told just in written form. They deserved to be heard straight from the mouths of their protagonists. I asked some of the participants I deemed to be the best storytellers to share their experiences on camera, at their homes (see figure 2.2). A written informed consent form invited them to make a collaborative documentary under a Creative Commons license. At the end of the process, the edited material would be submitted for their approval. My friends at Universidad Autónoma Metropolitana in Mexico ironized about this procedure, labeling it an "anthropological casting," since the workshops gave us a chance to test both interviewees and stories. The advantage was indeed to get clues in advance that would guide the shooting of the film before arriving at anyone's home. We interviewed twenty-seven people this way. The setting of the cameras and the script for the interview were quite free, open to the hosts' preferences. We always made a few suggestions to inspire potential topics, but these were soon substituted by the participant's own choices. For example, we once went to the home of a mother with two teenage daughters in Montevideo. Celina had shown generosity during the workshops, telling us about her risky pregnancies, which had kept her bedridden for months. She got used to eating, reading, and literally living in her bed, a situation that deeply resignified her relationship with the bedroom. When we arrived at Celina's home, I asked her where she preferred to shoot. She gathered strength and, after a short silence, suggested the bed for the interview. This king-size bed had become the center of that home, attracting mother and daughters with its magnetism. The interview was very emotional. From there, it became easy to evoke childhood games, like the girls making paper planes, evenings spent watching TV series on the computer together, and disputes about when and how to tidy up the mess of shoes that piled up around this essential place.

Sometimes, the interview corroborated something we had explored in a previous workshop. Other times, it ran in new and exciting directions. We met Irene, a young mother living in the center of Madrid, who spontaneously decided to breastfeed her child in the middle of the conversation, facing the camera. We were pleased by such naturality. At the end of the interview, I asked her permission to use the images, which she gladly granted (although objecting that she was "a very shy person"). This event had a deeper meaning. At that time, the core of this couple's life revolved around the kids. This is the only house I have ever visited that had no doors. They were also experimenting with cosleeping, so all four members of the family slept together. The whole organization of the space revealed these explorations in parenting.

On another occasion we visited Manuela and Tiana, a lesbian couple, at their shared flat. I had met Manuela in several previous workshops, where she had shown herself to be up-to-date with cultural trends and to have a sharp, quick wit. This time, the encounter had to be postponed because of the sudden death of her father. I was curious about things like the conviviality in a nonheterosexual home, their "coming out," the reactions from their families, and their activism on LGBTQ initiatives. Instead, I found a person immersed in mourning the loss of her father. Consequently, the interview revolved around that. A single daughter, she had inherited her parents' house, together with a legacy of heirlooms, photographs, and random stuff (including, she confessed, portraits signed by the dictator Franco). She did not know what to do with all that. To make matters worse, she had cut off contact with her father and his branch of the family long ago. As the interview progressed, I felt increasingly in tune with her troubles. I had been through the same situation—going through a father's things—just a few weeks before. What was initially intended to be a (potentially exoticizing) session on nonheteronormative couple-building happily turned into a (sympathetic) session on home liquidations and the strange burden of familial memories—something that eventually happens to everyone.

Filming at others' homes introduced three new dimensions in the research process: (1) the tension between ethnographic fieldwork and filmic recording,

Figure 2.2. Filming at Mexico City, September 2015 (courtesy of Jorge Moreno Andrés).

(2) the production of a choral voice, and (3) the poetics of space itself. First, my initial goal to visually document intimacies progressively made room for a more ambitious intent, shared with my colleague Jorge Moreno: to give it a narrative form that could be seen by a general public without being boring. The basic motto of film production is "show, don't explain," which in our case may translate to "tell a story, not a bunch of facts." What makes perfect sense in a scientific report can be tedious to the point of exhaustion in a filmic format. However, if we found the conversation with our informants fascinating, and their personal spaces so beautiful, why not try to convey this in the film? This effort had two consequences. First, we began to consider the cinematographic genre of the urban symphony as the most suitable scheme for our story. An urban symphony is a visual discourse on the modern city, which depicts urban life from a particular vantage point. Some of the classics in the genre, such as *Berlin 1900*, show crowds, traffic, rush, working machinery, political rituals, and mass movement in public places—something that erupted in the first modern metropolis and got fixed in the concept of "urbanism as a way of life" by the Chicago school (Wirth 1969). Instead, our choice was to tell the city from the inside. This point of view has rarely been adopted. We developed an indoor urban symphony. The resulting poetics are of a different kind. The big city does not appear as an anonymous locus of commodities, industry, and mass human relations anymore. It is rather an arena for personal assertion: quest, surprise, and self-discovery. The movie

focuses on how something beautiful and enigmatic emerges at our homes: an order of our own, a universe.

This pursuit of a filmic format entails tensions of a practical kind. Written ethnography impels the privileging of conversation: you abandon yourself to the liveliness of the encounter. Shooting a movie introduces stronger requirements. To be editable, the interviewee's interventions must be punctuated by silences. The recordings must be free of noise, including that of the interviewer's voice, in a series of sequences that can be easily rearranged afterward. My natural impulse as conductor is to let myself go when chatting, overlapping with the interviewee's voice and falling into digressions. At the camera, Jorge Moreno would discreetly tap on my shoulder to alert me every time I was talking too much—please, stop ruining good sequences. This tension between the logic of research and that of an audiovisual endeavor refashioned the timing and framing of the interviews, as well as my own attire. For the sake of script continuity, I began to wear the same blue shirt and brown pants in all the shots. I had become a character within the story.

Second, the starring role of this urban indoor universe had to be narratively forged. To function well for an audience, a documentary needs characters. Manuela with her heirlooms, Celina and her daughter on the bed, Irene breastfeeding her baby, Camilo ironizing on his dream house, Norma with her dejá vù: they were all characters in their own right. Yet it was necessary to edit those voices to braid them together chorally. Chapter 5 will analyze the interesting effects of meaning that such a montage produces. The most noticeable is the pluralization of the voice, which becomes collective. The juxtaposition, collage, and contrast of topics and reflections creates dialogic insights in a process of reciprocal enlightenment. This polyphony engulfs, of course, our own voices as well.

Third, the symphonic format has the power to embrace the space in its materiality. Ambiences, objects, terraces, sky, corners, plants, light, windows, street noise, all entered the flow of discourse in a way that is difficult to achieve in writing. This was important for two reasons. Nowadays, too many authors invoke matter, energies, affects, feelings, senses, and emotions, but few are able to effectively perform such a promise—we are more often left with mere blathering on those things than with convincing guidance on them. The audiovisual is, by contrast, the perfect medium for accomplishing this.

There is another reason to sensually include the space. Speaking of intimacy, spatial closeness and sensory evocation are of the essence. How could these key dimensions be conveyed without image and sound? We put our best into producing a series of visual sequences and an appropriate soundtrack. Jorge Moreno produced several still lifes from stuff and places referred to in the stories by the informants. They were not merely juxtaposed but were articulated to unfold a discourse in their own right—as it indeed happens in the real world, where things and rooms intervene with true agency in the drama of our lives. I also composed a musical soundtrack for the film, in the form of four Latin-flavored variations on a famous Cuban bolero, "*La última noche que pasé contigo*" (The last night I spent with you). Together, the still life series and the soundtrack entwine in a coherent thread throughout the entire documentary, adding our own say to the whole.

SCREENING THE MOVIE

The Order I Live In has been screened in the three cities where it was filmed. The first time, in Mexico City, we used a rough cut or provisional version. The participants in the interviews and a selected number of friends acted as guest audience. After ten minutes of screening, we realized with horror that we were playing the wrong file. We had to stop, and while Jorge rebooted the thing, I entertained the audience by singing Mexican songs with my little *jarana*. I learned some lessons from the experience. Every screening is a performance, a unique event. Each time you show the movie, it is reborn under a different light. Certainly, this rule applies to texts of all kinds, for a text is a living entity whose meaning partially depends on its actualization by the practice of reading. In film, the watching happens synchronically, in real time. You can feel how people are concentrated or distracted, nodding with pleasure or shaking their heads. Interruptions and interferences—barking dogs, opening doors, people chatting or fiddling about with their cellphones—eventually happen. Key technical details, such as the equalization of sound and color temperature, fail every time. All these things have a communicative impact on such an incredibly plastic creature.

You shot a movie, but you don't own it. You have carefully produced, recorded, and edited it. You have gone over the film master a thousand times, ad nauseam. Yet, the first time you show it in public, it is born anew. You feel it as something alien. It belongs to others: the participants and the public. This strangely distanced but at the same time affective experience of authorship is radically different from what happens with papers, books, and reports. Such an effect is probably due to the performative nature of the medium and the collective modality of reception. The act of watching with others has the power to profoundly redefine the actions, sounds, and images taking place on screen. It is curious to see how people laugh, or get emotional, at very different points. Why are the puns of certain story lines mysteriously missed, or received with an icy silence, while other times they are amplified by a collective approval?

After the so-called ethnographic critique of the 1980s (Clifford and Marcus 1986), anthropology has been dealing with the foundations of ethnographic writing, scientific authorship, and the return of knowledge to the sites where it is coproduced. We have become wary about the intricacies of the role of the author and the communicative circuits in which a monograph gets inserted. These are not petty methodological details but important matters that impact the value of the whole ethnographic enterprise. It is urgent to rethink ethnographic formats and their circuits in a situation in which the traditional flow of this genre of communication has become altered. How to give due recognition to the contribution of many voices? How to handle the second life that our cultural texts are given?

I will return to these questions in the final chapter to extract a few methodological learnings from this whole research process—including the CEWs, the transurban journey, and the making of the documentary. In chapter 5, I will address the complex editing choices faced by the ethnographer in the methodological process of juxtaposing and combining individual stories in order to forge a collective voice. The main point is that these textual operations are governed by the same poetics of displacement, signature, closure, and reverberation analytically proposed as principles at work in the informants' generativity and productivity. This is a reflexive stance. In the concluding chapter, I will apply it in a more tangible way by disclosing a few personal learnings on collaboration, empathy, and remembrance as key foundations of complicity in any form of research on intimacies.

For now, a few comments should suffice on the variety of reactions that the screening produced. Whereas we are tempted to consider the publishing of a monograph as the final point in the ethnographic process, the screening of a documentary is a great opportunity to go back to the field, to reciprocate for the gifts received, and to explore convergences and divergences of interpretation with participants and audiences.

Most of the interviewees were glad to see themselves on screen and pleased with the results. Some let us know they were moved. After the premiere in Montevideo, the whole group gathered for a family photo and a celebration over beers. Dialogic editing generates an effect of resonance among stories that surprised many. Some of them were positively curious about the participants in other cities. "This breastfeeding mother in Madrid," a participant from Mexico said, "I would love to know her. I feel we have a lot in common." Others felt hooked by the charm displayed by certain storytellers. "This girl who tells you how to clean a bathroom, she is so funny." Although we had no strong negative reactions to the film, one person expressed her disappointment because her daughter did not make the final cut of the film (due to technical reasons, hours of shooting had to be discarded). Two more people expressed in private some dissonance regarding their role on screen. One was a recent father who confided his feelings about having a child:

When you see a human growing up, you understand everything. Your childhood, the role of your parents, your mother's worries, the family structure, those conflicts among siblings. . . . Everything gets connected. Everything! And one says: "It is true, now I understand. Why it was this way, why I did not understand this before." I tended to blame everything on my father's shitty character, on these unforgivable reactions from my mother, on whatever attitude my sister had. . . . No! You realize that everything has its way of getting connected. You see yourself in the chessboard of life: "Here I was." A sensation comes over you like: Whoa, that was it. That was it.

I find Diego terrific in the sequence, monologuing like a Shakespearean character about the circle of life. True, the arrival of children gives you a mirror, a weird passage after which you fully understand who you are. "I see no problem with the excerpt," I said to him. "I love what you say." "The problem," he replied, "is that my father is actually such a nice guy. He does not have shitty character at all; this was just a manner of speaking. I am afraid that, if he eventually sees this, he could believe I am talking literally of him." I tried to dissipate his doubts with honesty. The discourse was clearly figurative. It was unlikely that his father would take it the wrong way. We agreed to relax about it.

Xochitl expressed remorse too, after contemplating herself in the film. In her sequence, she summarizes how important the role of a mother is, no matter the professional sacrifices it may embody:

Sometimes I wonder why I am not such a renowned dancer, or choreographer. I was in the scene; I knew all the big names! But my decision has been to also be a mother. I am convinced it is a great job, to help them grow, to help them understand—even those things you don't fully understand yourself. He [the son] is a philosopher, indeed. He often asks very complicated questions, for which I don't have an answer. You must be committed to it. And it may sound awkward, but it hurts me to see so many kids that don't have this. I say: "This cannot be!" Those children who lack love, or support, or anyone to tell them: "Look, things are so and so." This is essential to any human being, whether you are a choreographer, or a chef, or whatever. Over time this has become quite clear to me.

For Xochitl, the source of discomfort was an undertone of sadness that pops up throughout the confession. "I see myself so serious, so sad on the screen," she worried. Being a mother is important, but it is not everything. Xochitl is a choreography teacher. We knew this from the moment we entered her home, for the first thing you see on the wall is a picture of her, dancing on a stage. For people trained to have professional careers, parenting has a tinge of regret—or at least a wonder—about lost opportunities and alternative life paths. What would I have become, without kids? Such feelings are necessarily ambivalent, bittersweet, and difficult to utter without shame or guilt. I explained to her why I had picked out this fragment in particular. "You are so brave in the sequence. Somebody had to say it. Because every parent knows: of the many sacrifices we make in parenting, the biggest one is how it affects your career. Of course," I added, "I would have liked to be Max Weber or George Simmel too. But I am just Paco Cruces, a homemaker who spends half of his time in the kitchen, frying potatoes." She smiled with this exchange of confessions, then agreed to leave the sequence in the movie. While in other cases we discarded any potentially conflicting or harmful material, in these ones I pleaded with them to approve the sequences.

The premiere in Madrid was a highlight. It took place in CentroCentro, one of the emblematic venues at Cibeles square, the very core of the city (see figure 2.3). We gathered two hundred people, with authorities from the university and the city council, faculty colleagues and students, Madrid's CEW participants, old friends from out of town, neighbors, even my wife and kids. Jorge's wide network was also there. It was exciting. The youngest spectator was my twelve-year-old son. He asked for popcorn and gave me the best critique: "I thought I was going to get bored, but I didn't."

After Madrid, Montevideo, and Mexico City, the movie has been shown in filmic or academic venues in Toulouse, France; Zagreb, Croatia; Göttingen, Germany; Lund, Sweden; Santiago de Compostela, Córdoba, Valencia, and

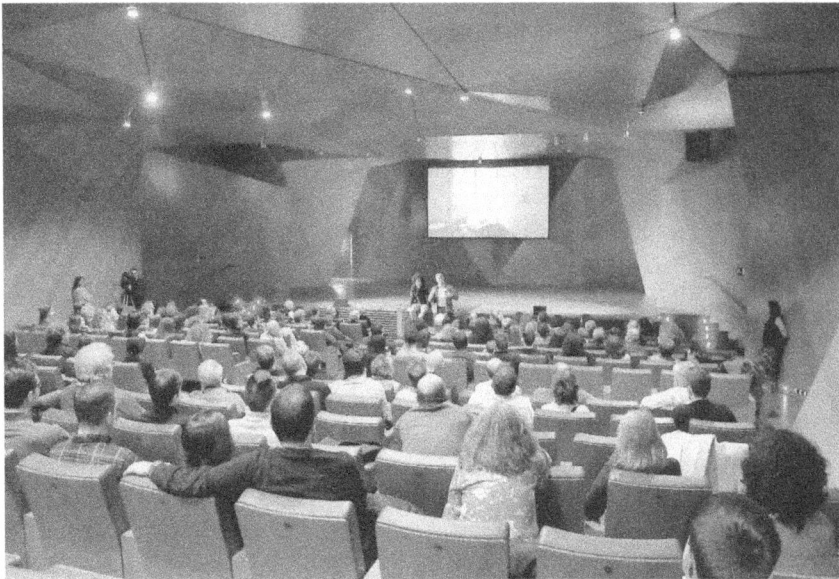

Figure 2.3. Screening of the film in the CentroCentro cultural center, Madrid, 2018 (courtesy of UNED).

Sevilla, Spain; and Berkeley, San Diego, and Irvine in the United States. Nowadays it is available on Canal UNED, our open-source university channel.[9] The reactions of the public have been moving. "It is like being invited to a late-night conversation in someone's living room," we were told. We are pleased that this invented format works well for a broad public, not just for anthropologists and colleagues. Our fear was that so much discourse on the details of daily life could turn out to be unable to hold the attention of the spectator for one long hour. What really happens is that people see themselves in the stories. In the Q&A, the most common reactions were the desire to know more about the real people behind the characters and the inclination to share their own stories.

In this way, this film born of dialogues was continued through further dialogues. This fact recalls a dialogical stance of a more general purview. "The importance of learning how to read does not rest on being able to read something written by others," Jesús Martín Barbero has explained, "but in being able to tell your own story" (Martín-Barbero and Lluch 2012, 38). The pains and pleasures linked to the exposure of intimacy relate to this "drama of self-recognition": the process by which you, happily or painfully, become conscious of who you are by contemplating someone else's story (Martín-Barbero 1989, 12, 165).

When inquiring about intimacy, the key problem is not how to explain it, reduce it, or reform it but how to join it—in the words of Deleuze and Guattari, "how to join the World, or to meld with it" (quoted in Ingold 2010, 10). The real challenge is to recount intimacy without destroying it. Because, as something immensely delicate and brittle, intimacy dissipates as soon as you touch it, like a butterfly's wing. What the screening process teaches us is that intimacy can be shared, and this sharing is a frank source of joy. Hence, we should consider intimacy to consist not so much of those precious things that people want preserved but rather of all those deemed worthy of being shared. Both the magic and the appeal of intimacy rest on this drive for sharing. It is a virtuous circuit, where we tried to contribute something of our own.

NOTES

1. The impact of digital technologies has produced a robust literature about online research. Hine 2008; Kelty et al. 2009; and Coleman 2010 are important references. Zafra 2010, 2017; Lasén 2012; Winocur 2015; and Lluch 2017 represent solid examples of this kind of work in Spanish. Regarding the penetration of the digital domain in intimacy, see the ethnographies by Kaufmann 2010a; Nippert-Eng 2010; Hochschild 2012; and Ehn, Löfgren, and Wilk 2016.

2. Matadero Medialab, https://www.medialab-matadero.es/en.

3. This first series of workshops in Madrid, Prosumers: Logics of Production/ Consumption in the Cultures of the Web, was coordinated by me with Amparo Lasén, Héctor Fouce, Fernando González de Requena, Karina Boggio, Fernando Monge, Montserrat Cañedo, Gloria G. Durán, and Sara Sama. A presentation video in Spanish can be seen at https://www.medialab-matadero.es/en/videos/presentation-prosumers -consumptionproduction-dynamics-network-cultures.

4. The two volumes of *L'invention du quotidian* by Michel de Certeau (1990, 1994) inspired the design of the workshops. We intended to document his idea of a "consumerist productivity": a proliferation of daily inventions that allow one to read, beyond the seemingly opaque activity of the subjects, their perceptive, valuative, and practical dispositions or "tactics." This entails defying the image of passivity and dullness currently attributed to acts of consumption in general and, by extension, to everyday habits and chores. Certeau's ideas displace the research questions from the "what" and "how many" to the "how." By means of idiosyncratic "*manières de faire*" or "arts of doing," specific subjects inscribe themselves in their quotidian gestures and routines, even under conditions of domination or submission. These ideas were applicable to the relationship between production and consumption in the online world, where, for example, the activities of reading and writing have become insepa-rable. In a second moment, they led us to understand in terms of genuine "action" the many relational, reproductive, corporeal, sensorial, and affective dimensions of intimacy-making.

5. I owe these suggestions on the situated character of interpretation to Honorio Velasco.

6. A final balance in Spanish of Metropolitan Intimacies, the second series of these workshops, can be seen at https://www.medialab-matadero.es/en/videos/metropolitan -intimacies-collective-exploration-workshop-inside-outside. The Tupperware Party workshop, conducted by Gloria G. Durán, can be followed in a video in Spanish at https://www.medialab-matadero.es/en/videos/workshop-tupperware-party-conquer -world.

7. The overseas sites were Centro Cultural de España, CEIS research centre, and Facultad de Psicología at Universidad de la República, in Montevideo; CENART Multimedia Center and UAM-Iztapalapa, in Mexico City.

8. This project was coincident in time with others with a sharper emphasis on digital life, including an online questionnaire for Mexican and Spanish internauts, used during our 2012 research on young urban creators (García Canclini, Cruces, and Urteaga 2012); interviews and participant observation in Spanish companies in the sector of the New Economy (Reygadas, Cruces et al. 2011); and ethnographies on forms of digital reading (Cruces 2017). The findings include new concepts of work at organizations and start-ups; a growing imbrication between the worlds of work and life, with a tendency to blur their conventional boundaries; new kinds of job and professional profiles by young creators that were employees or self-employed in the creative industries; trending economies of innovation; the impacts of connec-tivity on forms of time reckoning, subjectivity, and sociality; and the rise of online

communities and collaborative social movements mobilized for free licenses and cultural commons.

9. The film *The Order I Live In* can be accessed and downloaded in VOS version at Canal UNED: https://canal.uned.es/video/5c07ac67b1111f5b718bb727 and in Vimeo at https://vimeo.com/240680831?embedded=true&source=vi meo_logo&owner=5193433.

Chapter 3

Stories of the Self

TO TELL A STORY

In 1983, Susan Sontag and John Berger debated about the art of storytelling on the TV program *Voices*. Claiming that such an art form belongs first and foremost to the realm of daily life, Berger argues,

> If I think of somebody telling a story, I see a group of people huddled together, and around them a vast space, quite frightening. Maybe they are huddled against a wall, maybe they're around a fire. And, for me, somewhere in the very idea of a story, there is something to do with shelter. The shelter perhaps of the voyager, the traveler, who has come home, who has lived to tell the story. Or the soldier, who's come back, who has survived. So, there is this almost physical sense of shelter, where the story gets a kind of habitation, a kind of home. But then, inside the story, there is another kind of shelter. Because what the story narrates and tells is sheltered within the story from oblivion, forgetfulness, and daily indifference. (Berger and Sontag 1983)

Berger proposes the example of the death of a shepherd who was his friend. After his passing, Berger felt moved to write about his life. Telling stories is, Berger says, a way of demonstrating that a particular human life took place, was fulfilled, and had meaning. It fights back against oblivion and the absurd, affirming life at the very moment of its loss. This is why the writer, like the storyteller before, is "the secretary of death," and every story is "a rescue operation." Beyond their existential content, these remarks draw attention to something formal: the importance of endings and beginnings, both in life and in stories. Berger (Berger and Sontag 1983) goes a step further by proposing a link between the two: "Stories begin at their end. I mean, in life. The story of Romeo and Juliet in a sense begins at their death—that is when their story is given form. The end is not always death, but it quite frequently is." This never-ending bond between life and story might actually be characteristic of Berger's own literary and critical work, where the flow of living and the acts of narration so often become entangled.

Throughout the conversation, Sontag resists this vision. For her, this narrative model excessively privileges life story over other more modern, sophisticated, and polyhedric ways of telling a story in print or film. She makes it clear that this is just an archaic conception, one based on the proximity of the teller (or writer) to the community where the act of relating is doomed to return. Such an oral model contrasts with a modernist literary conception, closer to novels, journals, and cinema, that considers the story an author's original creation made for an anonymous readership. The purpose of this recounting is not to have one's experience recognized or mirrored but rather to enlarge the worlds in which one lives. We don't need stories to reproduce experience but to escape from it. Not to see our life reflected but rather to explore the possibilities of living a thousand lives in a thousand places.

In their discussion, Berger and Sontag enact this conceptual opposition. They capture technical dimensions such as the handling of time and point of view, the continuities/discontinuities between oral and printed forms of stories, and the responsibilities of the author toward their audiences. Berger, unlike Sontag, tends to blur any radical line between essay and fiction. "Real" and "imagined" stories share common roots, regardless of the notion of "truth" on which such a distinction is currently based. In the end, this attitude has to do with the significance of life as a model for storytelling. "There is no intensity in the story which actually matches the intensity of what is lived," Berger confesses. "And I think we have two different views, because in a way you say you want to be carried away by the story. I am saying: I want the story to stop things being carried away into oblivion, and into indifference."

"MOM, I AM TAKING THIS PHOTO FOR YOU"

Whether the Bergerian conception of life as narrative model extends to other forms of narrative practice (as Sontag rightfully objected) or not, this conception certainly sheds light on the microstories collected throughout our fieldwork. It applies to an aspect that I find particularly intriguing: the connection between good form and moral content. The notion of beginnings and endings is, in this respect, akin to the folklorists' poetic justice introduced in the first chapter: a surprising twist (too good to be true) by which we grasp the existence of a deeper meaning in what has been told. These forms of narrative closure connect a story's good form with its overall sense.

This connection came to the fore during Do You Recall?, a workshop on family photos held in Madrid. We wanted to re-create an activity that spontaneously takes place in everyday life: looking at photographs together and sharing stories about them. Prior to the advent of digital photography, family albums were an important cultural prop around which the household core consolidated a shared memory of its members, fixed key events, and asserted the continuity of generations. Our workshop aimed to explore the selection of photos and the characters portrayed.

Alba, a young schoolteacher from the north of Spain, stood out from the handful of participants. She was living with her fiancé while looking for a job in Madrid. As the youngest daughter in a large family, she had inherited a wooden box filled with photos, and with it, a whole family saga. She showed up smiling with the box under her arm, ready to share the treasure. As we will see later on in this chapter, family memories can be as much a blessing as a curse, but Alba felt lucky and proud. Her light blue eyes brightened when offering details about her private history, sprinkled with those of distant kin:

> This is the most curious [of my family photos]. Here is my aunt Amalia, with a suitor of hers who came back from America with my grandfather. He came back, fell in love with her, wooed her, but nothing. Nothing, she didn't want him. Then, on the very day she was going to say yes—because he had given an ultimatum: "Well, I'm leaving. I will wait for you in the fairgrounds. If you show up, all right. If you don't, I give up on you." And as it happens, this time she was going to say yes. But alas! Her little sister got sick that day. And she had to stay at home, taking care of her. Thus, he left forever. She never married. And she missed him very much until the last day of her life.

The loves that misfortune twisted up may come back at the end of our lives. Does Alba's account not materialize Berger's claim? Whenever a life is lived, a story comes to recount it. The family album is a place where lived lives mutate into something else: a recounted life, or rather a life to be recounted. This subtle transformation—from life to story—tends to take on a slightly ritualized form. And, in the common type of family saga, like the one contained in Alba's box, poetic justice often makes a sudden appearance—like in Berger's stories of peasants and shepherds. Poetic justice, so typical of happy endings, may be at work too in tragic, unhappy ones—with round endings and paradoxical shifts. In this way, we see how the careful recollection of photos, a task that women have traditionally taken on, orders the lives of the members of the family in such a way that they can be understood as significant narratives: meaningful lives, twice-told for others. Poetic justice extends from a particular life (with its comings and goings, ups and downs, longings and fulfillments) to the family album as an exemplary model.

Nevertheless, the photo album's significance goes far beyond the handing down of stories from one generation to the next. More than a mere repository of the past, it is a virtual place where those story lines crisscross and where everyone's gaze is expected to meet, sooner or later. This is the reason why Alba's recounting of Aunt Amalia is pertinent to her own self-understanding. We got this with the next photograph:

ALBA: This other one is from my graduation trip. We went to Rome. I had previously seen a photo of my mother when she visited there. She was standing on the stairs of Piazza di Spagna wearing this same skirt. So, I wanted to take a similar photo myself. I packed my mother's skirt and brought it with me [to Rome] and posed, more or less as she had done [in the photograph], on a similar stairway in Trastevere.

CONVENOR: For whom did you take this photo?

ALBA: In some sense I took it for her. It was like saying, "Mom, I am standing where you stood, seeing what you saw, even when you had no idea that I was going to be here."

Standing on the stairs, disguised as her mother thirty years earlier, Alba makes a remarkable use of photography to build a narrative that can be shared with others. She enacts the very notion of the family album as a place where the gaze of family members meets. As she declares, this is a mirror-photo. The mother will be able to recognize herself in the daughter's disguise. Reciprocally, the photo shows Alba looking directly into the camera, anticipating her mother's future gaze. So it is a time tunnel too. It binds three different moments: the first, the remote instant when the mother originally posed; the second, the present moment of taking the photo, when the daughter replicates the same gesture in Rome; the third, an anticipated moment, still to come in the future—but actually contained in the way the model gazes straight at the lens. The photo captures the daughter imagining herself looking at the photo with her mother, perhaps blissfully recalling that shared past together. Time collapses in this overlapping of mirroring images. In a ritual fashion, this photograph enacts a sophisticated narrative that asserts the common identity of mother and daughter as well as the permanence of their loving bond beyond the passing of time.

STRIVING FOR STYLE

Of course, not all storytelling contains Alba's sophisticated treatment of form. In natural speech, scripts tend to be hybrid, indefinite, and sketchy. The narrative structure is not to be found in the story itself but in the understandings built between narrator and listeners in an open-ended process of conversation.

Hence, structure belongs to the order of dialogue rather than to the text itself. Nonetheless, many of our collected stories bore a family resemblance to classic literary, dramatic, and cinematographic genres (comedy, parody, drama, tragedy, allegory, etc.), as well as to love stories, filthy stories, travel and personal journals, lyrical arias, and urban legends. (About the surprising continuities of classical narrative plots in contemporary cinema, see for example, Balló and Pérez 2006). This formal resemblance includes beautiful, pleasant endings, which imprint a convincing moral strength on the stories.

In the preceding chapters, I mentioned some of the stories from collective exploration workshops (CEWs) and filmed interviews. Like Alba's, they were exchanged in a lively give-and-take, with much laughter and emotion. Let us remember, for example, the stories from our Housekeeping workshop. We had the girl who resented her family's rules; the girl who instead grew up in an apartment filled with books but with no rules; the man who inhabited "an uninhabited home"—because he was unable to finish a seemingly endless refurbishing of his house; the young man who quarreled with his girlfriend about the right way to do their chores; the woman whose boyfriend made her feel like a messy person; the amateur artist looking for the hidden beauty of a laundry basket; the young woman with a strong drive for chaos growing inside her heart.

This is the kind of material that nourishes our corpus. We can call them *minimal stories*, short expressions that meet the minimum basic requirements of a story (Gerald 1973). We mentioned some of these elements apropos of Finnegan's (1998, 9) monograph on urban tales: (1) a protagonist, (2) an event or action unfolding a plot, (3) some facilitating or impeding actants, (4) a temporal scheme, (5) some internal principles of evaluation and moral coherence, and (6) a set of performance conventions. Many of our stories contain these six components. However, a substantial part of the interviews and workshops consisted not of stories properly speaking but of other genres of discourse, such as dialogues, descriptions, arguments, statements, questions, and volitions. How far should we go in treating all of them as "narrative"? Some contemporary narratologists convincingly favor a broad use of the term, arguing that what counts as narrative in a specific context may vary greatly and take many forms on the surface (Herman 2009; Herman and Vervaeck 2005). What a narrative essentially provides is a set of causal and temporal connections between events in the world. This can be arrived at by means of the kind of explicit temporal statement linked to the occurrence of a past event that Labov and Waletzky (1967) called "oral accounts of personal experience." This is the canonic model that, after their pioneering essay, has become the morphological ideal type for narrative research. But temporal and causal connections have a broader, more general range. They can also be achieved by implicit means, such as when some of the basic components of plot, action, or temporality within a story are elided or merely presupposed; or whenever a subjacent narrative understanding seems to be superimposed (as a subtext) over a set of accounts deployed in the form of images, descriptions, arguments, or factual assertions. Here I will not adopt a formalist, restrictive approach but instead consider narrative in its broader sense, as a diversity of discursive schemata that provide temporal, causal, and inferential connections. As we will see, in some of the microstories considered, the elements may only be implicit, or they may appear in combination with other genres in hybrid modalities of discourse. And yet a genuine narrative quality can be perceived and documented through them.

Of course, the dangers of an overextended use of the term must also be considered: not everything is narrative. And there are good reasons for this to be so. A pan-narrative view on human cognition misses other forms of well-documented ways of knowledge and consciousness that make up reason, communication, and mind. It also falls short of a thorough consideration of the totality of means by which human beings inhabit the world and give meaning to it—not just through stories but also through sensory experience, mathematical calculation, logical inference, and systematic experimentation. Moreover, it is the very proclivity of human imagination toward narrative forms, the fact that we are so hardwired for them, that gives narrativity a dangerous dark side—the one that critics of "post-truth" regimes of public communication have expressed concern about in recent times. Nigerian novelist Chimamanda Adichie (2018), for example, warns against what she calls "the dangers of the single story": the one-sidedness that comes from resorting to a single, overarching, and reductive explanatory scheme for all unknown realities. Tyler Cowen (an economist specializing in marginal cost analysis; 2009) has also given clever reasons to be "suspicious of good stories," among others their potential for oversimplification, Manicheism, and pan-explanation. Yet, I think that such dangers can only be countered by pluralizing our sources of storytelling and by revising their scope and limits—never by underestimating their power.

What is the form of these stories? What do they talk about? These are the two questions addressed in this chapter. The two questions are connected: in line with the Bergerian motto that life and stories pertain to each other, I will examine how issues of form, style, rhythm, and performance are bound to a story's cognitive, emotional, and interactional value in the context of intimacy building. It is precisely because of their performativity in daily life that questions of form and style, on the one hand, and those of content and meaning, on the other, have to be tackled together. My key argument is that poetics—the narrative and figurative use of language—is not an ornamental, displaced, roundabout way of speaking about things. It is integral to everyday life itself. Narrating, commenting, imagining, and naming whatever happens to us is an essential process that gives form and meaning to our lives, identities, and futures.

I focus on three traits that can be found throughout this narrative corpus: (1) a remarkable, albeit minimalist, search for style; (2) the conventions of modern living as an unnoticed background; and (3) the starring role of ego as a character in a plot governed by the agonistic task of making a space of one's own.

First, these stories have good form. They show a remarkable search for style, in the sense of a purposeful selection of expressive resources. In some of them, the narrative structure may be explicit, while in others it is incomplete or sketched out. Yet the listener can sense the storyteller striving to frame the account in a convincing way. One method for doing this is by using what the theorists of oral tradition have called "generic intertextuality" (Bauman 2004): by recalling, remaking, or even parodying scripts from a variety of genres, either oral or artistic. The frequency with which poetic justice is found in certain stories is also a good example of the search for good form. Typical sequences like "the hunter is hunted," "winner by accident," "happy ending," and "what bad luck" contain concluding formulas that, by surprising the listener, bring out a hidden rationale from the story. Certainly, poetic justice is one of the formal traits that make urban legends and other traditional genres recognizable (Brunvand 2001), but it also seems to be somewhat present in our daily conversation.

Second, these stories focus on a specific topic: the conventions of living. Through them, different ways of living are portrayed, discussed, understood, and negotiated against the unspoken background of modern living, which is a subtext that is mostly taken for granted. It consists of shared cultural values, practices, and assumptions. Ideas of comfort, decorum, and the art of living are at the heart of this complex, which pervades the uses and conception of domestic space and its technologies.

Third, these stories are oriented from a speaker's perspective. They are indeed tales of the self: of one's own deeds, vicissitudes, and predicaments. In order to articulate a plot, the speaker takes on a leading role in an action that requires the intervention of a multiplicity of other characters: their partner, parents, family, friends, landlord, furniture, domestic objects, electronic devices, kids, pets, fate, and so on.

These three aspects appear to be somehow conflated, a fact that calls for the consideration of this kind of microstory as a speech genre in its own right. Together, they define the minimal story. The reader will find tokens from a larger sample selected with a criterion of relevance, not statistical representativity. The cases illustrate the silent poetic processes at work: displacement, closure, signature, and resonance, which will be explained at length in chapter 5.

MY LIFE IN A TWEET

Could this stylization of speech also be expected in shorter, written microstories like those of contemporary mediated interactions via Twitter or
Instagram? We introduced a question on this topic in an online survey for a
research project on young urban creative producers in Madrid and Mexico
City (García Canclini, Cruces, and Urteaga 2012). "Put your life in a tweet"
was our request to around a thousand young Internet users, asking them to
summarize their lives in 140 characters or less. The challenge was productive. Although the limitation of space forces the answers to be simple and
stereotyped, the poetics of evocative stylization, metaphoric elaboration, and
generic intertextuality are at work.

> Calm, balanced, funny, loving, cheerful, centered, mature, stable, peaceful, ten-
> der. (Mexican woman, thirty years old)

> Good, beautiful, inexpensive. [*Bueno bonito barato.*] (Spanish man, twenty
> years old)

> I am the nicest healthiest most successful millionaire happy cheerful honest
> positive handsome sexy positive desirable loved and cared girl of the world.
> (Mexican woman, thirty-three years old)

> I am a successful and lucky guy, I work hard and do my best in everything I do.
> (Spanish man, twenty years old)

> Everything goes as planned, my universe is aligned in order to succeed in every
> aspect of my life, my family is great. (Mexican man, twenty-four years old)

> My life is happy, complete. I learn from mistakes. I grow. I smile with the good
> things. If I fall, I get up. I move ahead. No surrender. I take on challenges.
> (Mexican woman, thirty-three years old)

> A happy person who has enjoyed wonderful moments in life. The only thing left
> is to give thanks to God. (Mexican man, twenty-five years old)

> I want to stop being a conformist and begin to live a life that pleases God.
> (Mexican woman, twenty-three years old)

> A shitty life (with nothing) or almost nothing. (Spanish woman, twenty-two
> years old)

> [My life] is shit. I will never become anything that I really like and that gives
> me enough to eat. (Spanish woman, twenty-one years old)

[My life] is a mistake that should be ended. (Spanish man, twenty-five years old)

You must know me before criticizing me! For you indeed do not know what I'm like. (Mexican woman, twenty years old)

What a disgusting life. I want a job. I want a future! (Spanish woman, twenty years old)

Hello I wanna study fashion design but I don't have money. (Mexican man, twenty years old)

I am a 24-year-old girl. I love learning. I am very convivial. For me to live without friends is like being a garden without flowers, LOL. I am very competitive, both when it's time to work or to study. I like to give it my all. (Spanish woman, twenty-four years old)

I am passionate about sports, I love Barça, living with my partner and my family, to travel and enjoy and to have a job in accordance with my professional skills. (Spanish man, thirty years old)

I am a very creative person, witty, amiable, honest, sincere, uncomplicated, intelligent. (Mexican woman, twenty-three years old)

The result is aphoristic, following a remarkable aesthetic of brevity. The tone swings dramatically, from detached irony to confidential innocence, from humor to despair. Some of these tweets are reminiscent of a variety of contemporary rhetoric styles, including self-help literature, religious preaching, sitcom dialogue, dark humor, job interviewing, corporate mission statements, traditional sayings, protest slogans, customer complaints, and other genres, written and oral.

However, these online "selfie-tweets" seem, by comparison to the richness of the life stories gathered from workshops and interviews, a poor reduction of the topic. Here we remain ignorant to almost everything about the emitter, including their background, the circumstances of their enunciation, and their communicative intentions. Most of the answers take on the form of descriptions (by adding adjectives as attributes of the self) or short statements (like plans and intentions) rather than narrative frames properly speaking. However, in many of them the seed of a story can be glimpsed, whether they introduce ego struggling after goals of self-fulfillment, emphasize the obstacles and difficulties found along the way, or convey bitter sentiments of frustration after failure.

Some tweets economically resound various social discourses. Let us consider the first three. Do they not adopt the style of a classified advertisement?

The subject is described in a raw way, by means of a juxtaposition of adjectives, very much like in newspapers' personal ads section. The effect is ironic. By counterfeiting a commercial discourse, it presents someone crudely selling themselves in the open. Irony can be defined as a trope consisting of the displaced use of an expression in a situation when it cannot or must not be taken literally (Fernandez 2001). Confronted with ironic speech, the receiver is compelled to question the seriousness of the assertion and to look for alternative decodings. In the most radical example, the ironic utterance, due to its inadequacy to the context, can be given sense only by attributing to it an entirely opposite meaning. Irony is at work to various degrees in these three tweets. The first of them ("Calm, balanced, funny") matches the form of a classified ad quite literally, to the point that we cannot know for certain if such a calm, balanced, funny, loving, and cheerful Mexican woman is mocking us—rejecting the request as impertinent and indiscreet—or being extremely adamant in fulfilling it. The second and third tweets, though, do not leave room for doubt. "Good, beautiful, inexpensive" (*Bueno, bonito, barato*) is a Spanish commonplace for cheap things sold as great. It originates in the cries of merchants who voiced their goods out loud in popular markets and fairs. Such semantic borrowing has a twofold effect. On a literal level, it seems to affirm: "Ladies and gentlemen, come and look. I have great value." On an ironic level, though, the sentence subtly alludes to the devaluation and hardships currently suffered by young people in Spain. It does so by comparing the speaker himself with cheap merchandise. In some respect, this is in line with the angry complaints that depict Spanish youths' lives as "shitty" or "a mistake." It is important to note that this survey was conducted just a few months before the political revolt of 2011 (known as 15-M) by young protesters throughout Spain. But unlike other tweets, this last one does not choose a literal language of resentment and denunciation but a semantic detour through a rich mental association with the deceitful bargaining typical of trade contexts. It thus contains a micronarrative. Finally, the third one of these tweets pushes the irony to its peak by resorting to another trope: hyperbole. In the first tweet, we encountered someone "balanced" and "funny"; in the second, "good" and "inexpensive." What are we driven to think of a person who claims to be "the nicest healthiest most successful millionaire happy cheerful . . . in the world"? Exaggeration works by knocking down every limit, making the expression impossible to believe. We may recall here Cintron's (2009) contention that the ethos of modernity is hyperbolic in essence, because it compels us to create never-ending novelties by a continuous breakdown of the boundaries of what was formerly considered real, in a dialectic of excess. In this particular case, hyperbolic immodesty is produced with the help of style markers, like the suppression of periods and the repetition of words. It has a comedic effect: the insane denial of any personal constraint, including the hardness and suffering, resented so much in other young internauts' selfie-tweets. This person's self-assertion is (rhetorically) beyond limits, a superhero capacity that makes her immune to any obstacle coming from the real world.

These three tweets intertextually refer to social discourses in order to ironically undercut their own credibility. Conversely, others look for external sources of legitimacy and trustworthiness. The person who states "my universe is aligned in order to succeed," like the one who "does his best in everything," or the one who "gives it her all," seem to be appropriating widespread, *prêt-a-porter* discourses from positive psychology, emotional management, and self-help literature. (A comparative analysis of these narratives can be found in Guaderrama 2012, 273–298.)

All this suggests how the construction of a life story, even the extremely brief kind contained in a tweet, is always a creative patchwork that comments on pieces taken from other sources. Any life story is paradoxically polyphonic and intertextual in this way, following Bajtin's dictum about heteroglossia: our accent is always borrowed from someone else.

The examples taken from Alba's box of photographs, the Housekeeping CEWs, and these selfie-tweets clearly indicate a stylistic search for discursive coherence. However, this fact should not be overstated. Their relation to the great canonical and literary forms does not go further than a family resemblance or an opportunistic evocation. They are kept, by definition, tactical and inconsequential. They were not made to last but to be exchanged, to present rather than represent. Structure is always in the making. It is a bridge, so to speak, built by the teller and the listener, negotiated between the schemata that the teller has in mind and the responses that they are able to anticipate from the audience. This exchange provides a disposable ephemeral structure, reminding us of Bakhtin's conception of dialogue as "the simultaneous unity of differences in the act of enunciation" (in Holquist 1990, 36). These scripts do not abide by the strictures of a specific genre; rather, they follow the speaker's poetic strategies to communicate to others the speaker's position in life and to give a coherent account of their singularity.

WOMAN AT THE WINDOW

The composition of the household has been a key factor among the people interviewed. Families in different moments of their cycle, couples with no children, people living alone, and students living in shared apartments were the most typical groupings. There were still others, often described as transitional arrangements, "in between" the more conventional ones. Most of our interviewees recognized having passed various stages before arriving at their present situation. The types of home were quite determinant of the practices and concerns of the dweller and steered the path our conversations took.

There were several students sharing apartments. Iago, a young Italian artist, was living in Madrid with four other people, including Spaniards and foreigners, in a neighborhood near the university. His interview revolved around the high rotation of people in the house, the emergence of rules for living together, and the inheritance of a few bizarre objects left behind by former dwellers and kept as decorative souvenirs: a carbonized piece of pizza that had been thrown on top of a lamp after a party, which was still there, covered in dust; five big armchairs to watch TV in the living room, one for each roommate; a rope with which one of them used to (comically) threaten to hang himself, in case he did not pass the course; and an old piggy bank filled with coins to be used for a fantasized collective trip that never took place. The difficulties of housekeeping and these emerging symbols of fraternity were key topics for those students.

In the case of Samuel and Jonas, a gay couple with Jewish roots living in Mexico City's *zona rosa*, the focus was different. The history of their relationship notably overlapped with that of their dwelling in the apartment. It is a story that began by wrestling with their families about the decision to come out of the closet and move in together. It continues with the struggle to find an affordable place in the hyperexpensive city center. It then goes on about the joys and sorrows of having to share the space with unreliable tenants. It concludes with a happy ending, when they finally found a woman who fit in smoothly in the always complicated puzzle of sharing a space.

The most remarkable among our students' narratives is that of Norma, the girl who signed her name inside closets. She had already told two interesting stories during Personal Objects, a CEW in Mexico City. On that occasion, she mentioned her recent struggles with a rare type of diabetes. It was also a delight to hear her reminisce about her childhood memories, with the anxieties of constantly moving to new family houses and the comforting solution she found of signing her name, with the dates of their arrival and departure, deep inside the closets. As I will argue later, the very idea of signature is a key component of the poetic operations put in motion in the process of owning an intimate space. I think that Norma, a young anthropology and film researcher, was fully aware of this idea. She was giving an elegant narrative form to it.

This entanglement of reflection and storytelling came to the fore when we visited Norma in Colonia Narvarte. Here she shares a big apartment with two male roommates. "Hello. Come on in," she greets us happily at the door. The living room is ample and quiet, connected to an open kitchen. In the sink, a pile of recently washed dishes. The living room, modestly furnished, is the only common room in the house: a big couch, a couple of armchairs, a lamp. Her bedroom, in contrast, is bright and carefully decorated. We decide to have the interview there. In our movie, Jorge's keen eye opens the shot wider with each sequence of her testimony, revealing the full range of the bedroom's beautiful shades of light. Once the camera is set, Norma begins her monologue.

We are very comfortable here, especially with the neighborhood, you know? The feeling of such a chaotic city leaves you so exhausted. . . . You simply arrive home, and you know you can relax here. Because, although there is some noise, it is nothing compared to the rest of the city, which is deafening. Where I used to live in Xalapa, only women lived in the building, just women. Mostly widows. The ones that weren't were divorcées. And me, alone. So, it was really quiet, also because you had to walk down a long corridor; the apartments were at the very end. You could not hear any noise from the street. Only around noon, one could listen to the old ladies chatting: "*Ay*, look how my orchid has grown," "*Ay*, here's the recipe for this or that." But after six in the evening, not a peep. And they were always looking out for me to make sure that I got home safe. At first it was uncomfortable, you know? Like they were invading my privacy. But then it was like, "If anything happens to me one day, these women are going to go look for me immediately." Then, it was OK. But it also was like, "Hey, you got a postcard from your sister. She says she is OK." What? Why did you read my sister's postcard? [laugh] . . . After a year and a half living here, I still haven't met my neighbors. You run into them in the corridor like this [hanging her head], "Good evening," "Good morning," and they don't even look at you. It feels weird, after having had neighbors who read your postcards, very weird. In Veracruz, people are different. They like to touch you, you know? I mean, you may be in line to buy potatoes, and then the lady at your back: "*Ay, mija*, what lovely hair, blah blah blah," and she touches you [caressing her hair], and "What lovely cheeks," and stuff and "Come on, please help me with that." Plenty of contact, see? Here [in Mexico City] there is also a lot of contact, but a different kind. I mean, you take the subway and cannot help but be touched. Contact by overcrowding! Because you go [crammed] this way, you have someone's armpit here [in your face]. And in case someone here touches you the same way that they touch you in Veracruz, you'd better worry because it is not normal. [In Veracruz] people at the stores are extremely kind. You can be in line to buy tortillas and you learn about the life story of the person in front, the one behind, the one at the counter. . . . And here [in Mexico City] nobody talks to strangers. Once, in the subway I went to the cashier and said, "Good morning. I would like so and so." The lady almost burst into tears. She tells me, "*Ay, mija*, thank you so much." "Why?" "Well, here nobody says good morning to me. I really appreciate it." And this shocked me, you know? You say good morning, good evening, and maybe they don't even look at you. But this lady almost burst into tears because I said good morning! Which in Veracruz is totally normal. . . . After seven years in Veracruz, we got used to a lot of warmth. This is something you really miss here. Talking to a stranger with no worries. Asking for directions. I don't know, when you ask for directions here, people feel obliged to give them. Even if they don't know where you wanna go, they give you directions anyway, and you get lost. In Veracruz, if you get on a bus and you ask the lady sitting at your side, "Excuse me, ma'am, where is the stop for the Anthropology Museum?" "*Ay*, I don't know, but you can get down here," and suddenly someone behind you chimes in, "No, you better go that way," and the next one. . . . All of a sudden, you have the whole bus giving you instructions! This is beautiful. It feels like a big hug. But here people are always in a rush and do this very impolitely. Most often they give you directions no matter if they don't know where you are going, and they only make you more lost. This is weird for me. It would be better if they just tell you they don't know.

Norma is taking a very roundabout way to address the history of her apartment. This is so because, in order to make sense of it, she finds it necessary to take a step back. (Humans live toward the future, but they understand toward the past.) She recalls other stories that came before: the origins of her friendship with Marcos, their struggle to find a place together and to be admitted as tenants in Mexico City, their former experiences in Xalapa and Veracruz, the contrasts between those eastern cities and the capital. Although all these stories intermingle, it can be noted that each one has a well-defined script. While "Getting This House" is told mostly as an episode of struggle and conquest, "Coming to the Big City" can be read as a longer epopee of travel and adventure. "This Is My Room" is like an intimate diary of creative self-discovery, and "Doing Chores" is a tale of community building, where the emergence of the other and the revelation of the self go hand-in-hand. Sometimes she makes these scripts very clear, for example when recalling how, during the interview with their landlord, a travel agency owner, she and her friend intentionally performed the old cliché of "young students coming from out of town, with our cartons of eggs and our luggage filled with dreams." In other moments she is able to distance herself from the parochial stereotypes about dwellers of the capital city, commonly considered "rude, impolite, and intractable"—regardless, she resorts to such commonplaces from time to time. Narrative schemata intermingle because all of them work as putative answers to a particular situation of speech (what pragmatologists call a question under demand, or QUD). In this case, the QUD is intrinsically ambiguous. As we had requested Norma to share whatever she found interesting, it is not surprising that so many different things came together.

Narrativity affects discourse in two distinct ways. On the macro level, it frames the whole speech, scaffolding a variety of other forms of description and argumentation. As shown above, Norma resorts to historical schemata (tales from the past) in order to bring together in the present the disparate pieces intimate life is made of. On a second level, narrativity works by introducing brief flashes of anecdotes, images, and even dialogues that incarnate the main argument. Norma proves to be incredibly good at this. As she is proceeding to describe the conviviality in the house, the distribution of chores, or the contrasts between Xalapa and Mexico City, she intersperses microstories, both real and fictional, that encompass things as varied as a crowded bus where everyone chimes in on others' private conversations, a subway employee moved by Norma's politeness, and the ephemeral glances exchanged with nasty neighbors in hallways. This second modality of storytelling is embedded within discourse instead of overarching it. It has the tactical purpose of persuasively reinforcing a point that is at stake. But it also contains a sensorial tone that insufflates lived qualities into an otherwise abstract and dry account. Flash-stories of this kind work "as if": they recount not only actual events but also potential and fictive ones.

How does dialogue interact with narrative framing? While narrative forms are typically sequential and temporal, dialogue can be conceived of as an exchange of questions and answers. During an interview, we can observe different ways in which these two kinds of schemata become ingrained. My questions along the conversation with Norma seemingly open and close the cycle of microstories by pushing her to explore and interrogate their internal relationships as well as their external links with unmentioned elements of the context. For example, at a certain point I ask whether one's roommates may become "a family" of sorts. Her initial answer is argumentative:

Yes, they are my family, because they are the ones who are here when I need them, aren't they? If [when living in Xalapa] I fought with my fiancé, if I was devastated because "He said this, and he did that, and then I don't know if I can stand him anymore," then I went to cry my heart out to Marcos, as I used to do with my sister before. Because now both he and I were alone in this city, and in the end, this was a way for us to keep each other company. Now it is more or less the same. I mean, when I was a kid and I would come home from school, the first thing my mom would say was, "How was your day?" "OK." I always answered OK; it did not matter how it had gone. Here, they [Marcos and Brian] are the ones who ask me "How was your day?" when I come home. So really, they are my family, because they are the people who live with me day in and day out in this city. They are my family for intimate things and everything else that happens behind closed doors. The people I can trust when I feel troubled. The people who care about my well-being, the ones who ask me "How are you doing," the people who realize if I did or didn't come home at night. So, family is not just bonds of blood. Family is whoever is with you, whether they like it or not. And this is what happens here somehow. They are with me, whether they like it or not, rain or shine. And I am here for them just the same. It's no coincidence that one of them is my emergency contact in case something happens to me.

Our conversation meanders on about the distribution of chores, the reasons why she prefers being in charge of the cleaning of the bathroom instead of other tasks, the difference between living with male or female roommates, how she placed the furniture in her bedroom, and what her favorite objects are. With this last aspect, it becomes clear that every personal object in the room points to someone important in her life: the postcards on the wall, her sister; the books on the shelves, her father; the decorative toys, her brother. And a photo of her dog, who recently died at eighteen years of age:

> After so many years, she was more like a relative than a pet for me. She was my sister-dog. When she died it was difficult, plus I was here all alone, writing my final university essays. So, the burden of putting her to sleep fell on my mom. As soon as she phoned me: "Wahhh!" [crying loudly]. The worst thing was being alone. Marcos and Brian were on holiday. Everything converged: I was alone, I had a dreadful flu, my dog had died, and things had gone awry with a boy I was dating. Four things, far too much. Had they come one at a time, it would have been OK. But all together? I couldn't sleep, I was sick, with signs of having cried, and so on. Devastated. And alone! No one to cry "Boohoo" to. No one to care for me. Just the worst. Then Brian, who had gone for fieldwork in Guerrero, returned for one night. He had to leave for Xalapa immediately the next day. Then he saw me and said, "You look really awful." "Wahhh!" I began to wail. And then [everything was] OK, you see? He hugged me, we talked, he showed me photos from his fieldwork, and the next day he left. Wow, what a relief. I mean: this is what family does. It was not about me telling him all my sorrows. It was simply about having someone to tell you, "What's going on? You look horrible!" And to hug me, and to distract me with anything [her eyes welling up]. This is what they mean to me, don't they? Somebody who doesn't have to act like a mom or dad, taking care of you, or anything like that. But people who are gonna do it, in case they have to. And they do it because they want to. This is the beautiful thing: it is a family that you have chosen by yourself. Not a family that you won in a raffle. I mean, you cannot escape from the parents you have been given. But you can select the friends you live with. You can choose the person whose support you are going to look for when in the span of one weekend you get sick, you can't sleep, your dog dies, and on top of all that, your boyfriend dumps you. This is what they are to me.

Let us note how the QUD "Are roommates like family?" returns here in full narrative version. Dialogue opens and closes a variety of narrative plots throughout the conversation. By interrogating the relationships between elements that can be dropped or revisited at various points of the encounter, dialogue activates the narrative framing in many directions, bringing this framing to the fore or, on the contrary, sending it to the background.

In addition to overarching "frames" and inserted "flashes," there is yet a third type of narrative component: marked stories, in the sense of them incorporating metalinguistic signals of stylization and performance, which are intentionally told as such. They are easy to recognize because they appear segregated from the flow of conversation. They are obviously twice-told and meticulously performed. The characters are fixed from the onset. The rhythm is artfully managed by the slowing down and speeding up of the pace of the action. The closure is announced and carefully executed. "Signing Inside Closets" belongs to this category. At the end of our interview, we asked Norma to perform it in front of the camera. We had already heard it during the CEW. The story has two parts. The first recounts the foundational moment when she, as a little girl, inaugurates her secret personal ritual of etching her name deep inside the closets of the many houses she lived in. The second episode takes place years later. She has now become a woman. The event takes the listener by surprise—much like it must have surprised the narrator herself:

I was now eighteen and had returned to León. No, I was nineteen; by then I had already been living in León for over a year. Again! I was studying something I really didn't like. One day, a classmate was having a party nearby. I went. From the very beginning, I noticed that everything felt very familiar. I thought, "I must have passed by this place when going to the grocery store, or whatever," since I was not far from home. But then we went in, and I sat in the only armchair there was. I felt weird. I looked at the corridor. Weirder. I looked around: it was familiar. So what? It was not something odd enough to ask about, but I couldn't ignore it either. Then I walked to a small bathroom; the door to it had tiny wooden blinds. . . . I opened the door.

Then it hit me.

I was little, in my parents' bedroom. I had a fever and stayed in their bed that day. And I got up to go to the bathroom.

As I gripped the door handle, everything came back. All the memories. Here I was, with the door handle in my hand. I had lived in this house during the 1995 crisis! I rushed upstairs and ran to the closet. There it was. My first signature. Out of all the closets I have tagged in my life, this one was the very first.

"Signing Inside Closets" falls in the category of unique story. Unlike frame-stories ("Youngsters from Out of Town with Their Luggage Filled with Dreams") and flash-stories ("The Subway Clerk Who Burst into Tears"), which are mostly instrumental for defending or illustrating a point, this other kind of story seems to be carefully crafted, because it bears a special significance. It has something to do with the singular biography and identity of the teller. This is made noticeable by means of the careful setting of the plot from the onset and then at the end through the poetic justice of an unexpected twist.

It summarizes a crucial experience for Norma, her coping with the anxieties of mobility and volatility, and the brilliant solution she found as a girl for overcoming such existential feelings. It is genuinely a "story of the self," for it was precisely in the very process of becoming a person—giving herself a name and a place to inhabit in the world—that the story was created. It is the personal myth of a personal ritual. The ritual manipulated two metaphoric elements of the self (name and dates) in order to metonymically fix them to a symbolically marked space: to set them in stone. The young Norma was building a little memorial outside the purview of the adults. The story is myth-like because it recounts something beyond a childish wish to stop linear time with a magic gesture, by etching indexes of oneself on the wall. It goes as far as to suggest a mysterious efficacy in doing so. The signature had been calling to her from the past: it drew the protagonist back to her origins. Is this not exactly what is expected to happen in a foundational myth? Time becomes circular, a sacred time-out-of-time, alleviated from the irretrievable condition of life in the secular world. During these breakdowns of linear time, we experience the past in the present, like what happened during her déjà vu. Rituals do not merely evoke past times; they reenact them (Connerton 1989). This story line reminds us of Alba in the guise of her mother, in an imaginary continuity of their lifetimes. Norma's tale suggests that the child we were somehow remains in the adult we are—or, in Bachelard's (1994) phenomeno-logical words, that one always dwells in one's first home. You may change houses, but a part of you will forever live—poetically at least—in the place of your childhood.

During the interview, Norma had explained the placement of the furniture in her bedroom. First, she had placed her desk below the window. So then, the big bed had to go to the opposite wall. The rest of the elements (bookshelves, a stationary bike, clothes, chairs, photos, souvenirs, notes, and postcards on the wall) had to be placed accordingly. I noticed a postcard fixed to the window frame, the famous *Young Woman at a Window* by Salvador Dalí. A window on a window? "Your room has a lot in common with this painting. You truly are this very woman at the window, aren't you? Everything is placed here in order to make it possible for you to look outside."

She assented with a smile. We had found an elegant circle to wrap up the conversation.

SINGULARITY AS ENTANGLEMENT

"Woman at the Window," like "The Daughter in Mother's Dress" and "Signing Inside Closets," testifies to the singularity of a life. When we sum up the character of someone as their "world" or "universe," what we have in mind is this holistic quality. Singularity is an obvious fact, but how do we grasp it? It can be perceived through the temporal lens of memories. It can also be spatially fixed, as when describing someone's room as an "atmosphere" or "ambient" with a certain quality. It is quintessentially inscribed in the body: in its movements, marks, and gestures. Gesture is a useful unit for the analysis of intimate life, for it condenses the singularity of someone in a unique pack that connects deep time with the spatialized here-and-now (Kaufmann 1997, 26).

Certainly, when considering elements one by one, there is nothing truly singular about anyone's body, nor anyone's home, nor, for that case, anyone's life. But singularity lies in the whole. The relational tangling of elements (some specific persons, their bodies, histories, past and present circumstances, possessions, relationships, activities, habits and routines, bents, and obsessions) forms a constellation, something we can call "a world of their own."

How should singularity be understood? On the one hand, singularity cannot be taken literally, as a matter of radical and incommensurable difference. Difference is never absolute. It is, as Bateson (1979, 68) put it, "unlocatable," a nonsubstantial perception, a categorical distinction that must exist in a certain mind: "a difference that makes a difference." True, one's life is somehow unrepeatable when compared to anyone else's. But this uniqueness should not be overemphasized because, at the same time, our commonalities constitute an undeniable sociological matter of fact. Most of the time, in most respects, we are mostly the same. A paradox can be found here. Difference matters not because it is massive but precisely because it is "infinitesimal"—as the philandering main character in *The Unbearable Lightness of Being* put it (Kundera 2006). Factual differences between human beings are meager when placed on the background of our basic vulnerability and nakedness, a condition that is, for Pardo (Pardo and Lasén 2020), the foundation of intimacy. Perhaps this is why unique details become so precious.

Singularity is holistic. It is about relations in a whole: composition, cosmos, patchwork, knit fabric, enmeshment. The holistic character of the intimate realm can be theoretically elaborated through concepts like entanglement (Löfgren 2014) and "throwntogetherness" (Massey, in Löfgren 2014). As mentioned above, this concern with the proper understanding of a whole was already present in the classical work of Bateson (1979), as it was also included in early Darwinian descriptions of the ecological medium of the tangle in *The Origin of Species*.[1] *Entanglement* refers to the intricate but hidden connections between all existing beings. It urges us to think about the material reality of things—and living things in particular—by taking into account their many forms of copresence, imbrication, codependence, and agency, in tight relation to other entities surrounding them. While the concept of identity underlines the edges that maintain differentiation between beings through time, the idea of entity underlines their coexistence in simultaneous spatial contiguity (Massey 1999, 8). In "Bringing Things to Life: Creative Entanglements in a World of Materials," Ingold (2010, 3) has recently advocated this relational way of thinking, opposing it to the halo-morphism of Aristotelian tradition, with its privileging of form over substance. He stands for a comprehension of objects as things. If objects are usually categorized by their artificially defined surfaces and boundaries, things are entities involved in a never-ending process of movement and redefinition, in flow with their environment. In a similar vein, Jane Bennet, a political scientist, has questioned in *Vibrant Matter* (2011) the notion that matter could be inert at all, an idea that she attributes to a Cartesian mechanistic tradition. Material things are always actively engaged with the rest of the biosphere. To analyze this fact, she proposes figures such as the "thing-power" (a paraphrasing of Foucauldian power/knowledge) and "the parliament of things" (a Latourian invention). These concepts are guided by a monist materialism that stems from Spinoza and has been updated by philosophers such as Deleuze, Ranciérè, and Latour (Bennet 2011, vi–xi). Thus, the notion of entanglement goes beyond a mere way of speaking. It subtly introduces an ontological stance with the ambition of blurring dualisms dividing form from substance, human from nonhuman, natural from man-made, and organic from inorganic.

There are indeed rhetorical excesses in the posthumanist trend to see matter "vibrating," things "thinging," and actants "acting" everywhere. I am not convinced that neomaterialist ontologies committed to an "emancipation of objects" are actually supported by state-of-the-art scientific biology. It is true that many foundational categories in this science, like "species," "organism," and "life," have recently come under review (cf. for example, Lenton, Dutreuil, and Latour 2020). But, I must confess, this is beyond my reach as a modest ethnographer of everyday life. Be that as it may, the productivity of these ideas lies somewhere else. If a realm exists in which the argument of a deep entanglement among living entities fully applies, it is, no doubt, that of the intimate sphere. The making of human intimacy entails all kinds of dense relationships, material links, spatial derives, semantic displacements, symbolic contaminations, evocative powers, affective tides, sensual crossovers, and powerful undercurrents of action. These entangling effects are silently contained in objects, ambiences, atmospheres, corners, gestures, routines, memorabilia, and people. The intimate world is relational. And so, the arguments of this critical posthumanist ontology tend to apply in a subtly reversed form. Perhaps it is not our intimacy that mimics a world of entanglements. It could be the other way around. It is precisely because all humans experience living and growing amid a meshwork that we can easily get in tune with otherworldly, nonhuman forms of entanglement, flow, and density.

The meaning of singularity in our informants' stories points to this holistic character, difficult to summarize or even name, that lies in the synesthetic and synecdochic entanglement between people, places, actions, objects, and affects (Löfgren 2014). This singularity becomes immediately evident to the participants both in our CEWs and interviews. When they chime in during the exchange of stories, they often announce that what we are about to hear is very "personal," "particular," "atypical," "special," "unusual," "out-of-the-ordinary." Really? Is everything so extraordinary? Maybe not. But at least this should make the listener refrain from jumping into easy generalizations about how different people—"millennials," "single women," "couples with kids," "elderly," "Europeans," "heteronormatives"—conduct their lives. Certainly, these stories present things that are special to the narrator but in no way unrepeatable: trips to Rome, families relocating, lovers who could never marry. If they are told as unique, it is because they testify to the unalienable universe of the teller.

It would then be fair to say that stories reverberate in the ones told by others. In the trading of tales, everyone seems to think, "This could be me." So, the recognition of singularity does not make experience uncommunicable. On the contrary, daily life conversation is founded on the expectation of reverberation among singular stories. This highlights something important about the nature of intimacy as an act of storytelling: intimacy is built on the sharing of unique experiences. We all think of ourselves as subjects who are simultaneously unique and capable of being reflected in others' stories. This can be appreciated in literary versions of this genre, for example, the compilation of short stories *I Thought My Father Was God* that Paul Auster (2002) made from microstories about American life sent to him by his audience.

REJOICING IN ONE'S SELF

Everyday life stories can be singular and shared at the same time. This is the source of the intense pleasure that emanates from the daily life anecdote and the personal experience account as genres. It is for pleasure that we chitchat all the time.

The pleasure of recounting is a basic finding from this research and the main reason why we decided to give it a filmic form. Too often we take for granted that writing down stories and arguments is the best way to improve them. Actually, in such transcription we lose gesture, tone, and emotion.

What is the source of this pleasure? On the one hand, it springs from a verbal proclivity. Humans are not only *homo ludens* (Huizinga 2002) but also *homo narrans* (Fisher 1985). The pleasure of recounting counts. We trade in stories. We find it fascinating to know what happened to the neighbor, what is going on in the political arena, what dark past hides behind the main character of our favorite TV show. This proclivity is quite indifferent to the content of the story. In genres of discourse centered on blame, suffering, or anxiety, like grumbling about illness or complaining about politics, one may find relief in discussing painful details of a medical treatment as well as in denouncing outrageous misdeeds by civil servants, expert systems, and bad government. The pleasure of recounting is not necessarily related to positive thoughts and emotions. Those genres allow us to find a place in discourse for bodily afflictions and social frustrations.

However, regarding intimacy, there is something else. The joy is not just about recounting but also about sharing something valuable. As we have seen, Berger termed it "a rescue operation" from oblivion and irrelevance—an operation continuously applied to the many petty things that nourish our daily lives. I also find the expression *jouissance de soi* (rejoicing in one's self), which Simonet-Tenant (2009, 43–47) has applied to the history of intimacy in France, revealing. As symptoms of the rising attention to the body and intimate spaces among the French bourgeoisie and aristocracy around the late eighteenth century, she mentions urban phenomena like the growing specialization of rooms in the home; the diminishing of the threshold of tolerance to odors; the invention of the toilet and the boudoir; the proliferation of mirrors, locks, and clocks; the inviolability of private correspondence; and the emergence of the personal diary as a literary genre. The joint evolution of these cultural traits reflects a new set of dispositions: the possession, mastery, and enjoyment of the self. They entail a taste for closures, an affirmation of ownership, and the right to rejoice in that special relationship that every individual maintains with themselves.

The right to intimacy is a bourgeois conquest. It came associated with the generalization of domestic technologies and the desire to enjoy one's self. During the twentieth century, this desire has become democratized and universalized. At the beginning of this book, I tried to convey this by saying that intimacy is too good not to be true. Many of our stories adamantly predicate this: that intimacy is something extremely valuable; that it is worthy of being found and fought for; and that, whenever it takes place, the allures of intimacy invite us to distribute them. Intimacy is a secret begging to be shared, a closure wanting to be opened. Or better yet: a secret and a closure generated steadily in the very act of being shared and opened, through complicity and confidence.

Regarding the right to secrecy, Simonet-Tenant (2010, 47) notes,

> The rejoicing in one's self entails the possibility of not telling everything about you, or telling it to freely chosen interlocutors. The eighteenth century, which as we have seen was the century of blindness, is also the age of the possible secret.

For, what is a secret if not a restricted blindness? Secret is an ambiguous term, since it may cover both the forbidden word or absolute silence as much as some form of communication among initiates, that is, a certain kind of sociality built upon the sharing of intimacy. Among the bourgeois young girls and boys it was so: privileged friendships in which the juvenile confidences and the intensity of emotions are exalted blossomed since the second half of the eighteenth century.

In other words, intimacy is the place of a truth of the subject. This "truth" cannot be thought of in objectivistic terms, in the same way that we judge the truth value of empirical propositions about events in the world, assessing its correspondence with facts. Conversely, we should not think of this truth in an essentialist way either—a perspective so much demoted by critics like Pardo (1996)—as a "pure interiority," an ineffable and uncommunicable authenticity, a dark reality that hides deep inside the subject, knowable only to oneself. Pure objectivity or pure interiority are equally inadequate parameters. Judging from them, intimacy vanishes. It appears either as a bunch of lies, self-deception, and mythology, or worse, as a locus of oppression and violence. A smokescreen. A romantic and individualistic fiction.

The truth contained in the intimate narratives has to do with this *jouissance de soi* that imposes itself on the subject as evidence whenever taking charge of one's own life: one's stuff, activities, feelings, times, experiences, loves, spaces, body, plans, desires. This evidence is akin to the concept of veracity in Habermas's (1994) linguistic ethics: not the correlate between what is said in words and the thing itself (truth value) but rather the existing relationship between what is said and an honest self-perception of intentions and motives on the part of the speaker. Unlike truth, veracity is a pertinent parameter to assess intimacy. It can be defined as the degree of accord between a speaker and what they are telling. Certainly, we cannot easily assess the truth of an intimate story, but we are capable of judging to what degree someone believes in it.

This was the thread with which the film *The Order I Live In* was weaved. We were less interested in the truth value of microstories than in their veracity regarding this "rejoicing of oneself." Not because our participants had no problems or because their lives were happy and simple (some of the critics of our documentary wondered why we didn't talk more about housing scarcity and urban crisis). Among the many themes that sprang up in a conversation held with dozens of people in three cities, the one that spontaneously came out was the many ways of enjoying one's own space. Of course, participants wanted to talk about their troubles too. Nobody told us their life was easy. All of them had wounds, which they carefully navigated during the conversation. Sometimes I voluntarily escaped through a diverging path whenever the couple's disagreements, the professional frustrations, the health and money difficulties came to the fore in tones that were too bitter. One of the interviewees had suffered an express kidnapping in Mexico City, no less. The parents of two others had recently died. Many of our informants were passing through economic hardships; some were unemployed. Two spouses did not conceal their harsh differences; they divorced shortly afterward. A young informant was a close friend of a journalist who was killed in the vicinity of the neighborhood where she lives. Some of these topics were commented on, mostly off the record, before or after the shooting of the movie.

Nevertheless, the rejoicing of the self was in one form or another at the center of their attention. This was particularly noticeable in the encounters with young couples that were moving in together as well as with people emancipating from their parents. Yunes and Martin, students in their twenties from Montevideo, worked in a homeless shelter in the city center. A few months after beginning their relationship, they moved in together into a little house in the suburbs, in beautiful green surroundings near the coast. The modest furniture was still to find its place. In a tiny yet bright interior, with chirping birds, mattresses on the floor, and a single pan, they explained enthusiastically why possessions were of minor importance:

> YUNES: When we moved in, we didn't have a refrigerator or a stove. We had a mattress and a few other important things. The heater was brought in on the first day. But we didn't have a stove, so we ate sandwiches and drank lukewarm water, like children do.

> MARTIN: It was a need to inhabit the place, to settle down, not to get loaded with things, to have pots, or things like that. Yes, they are necessary though. We were cooking with cold water in a single pan. We had to clean it and then keep frying. . . . But the need to inhabit the place was much stronger.

Scarcity is taken more as a promise than a problem. Yunes and Martin expected that, like a metaphor of the organic growth of their life in common, this interior would get filled with all kinds of wonderful things, without much previous planning. Of course, the openness to tomorrow does not exclude subtle negotiations about how much of your past (clothes, stuff, memories) you could bring to the empty house. For example, they joked about how much of Yunes's well-stocked wardrobe would be "too much" to bring from her parents' home. The joy of this moment, when two lovers inaugurate a new dwelling, is constitutive. Like in the summer-love movies by Eric Rohmer, the promises of the unknown materialize in the ambiguities of things still to come: empty spaces to be filled, walls to be painted, rooms to be occupied, words to be said, dreams to be shared. The situation pushes simultaneously in the direction of the revelation of one's self and into the discovery of the other, since the two processes are contained in the invention of a "we." Of course, these anticipations of a good life in common were already present in traditional forms of courtship and marriage and symbolically enacted during their rituals with rich imageries of abundance, health, and mutual devotion. Now, our modern first homemaking elaborates on these same ideas through less trodden symbolic means. Invented and idiosyncratic microrituals emerge around activities like moving in, buying furniture, decorating the house, and communicating the new situation to peers and relatives. They symbolize not only the promises of the common life to come but also the freedom of the spouses, the equality among them, the openness of their situation, and the uncertainty of the outcome. In an age of *Liquid Love* (Bauman 2003) and *The Normal Chaos of Love* (Beck and Beck-Gernsheim 1995), such rituals are not fixed but are partially cobbled together by the members of the couple with the help—or obstruction—of their inner circle (about new emerging rites of online dating, see Kaufmann 2010a and Hochschild 2012).

The enjoyment of one's self can be associated with all kinds of quotidian practices: from lonely study to playing with children, from dinners with friends to smoking at the window. For Lila, the weekly cleaning of the bathroom could provide a great source of joy:

> Then you abandon yourself, as if you were possessed, and . . . you do deep cleaning! As if you were letting go of all your rage. You start cleaning! With plenty of water, scrubbing, getting soaked, it doesn't matter. In normal life you say, "My gosh, I got wet precisely when I had to go out." Now it doesn't matter. Nobody is gonna see you. It is so great to be cleaning the bathroom. You take the shower sprinkler like a gun and begin to splash: on the walls, the bidet, the toilet, the sink. Spectacular! Cleaning the bathroom is like therapy.

The house can be, of course, a privileged object of desire. At the time, Lila was living between her parents' apartment in Montevideo, where she traveled weekly to study at the university, and her great-uncle's large house in the province, where she had borrowed a room with her husband after the death of her grandmother. She was not shy about her daydreams of owning a family house in Carmelo, her town:

> The house I will live in until I die is already super planned out in our minds. We have sketched it out a thousand times in notebooks, figuring out the spaces, the colors . . . We are far from having it, and yet it is already done in our minds. We want a hall, so when you enter the house, you cannot see the kitchen or the rooms. We want a fireplace; we love fire. We do love it! The kitchen has to be spacious: a large kitchen and a small room.

This daydream about *la casita de hasta cuando me muera* ("a house until I die") was not connected with mere ownership but to the kind of intimacy that can be deployed in it. This becomes transparent in Lila's design of a projected *patio* (yard):

> You own this yard, then. Nobody sees you. There you can lie down, like a real slob. In your underwear. The intimacy of being with your kids, your dog, your things, saying, "Who's a good boy?" Men are sometimes ashamed of this. "My baby, my everything . . . " These funny things you do when nobody is watching. We enjoy this freedom to behave like fools, very much. Someone may think you look silly cuddling with your dog: "Oh my baby!" It is really important to have a house that allows this intimacy. Important for being ourselves.

BEYOND "I"

To rejoice in oneself is, mysteriously and imperatively, to rejoice in the life of others. Pablo Neruda (2017, 5), Chilean poet, put it beautifully: "Maybe I did not live in myself, maybe I lived just the lives of others." If intimacy is defined, as we have done, in terms of experiences of both proximity and familiarity, it is then an essentially relational phenomenon, having to do with a self in relation, not with the experiences of someone locked in their interiority. The intimate world is constructed through personal attachments that make sense in concrete spatial settings. In interactionist jargon, the self can only be seized and performed through "participations" and "belongings" (Goffman 1972). Participation extends personal identity to bigger social wholes of which one is just a part: a household, a family, a group of peers, a class, a church, a company, a political party, a union, a club, a gang, a city, an ethnic group, a nation, a civilization, humankind . . . Conversely, belongings are partial entities (possessions, body parts, objects, territories) used as markers of the person's overall individuality (my hand, my bike, my room, my name, my wallet). We find here a significant *chiasma*. On the one hand, the term *in-dividual* denotes that the person has constitutive integrity and unity. It cannot be divided without destroying it. On the other hand, the relational self is processual and in-becoming: only defines itself by flexibly remapping its limits by a complex play of grammars of alterizing/identifying with some others (Baumann 2004). This interplay of participation and distance continuously remap "I," "you," "we," and "they," as well as their frontiers (cf. also Hall 1997).

This tension is at the very center of everyday life, which appears at the same time as the factory of common culture and the realm where individual character and needs find their best expression. Sociological literature on reflexive modernization underscores the singularization of the self due to accelerated processes of individualization and institutionalization (e.g., Giddens 1991; Bauman 2001; Lahire 2006; Kaufmann 2004; De Singly 2016; Bourdin 2005). At the same time, the ethnography of domestic life reveals the power of this realm for inexhaustibly producing commons, shared values, and rules of its own. Douglas (1991, 304), for example, has noted the strange moral economy that regulates the idea of home when compared to a capitalist point of view like the one that runs a hotel. Hochschild (and Machung 1989; Hochschild 2012) has framed the domestic economy in terms of "gift" circulation and "value creation." Highmore (2010) underscores the "ordinary" character of what is produced in this context, transversal to class and other social differences. Elaborating further on "moral economy," Löfgren (2019b) translates it as a continuous and ambivalent passage between "mine" and "ours," the "I" and the "we."

This last point is noticeable in our stories. As intimacy happens to be shared, it imposes the continuous and subtle passage from the individual to the collective, from me to us (and vice versa). As the poet wrote, "*Je suis un autre.*" Although the discourses gathered in our thematic CEWs and film interviews were very much self-centered, the slippage from the protagonist to other actants of daily life—personal and impersonal, human and nonhuman—was pervasive. Later I will say more about the narrative plot in which those various actants contribute to the recounting of the adventures of ego. Suffice it to say that this continuous movement back and forth between the self and its entanglements set two things up. On the one hand, it allows us to fully grasp the discursive strategies of a subject enmeshed within their social and material environment. On the other hand, we tried to reproduce this effect on film by creating a collective choral voice in which the dialogue of the selves with their significant others could be performed.

Among the topics beyond "I," some are prominent. First, the importance and difficulties inherent in living alone. For many of our participants, the goal of getting "a place of my own" was at the center of their stories, with dilemmas, troubles, and joys. Under the label "The Club for Those Who Live Alone," we gathered an array of these experiences in the film. They include things like someone who created a club for singles in order to have the possibility of dining at least once a week in good company, the humorous dynamics of partying and disorder typical of apartments shared by students, and the frictions brought to this kind of residence by the diverging needs of couples who see themselves forced to share with singles.

Second, we explored the relationality that the self maintains with objects, under the title "Dancing with Things" (following Kaufmann 1997). Mirrors, refurbishing, king-size beds, streetlights, serving plates, towels, windows, frying pans, baby bottles, and old toys have their say. They impose a silent but efficacious agency of their own, intervening in social relations, fixing certain meanings and displacing others. What we called "The War on Stuff" was of particular interest. Muffled frictions and annoyances set their ambush around the use or possession of certain spots and appliances in the home: the remote control, the big easy chair in front of the TV, the cellphones, the mattresses, the bikes, the favorite mug, a certain place at the table, laptops, backpacks, the coolest corner for having a nap.

Third, by including couples with children, the film shows the work of care during that key moment that Kaufmann (1997, 89) calls "domestic mobilization" and, beyond that, the magic joy of seeing yourself mirrored in your children. Children may or may not resemble their parents in many respects, but they always bring back to them a forgotten, dormant part of their past, which is actualized and revived. People sing lullabies, play games, paint dinosaurs and bears on the wall. By doing so, they resume a fragment of their own histories.

Fourth, in "Ulysses Syndrome," we elaborated on the relationality that attaches the self (or not) to particular places. It does not matter whether you live in Madrid, Mexico, or Montevideo. More than cosmopolitan heroes from nowhere, in times of globalization there are plenty of people who belong to more than one place. As in Homer's *Odyssey*, the contemporary self is made of journeys. The outcome is ambivalent. Leaving the motherland leaves traces, memories, and attachments. Homesickness may appear, or not. Roots may be—or not—missed, forgotten, idealized. This mobile condition was commonplace among our interviewees. Some were caught between the hinterland and the capital city, others between Europe and Latin America. There were plenty of languages and places of residence. The "Ulysses Syndrome" (borrowing this expression from the Mexican Alejandro Reyes 1956) illustrates the complexities and tensions that constitute urban subjectivities.

Finally, under the title "The Burden of Memory," our film wondered about the place of familial memories in times of a regime of quick obsolescence, an exploration I will readdress later in this chapter. There is a component of serendipity here. Some of our informants had lost a close relative, having to clear out the house after the passing. This painful task, which entails the evaluation of what is worth keeping and what is not, was an occasion for them to reflect on the value and fugacity of the past and for us to inquire into how modern dwellers cope with the duty of administering this burden under pressing conditions of rapid obsolescence, scarcity of space, and lives projected into the future.

WILL THERMOMIX BECOME THE NEW NORMAL?

To make sense of a discourse, it does not suffice to pay attention to what is said. It is equally necessary to note what is not said, whether because it is too obvious or, on the contrary, simply unthinkable. Throughout our research, the former was the case for the dwelling conventions of the modern habitat, things like the distribution of space in contemporary apartments; the technologies and services installed in them; and certain values of modern dwelling, such as comfort and connectivity. The fact that these conventions tend to go unnoticed proves that they have been fully naturalized and interiorized.

The structural conventions of our indoor spaces have a long history. Monique Eleb and Anne Debarre, respectively a social psychologist and an architect, have researched what they call "the invention of modern living" by analyzing building plans from different periods in Paris as well as architecture magazines and treatises on urbanity, understood as guides for good living (savoir vivre). Some key elements in such a system of conventions are comfort and hygiene; the division of rooms according to their function—representation, privacy, or service; and the incorporation of technologies today rendered invisible: running water, electricity, gas, telephone, and elevator (Frykman and Löfgren 1987; Eleb and Debarre 1995; Cieraad 1999, 2021; Eleb and Bendimérad 2010).

The naturalization of this set of conventions becomes clear when contrasted with the position of a more recent generation of technologies, as mobile communications, home automation, and the Internet of things. Nowadays, smartphones and laptops occupy a key position in the hierarchy of technologies, as extensions of the self. They easily become identity objects. This was noticeable in the sessions devoted to appliances. For example, given his love for the latest gadgets and electronics, one of the participants humorously introduced himself as a *ciberpijo* ("cyber-preppy"), adding that his living room is unconventionally furnished with three connected megascreens plus a freezer. This self-presentation makes sense only when set against the background of the standard living room in Spain since the 1970s, with the TV set regulating family coexistence and being the predictable centerpiece of the room's furniture. On the contrary, in the socially desirable discourse of the younger participants, television has become an object tinged with anachrony and alienation, an inheritance of outdated times. The most glamorous technologies—those that open life to the future—include the Thermomix kitchen robot, "the fancy of a magical cook," as someone put it. A woman told us her personal story in these terms: provincial parents send a present to their young daughter, who is making her way alone in the big city. She receives the package. She unwraps it, expecting to see the dreamed-of Thermomix, just to find . . . a small and disappointing TV set. Shortly after that story was told, another participant told practically the very same plot:

> Thinking about TV . . . When I celebrated my thirtieth birthday, I did not have a TV at home either. So [my parents] gave me a television set plus a blender. But what I really wanted was a Thermomix [kitchen robot]! I did want the Thermomix, but I was rewarded with a TV! . . . I definitely did not want it. It was like, "Wow, you don't know me at all! Don't you see I do not want this?" By giving me a TV, it was like they were intruding on my personality. But nowadays I watch it a lot. The computer is what takes up more space though.

AN AGONISTIC PLOT: THE TASKS OF EGO

This story entitled "The Dreamed Food Processor," which overtly opposes the Thermomix versus the TV set imposed by the parents, finely illustrates another commonality in the discourses of our corpus: the structure of the story presents the person struggling for their self-making through tasks that compose an agonistic, and sometimes antiheroic, allegory. In the narrative deployment of this plot, other characters, relations, ambiences, and singular objects appear in the role of facilitating or obtruding actants.

The goal of finding oneself, of establishing autonomy and affirming one's own space, provides the rationale for the unfolding of events. The singular "I" develops its action in what we could call, in Hegelian fashion, "the fight for space." The subject struggles with an alien order as they try to build their own. Sometimes the purpose of the action is not so much the making of space but the need to find it, or just to keep it unchanged. Various figures or events can play the antagonist role: the anonymous urban order, the landlord, the lack of money, loneliness. As shown by Camilo's experience, one can be one's own worst enemy in the fierce battle against the vacuum brought about by the struggle of inventing oneself, of producing *ex nihilo* an independent but meaningful urban existence:

> Then I went to live alone. I had been told that living alone was something great, fantastic: you did whatever you wanted, whenever you wanted, the way you wanted. This was odd for me, because until that moment in my life it had not been this way. There was always someone else. Then I remember some friends telling me, "Nooooo, you prepare a nice dinner for yourself, with candles and everything, then you just sit down and enjoy." On my first night alone, I came home after having done my shopping and I recalled my friends' advice. So, I said, "OK, let's do this." I prepared dinner, lit candles, a tablecloth—I usually don't, but I wanted to re-create that ritual a little. And I got ready to eat. In less than seven minutes, I had already devoured all my food. And there I was, seated

and telling myself, "Now what? When does the fantastic thing come?" But there was nothing. So, that same night I decided to invent something called the "Club for Those Who Live Alone."

Partners, friends, siblings, and roommates can be seen as facilitating or obstructing figures. But, for the younger interviewees who were in the process of looking for "a place of their own," parents are the preferred antagonists:

> I began to understand that I was in need of a place of my own. Then I looked for my own space. Of course, it was not my parents' home. There, I looked around and said, "This is not my place. It has no light. I don't like the furniture." But I couldn't tell my mother, "Leave the house to me and I will do whatever I want with it." No. Therefore, it was like: "I have to look for a space of my own."

This view of parents and older kin contains a very ambivalent element. They may well be the gatekeepers of a normative world of impositions, restrictive norms, dubious taste, and empty, meaningless conventions. However, they are also supportive of the subject in their worst struggles, no matter what. Even more poetically relevant is that in the interplay between modernity and tradition, they are the guardians of the subject's roots: beloved childhood memories, cherished recipes from Grandma, indelible experiences of the first explorations of a pristine universe.

The partner in a couple may also play this role of the antagonist in the deployment of one's self. As in the case of parents, it is easy to understand this contradictory stance. Our other half is always, ineluctably, also a source of daily negativity and resistance. This becomes noticeable in the minimal, petty details as we are forced to negotiate even the simplest arrangement of, say, things on a table.

> I always read three or four books at the same time. I scatter my things all around: papers, pens, my phone. For me, this is not a mess, because this way I have it all in sight. But every time I return home, my boyfriend has made a pile with all my things and has set it on the kitchen table. This, I don't take so well, because I want the table cleared up. When he puts it there, he forces me to arrange it, so he interferes a little in my own chaos. But I get on very well with my chaos!

Natural ambivalence may easily give way to the confession of a deeper disagreement. From a joking tone we can pass to a bitter one, from affection to rage. Be that as it may, the majority of what we call "wars on things" does not lead to anything other than a celebration of every detail of the otherness that cannot be ultimately reduced. This singular difference between members of the couple, family, or household can be minimal; but precisely for that reason it is sacred. It cannot be called into question. A joyful example of these "Wars on Things" stories was shared by Iago, an Italian participant, speaking about his parents. In the heat of the Tuscan summer, they used to move from room to room looking for the coolest mattress on which to take a nap.

> Around this issue of beds: we have plenty of room at home, and about ten years ago my parents decided to change the mattresses. Then, the dispute came: softer mattress, firmer mattress . . . They decided to go with a firmer mattress, because it is healthier. But the old softer one is actually much better, qualitatively speaking. Then we could not throw it away, so they moved it to another bedroom. But one room is warmer. What is happening now? It happens that during the summer the warmer room gets too hot, so my father cannot sleep over there. Then he moves to the other room, and when it gets cold, he goes back to the warmer one with my mom. My parents say, "Do we move to sleep at the summer residence, or at the winter residence?" depending on the weather. It is a real joke every day.

Objects play an important role as analyzers of human relations in our personal world. They are not passive or silent. They appear to be true actants. And this is not a merely discursive issue. If they are so important in the stories, it is because they have a strong structuring role in daily life. They play a crucial part in quotidian reflexivity, becoming central in what Kaufmann (1997, 17) has rightfully called "home action" (*action ménagère*) or, more poetically, "the dance with the things."

In our workshops and interviews, objects have proved to be extremely telling. They are reservoirs of memory. They impose their demands, rhythms, limitations, traces, and regrets. It is important to understand, though, that they do not act nor speak alone but only insofar as they are part of a chain of actions and relations that should be regarded as a system—a universe in which humans are the ultimate agents and primary force. This can be illustrated with the "Wars on Things" type of story. Objects make their appearance as key ingredients in a relationship among coresidents. Is this not the deepest meaning of the concept of home? As opposed to a mere enclosure or a contract or a group of cohabiting kin, home is a system of human relations that intensely depends on the vicissitudes of shared objects. For, as good as objects are in separating and drawing boundaries among the members of a group, they are equally good at uniting them. For example:

> When my grandpa died, my mother saw me playing with his pocket watch. She told me, "When you become a responsible adult, I will give it to you." I was eight. Years passed, but still, I did not feel I could rightfully ask for it. From time to time, I thought about it, because I loved my grandfather very much. When I returned home from military service—I was twenty-one—I felt brave enough to ask for it. My mother said, "At last, my son, you are finally a grown man." As soon as I took it into my hands, I could see that the watch did not work. "But,

Mother, have you been careless with it?" "No, son. It never worked." [laughs from the audience]

Ritual objects bind generations beyond death. Unlike this grandson, who believed that the watch "did not work," I think that this watch worked very well. In discourse and in action—in myth and ritual—it established a continuity among three generations. It provided a bond that denied a definitive farewell. In this story, as in so many others in which inherited objects play a role, time is not objectified nor measurable; it is a predicated, overarching entity that embeds the family history and subtly asserts its permanence.

This is probably why we have gathered so many touching stories about objects that maintain their capacity to act across time. Like the story of the woman who accidentally found a drawing in her deceased grandfather's wallet, hidden in a secret fold. She realized that she herself had drawn it, thirty years earlier. It depicted a little girl holding hands with an old man. Her grandfather had silently kept it throughout his whole life, close to his heart. Other stories tell of kids who appropriate their parents' toys. Others tell of widowed fathers who moved in to their children's rooms once they had grown up and moved out. Objects may be special or ordinary, trivial or high-tech, but through them all the relations across time among people living under the same roof can be felt, thought, and told. This is what the phenomenologist Alfred Schultz (1977), inspired by the musicians who routinely tune their instruments to perform together, called tuning-in relationships. He saw the model of human interaction itself in this coordination through time mediated by objects. The following statement from Ana also makes for an interesting example:

> This ring, I always have it on. It is made of gold and coral. It is my grandmother's, who always wore it. In my childhood memories, this ring is always on her finger. When she died, my mother took it. But she has never used it. When my son was born, my mother gave it to me, and I wear it, always. I am afraid to lose it, but still I use it. Whenever I go out, I put it on, and when I come back, it is one of the first things I take off and put aside. But if I go out without it, I feel its absence.

Objects have a magical appeal. Could this be why there are so many magical rings in fairy tales? They participate in the plot by whispering untold things to the actors. And objects can mark the body too. When they come from the past, they make themselves present through the body, which is the most here-and-now thing we have. Ana feels the absence of the meaningful ring on her finger. Throughout her childhood, Rafaela, another participant, had been accompanied by the chromatic accordion that now decorates her living

room; the length of her thumb and the strength of her young neck speak of
years of rehearsal.

ULYSSES SYNDROME

In another narrative type, the family features as a point of origin from which
the traveler departs in order to become able to recognize themself somewhere
else. For example, Iago, a young Italian artist, reflected on his surprise when,
returning home after years of absence, he listened to the accent of his mother
tongue, hearing it from the outside, so to speak. He suddenly realized that
this accent no longer belonged to him. Here, speech works as the analyzer of
a rite of passage. The sociolinguistic perception of your own accent from the
outside—listening to yourself as another—triggers the crossing of a threshold
from which there is no return.

As in the Homeric account, the end of the story of an adventurer is always
bittersweet: the subject returns to discover himself as a stranger in his homeland. In a memorable passage, "*La melancolía del viajero*" (The melancholy
of the traveler), the Mexican writer Alfonso Reyes (1956, 357) has re-created
the untold drama of the Greek hero, once safely returned at the side of
Penelope. He does not know where he belongs anymore. And he never will,
since he will keep hearing the sirens' song forever:

> You can escape from the seduction of the sirens, by brutally tying yourself to
> the mast. But how could you forget the sirens' songs? . . . Like anyone who has
> wandered much throughout the world, Ulysses no longer knows what to wish
> for, whether rest or adventure. A man who loses his center will never recover it.
> Alas! Those who travel by sea and land must have a saint-like spirit of renun-
> ciation and a heart made to withstand every blow of joy and sorrow. They fear
> returning to their beaches, but they desire them. Upon returning, they do not find
> what they had left. Where has the dreamed home and land gone? . . . Ulysses
> must keep going, like a condemned rolling stone. He pretends that the gods are
> the ones who send him. . . . Some of us rather believe that returning to the sinful
> Island of the Songs is what Ulysses truly wants.

This traveler's melancholy describes a certain way of being in the world,
fitting for cosmopolitan subjectivities. Many in our sample of participants
shared it. This disposition is certainly ambivalent because it entails the
determination to let things go—locality, family, possessions, flavors, friends,
books, music, lovers—in order to enrich one's biography through a direct
experience of the vastness of the world. But there is always the temptation to
return to cherished things abandoned along the path (like Ulysses's songs).
Is this not a cosmopolitan form of homesickness? Amanda, a Mexican

musicologist who has lived in Singapore, Madrid, Los Angeles, Santiago de Chile, Mexico City, and Querétaro, made it clear:

> If the migrating experience repeats, several places make you feel "homesick," right? When I returned to Mexico after Singapore, there were many things I missed. But I told myself, "This will pass." Then, after having lived some time in Madrid, I also missed so many things and flavors from Madrid. And with the USA, the same happened. When I moved to Chile, I missed LA; when we returned to LA, I missed Chile. It's funny. Do you know what we said in LA? "What I miss the most from Chile is your brother-in-law's Japanese sushi."

What Reyes refers to as "a spirit of renunciation" is the ascetic component inherent to this disposition, a calculated detachment from what we previously called participations and belongings. Norma, our woman at the window, traced this inclination to a family learning, tacitly transmitted by her parents:

> You attach yourself to places and things, but it becomes easy to let them go as well. You learn that what you need with you goes here [inside your head]. The rest is unnecessary. It might be OK, but you really don't need it. Perhaps this is the reason why there is nothing from my mom here. She is somehow present, because she is always moving, and she is the one who gave us her time. But she also taught us: "Carry only what you can."

With the passing of time, necessity turns into a virtue, and the cosmopolitan subject develops a Chilean pig skin (*cuero de chancho*). Yes, we may lose a bit of homeland, but in exchange we get the whole world.

> At a certain point, it became hard to get rid of objects. Especially friends, beloved friends: "Who knows when I will see them again." Then your skin becomes thicker. As they say in Chile, you develop a pig's skin. Afterward, you change your mind, and say, "I have a lot of friends spread all over the world, and I can go visit them."

FAMILIARITIES

What do our workshops and interviews speak about? It would be naive to sustain that they speak solely about "intimacy," understood as a unified, comprehensive concept—something that we could neatly contrapose to things public, domestic, and private. These discourses, actions, and gestures result from a dynamic interaction among very diverse people in response to an open demand. Their stories do not, then, provide a definition, much less a demarcation. The term that describes them best is *explorations*. Forms of intimacy can only be clarified in an indirect manner: by means of shortcuts and detours, through the agreements, disagreements, and interrogations that the group expresses out loud. They can be followed in their entanglements with many dimensions of urban life: physical space, economic survival, living with others, arrangements within the couple, family memories . . . In this list, significant absences were sex, shame, pain, failure, and dependence, although they can be sensed tacitly. Home service—personified by nannies, au pairs, and housekeepers—should probably be included in the omissions section as a topic that, being central to the lives of middle-class dwellers, tend to go by unnoticed in their discourses (Ehrenreich and Hochschild 2004).

In chapter 1, I exposed the difficulties of fencing the realm of intimacy. The participants in our CEWs coped with these troubles, hesitating about what to include in this category and what not to. This is reflected in the broad range of themes and tones of our filmed stories: dogs, travels, children, diets, bills, gardens, homework, cellphones, shopping, chores, commuting, holidays, naps, readings, cooking, love, neighbors, memories, and so on. Intimacy has a thousand faces.

These shared explorations do not authorize a categorial closure. Rather, they point to the extraordinary richness of the idea of intimacy and the slippery and flexible character of the contemporary experience of dwelling associated with it.

A good example was our CEW Make Yourself at Home. The session was initiated by inviting the participants to select a few things that made them feel at home. In Montevideo, someone synthesized her daily experience of returning home with this visual image: "Before I arrive home, I am already there." While still in her long commute, this woman anticipated the modest suburban house waiting for her at the barrio, at the end of a tree-lined avenue, with dogs barking welcome and the children inside calmly doing their assignments of the day. To this image, suitable to a working and property-owner mother, a younger woman—student and single—opposed her own daily routine of returning to a leased apartment, where she lived alone. She fully opens the windows (*"de par en par"*) and takes her time smoothly enjoying a cigarette while looking outside. This founding gesture opens the possibility of gazing at the street from there, as a kind of strategic vantage point. This same theme of windows functioning as powerful organizers of an intimate space was also found in Norma's evocation of the outside as perceived from her room (as well as in Dalí's painting *Young Woman at a Window*):

> The noises from outside are what actually calm me down. . . . I write better at night. No more roommates, cars, helicopters, vendors . . . But I cannot bear total silence. Three a.m. is my most lucid time. At 12:00 a.m., I hear the sweeping from the market stalls. They are closing. At 2:00 a.m., I hear the pots in the food

stall and the chatting of the cooks. I like this, because I feel comforted, in good company. Afterward there is a tremendous silence, until 6:00 a.m., when the gas man arrives and the market opens again. These are the signs that I did what I could: time for bed.

Camilo, the designer from Montevideo, summarized the experience of making oneself at home as being able to open the refrigerator without having to ask for permission. To this design-oriented definition, he added the confidence of actually having not just one but several homes: his own, his fiancée's, his parents', and a shared house at the beach. Like him, for many people the problem today is less where to live—the traditional "how to have a place of your own"—but rather the postmodern "how to make yourself at home." Of course, access to housing remains an economic challenge for most of the population, especially the younger generations. But factors of geographic mobility and affective trajectory complicate the biographical courses, adding complexity to the issue. In the traditional scheme of domestic reproduction, the locus of intimacy could be relatively taken for granted; today it is not. Familiarity understood as this ability "to feel at home" can be very much displaced, whether because you lack a place of your own, move it continuously, or (like Camilo) belong to more than one place. The frontiers of intimacy have become difficult to draw.

The ambiguities of the concept of familiarity embody the problem of how to feel at home. On the one hand, intimacy is something inexorably attached to space: it is about "closeness" and proximity (in space) and about routine and predictability (in time). On the other hand, the modern notion of intimacy entails the possibility (so frequently found) of carrying this space with you. Moving is not then "quitting the familiar" but "carrying it with you." The production of familiarity is very diverse. There are people for whom the mobile devices—laptops, iPods, tablets, cellphones—provide today the most fundamental experience of immediacy and self-abandonment. For many others, it is the family of origin that—as a first foundation stone—counts as an anchor against winds and tides. The techniques of the self—understood as a repertoire for self-control and self-design—have become extraordinarily enriched by resources of mobility and fixation. The possible articulations between these two poles are quite contingent, tactical, and opportunistic. Samantha, a Puerto Rican student in Madrid, reflected about her frequent use of electronic devices of all kinds for listening to music. She recognized that from time to time she needed to go back to her native home to recharge in her father's vast collection of vinyl salsa records. This kind of stock of sound, which works as a regional heritage—a Caribbean memory summarizing geographic and historical experiences in the form of rhythm, melody, and *tumbao*—is well commented in famous songs such as *"Barrunto"* ("One of the heart") and

"*La Abuelita*" ("The grandmother") by Willie Colón ("Remembering my grandma / the proverbs she said made me laugh").

Perhaps the most extreme example of this combination of absolute mobility (everything dispensable, ephemeral) and the need to keep some form of roots was given by Greta, a Madrilenian TV producer in her forties. She had spent her whole life moving from one job to another, from one place to another. She explained to us how much she appreciated the only photograph that she always carries with her: "It is me as a child. I pocketed it from my mother." During this long pillaging of time, she has kept this photo as her talisman, as the only evidence left of a foundational time.

All the subjects in our research expressed this tension between, from one side, the epochal exigence of continuous change and, from another, the psychological need of building in permanence. "Dwelling is recalling," Gaston Bachelard (1994) held. This classical argument presents the house as a basically conservative place, a locus where one could exert, beyond the basic functions of protection and shelter, those of memory, imagination, and daydreaming. Phenomenologically, we would always inhabit the territories of our childhood, the first home. But in metropolitan times, does the argument not run the other way round? Dwelling is forgetting. You are pushed to get rid of things, to recycle, to let things go, to always say farewell. It is for that reason that the questions of intimacy and familiarity appear so deeply enmeshed with those of memory, identity, and mobility.

THE BURDEN OF MEMORY

Family memory came as a gift to Alba, the young schoolteacher with a box of photographs. It entailed, though, a heavy responsibility: taking over the life stories of the family members. This delicate position—becoming the holder of a collective memory—is found among a number of young women of our sample, in the three cities we worked in. Circumstances vary, as does the personal attitude toward such an assignment. But all had this in common: the shock when realizing how much the family heritage would fall on them as a burden that entered in contradiction with day-to-day demands.

For Manuela this was clearly the case. We had met her in CEWs, years before. A librarian and feminist, she was great at spicing up a conversation with little stories. This time, there was no fun. Although we had an appointment to film the interview, she could not make it because of the sudden death of her father. Two months later we tried again. This time she received us in her tiny and tidy apartment in Usera, a working-class neighborhood in Madrid. Her partner, an "artivist" in her thirties, was with her. As mentioned in the second chapter, I had the expectation to address her non hetero home as well as the active role the couple was taking in the LGBTQ movement in the city. Instead, she received us dressed in one of her father's shirts, and from the very beginning, she led the conversation toward the events surrounding the death of her father, his mourning, and the material complications brought about by the inheritance of a big old family house in Santander, on the north coast of Spain, where heirlooms from more than three generations were all jumbled together. As a single daughter, she was the sole heir.

I detached myself so much from the family photos that now they are a burden for me. You acknowledge a certain emotionality in them, but the old bond is lost—those times when you said, "I never will get rid of this." What to do now? Here they are. They have come back to you. Some of them I didn't know still existed. Others got burned along the way. But I no longer have a bond to most of these objects, nor do they share the lightness of my life. . . . Whole cabinets full of porcelain, ivory, bone, and bronze figurines. It gives me the hives! Antiques, old books from those men with the triangle . . . Masons! It seems that a great-uncle of mine was a Freemason. And last but not least: portraits from Franco, books signed by him and Primo de Rivera [a Fascist Spanish leader]. My father inherited things from his grandfather and his great-great-grandfather. All that passed down to me from several generations. Some time ago, I was detached from it. I had even stopped talking to my father and other family members. Now everything returns: boom! In my face. . . . On the one hand, you don't want to burn it all. But this was unnecessary. No need [laughing]. And here it has no place. . . . During his last years, my father developed a Diogenes syndrome of sorts, hoarding paper and stuff. So, one of the first things to do was to throw away more than two thousand kilos of paper. I almost started a fire when switching on an old TV that started to burn. Then I realized this house was a real danger: "Let's start throwing things out." You opened the boxes and found—like Google: "Gastronomy," "Wines," "Hotels," "Stamps" . . . All the subjects he was interested in, boxes and boxes of papers and documents. Also "Economy," because my father was an economist. He even had the BOE [Spanish state official bulletin] from 1973, ranging by topic. A friend of mine says, "Do you know how valuable all this is?" "I don't know," I said. "But I'm gonna throw it away."

We think we live in the present, but this is a partial representation of ourselves. We live with the dead. Human life necessarily enmeshes with presences of the past as well as with anticipations of possible futures. This entanglement of times leads to various kinds of tensions, contradictions, and circles.

On the one hand, a house is made of memory. Not just an individual memory, with instrumental ways of reckoning and controlling the past, but a collective or social one. Social memory has ritual, body, and space as its main sites. This is "how societies remember" (Connerton 1989). First, enacting a ritual or a festival is resuming a never-ending time, brought back to the present by the action of dancers, singers, penitents, and celebrants. Celebrations and commemorations "bind the times" (Fernandez 1994, 145). Second, the body functions as a repository for all kinds of social dispositions and legacies. Belonging to a class, a range, a gender, a nation, a faith, a community is to retrieve perceptual and practical schematas able to reproduce an inscribed memory of gestures and preferences, originated way before the individual. This actualization of the past is highly mysterious. In the grace of a dance, the charm of a gesture, the taste of a wine, the accent of a voice, the unknown manifests itself. The performer, at the very moment of showing up in their best, seems haunted by something or someone. This is what the flamenco singers refer to as the *duende* of a song, or the jazz musician as the *groove* of a tune: forms of incorporated memory that can be sensed but from which it is impossible to ascertain the source. Third, all these body-oriented practices are firmly bound to space. A place is space endowed with a specific social memory. To dwell in a place is to invest it with the thickness of lived experience and biographical marks. To traverse a familiar route is to bring back moments, feelings, and events encoded in its corners, walls, and mobilia. Urban planners know how resistant this kind of spatialized memory can be. This is why the urban plan of old European cities is so difficult to change through restructuring projects. Space is resilient (Connerton 2009, 136).

Nevertheless, industrial economies build atop their own ruins. Consequently, modern society naturally tends to forget (Berman 1983; Connerton 2009). Or perhaps we should rather say that, in the making and unmaking of cities, streets, and homes, the imperatives of conservation and those of innovation collide. This is true for the public sphere, but it also applies, at a more modest scale, to the dynamics of home renewal. In the next chapter, we will look closer at this process by considering IKEA's global success. Let us just state that an interior is always the result of a compromise between keeping a collective memory and cutting away from it in order to freely navigate the present and the future.

Memory and forgetting clash in modern houses. On the one hand, no place incarnates continuity, survivals, and heterochrony like the home. The normalization of calendars and time reckoning in the public space (traffic lights, lines at the supermarket, strict turns patterning public speech) totally collapses at home. Objects of different epochs, styles, and origins are all packed together. The rhythms of conversations and actions meld. Furniture may be integrated in an ensemble, but normally it is not. From the walls, souvenirs, photos, calendars, paintings, and decorations evoke a patchworked chronotropy rather than a unified timeline. They witness heterogeneous time-lapses of individual, marriage, and family life when they do not result from hybrid combinations of dwellers in different periods. In a country house that my family and I have recently purchased, we are living with the remnants of stuff from the former owners. A secret (and slightly sinister) complicity exists with the otherness embedded in this presence that endures through mirrors, tools, boards, corridors, and plants. You feel obliged to respect it.

On the other hand, modern houses are very forgetful. Norma's mother put it this way: you carry what you can. And in an affluent, consumer-oriented economy, this disposition to throw away and let things go is complemented by its opposite: the excessive accumulation of stuff. One of the emerging problems of late modern homes is what to throw away—in Czarniawska and Löfgren's (2012) terms, "how to cope with material overflow." The modernist imperatives to remodel your home, invent yourself, and redesign your life have the dark underside of what to do with the leftovers.

This structural conflict manifests itself acutely at moments that show the contingency of any domestic order. Death and divorce are the most notorious. Biographical accounts often present these two events as cuts in a line or breakdowns in a structure: points of ending and beginning. Löfgren (2018) has noted how divorce shows the frailty of the everyday through the apparition of minor signals of danger. He uses the firefighter's metaphor of the "oxygen bomb": a housefire only becomes visible after the sudden opening of a door fans the flames. Fragility reveals itself in petty details like a discussion, a change in routine, an out-of-place object. The time-building repetition of the everyday becomes exposed. The death of a parent, the loss of a lover, the separation from the couple may not necessarily demolish the whole, but they certainly bring its fragile foundations into the open.

Claudia, a Montevidean psychologist in her twenties, recounted this story:

> I had to do it. My mother did not want to come back. To me it was painful too. Everything remained exactly the same: the rooms, the corners . . . as my grandpa had left them. It was hard. But in the end, I came back and did the job. Cleaning, emptying the house, choosing what to keep and what not. A hard time, but also moving. I found things! I found things that moved me a lot. My grandpa kept a couple of drawings in his wallet that I had drawn for him when I was a little girl. He and I were holding hands. It shook me. I had no idea my grandfather had kept them with him always, everywhere. In his wallet.

This personal account retakes an old family story. The house that Claudia and her mother were afraid to return to is her grandpa's house. An Italian who migrated to Montevideo in the 1950s, he was very fond of his granddaughter. Quarrels between the grandpa and the mother tore the family apart for decades. Little Claudia lost contact with him until, as an adult, she decided to look for him and resume the relationship. The old man dies, leaving her the modest house. The legacy was happily received, since Claudia was wanting to become independent from her parents. As in Manuela's case, with the house also came the painful task of taking stuff out. Here comes the surprise: the drawing she had made as a child, showing her and her grandpa, was always kept with him, in a hidden fold in his wallet. Here there is a recursive spiral between lives and stories. Claudia is not just the storyteller. She discovers herself to be—as we all are—a character in a story plotted by others, kept in the memory and the heart of others. The drawing found among her grandpa's stuff fits in as just one more episode, full of poetic justice, in the whole family drama.

Claudia changed the tone of her account when she introduced the participation of her mother in the story. Her mother initially refuses to cremate the corpse. Some time later, she makes a hasty request to spread the ashes in the backyard:

> It wasn't easy for my mother. For me either, but I insisted that my grandpa knew what he wanted. We had to do it. She finally made up her mind. By then, I had been living in the house for two or three years, with my friend Jacinta. My mother had the wish—after cremating my grandpa—to spread his ashes . . . at the back of my yard! The idea was to let him go in his own home, his house. But we had never talked about this again! She arrived at that idea on my friend's birthday no less. She phoned to say that she had made up her mind: she wanted to spread the ashes at the back of my yard. I told her, "Sorry, I have a birthday party right now. I can't throw Grandpa's ashes in the back!" She replied, "Please be cool. Can't you ask Jacinta to postpone it?" "No, Mom. I cannot throw Grandpa in the yard. I don't wanna step on him in the backyard." My mother got angry with me. She thought I was mean or something, that I didn't understand her. But actually, I cannot throw Grandpa in the back and sweep him away! No.

Claudia's mother imagined the yard as a place of memory, where the presence of her father could be fixed. Rosa, a Mexican woman, found such a place in the rooftop terrace, where her deceased father grew plants:

> Then I said, "What do we do?" One of my dearest aunts said, "Let's go see them." "Ah, this is a Moses' cradle; it should not be exposed to the sun. And this one is a *siempreviva* [in Spanish, 'ever living']; it doesn't need a lot of water." There was a little bush of chili peppers that my father harvested several times. He made hot sauces; he loved them. It pleased me to keep my father's plants alive: a living, green presence that belonged to him and that he cared for.

Even Manuela, after all her declarations of detachment from the inherited heirlooms and stuff, explained,

> This shirt is my father's. It has embroidered initials, as he was so classical. I don't know. With the clothes it gets very difficult. Soon I won't be able to throw

it away. Why? Because of the image I remember from my father. It's not about his belongings or stuff. It's about him. With his clothes.

These stories elaborate the tensions between honoring the past and living in the present at a symbolic level. The narrative resources are diverse. Manuela works with irony: the unexpected return of the remnants of a rejected past brings to light the actual impossibility of integrating them into her current life. Claudia's story bounces between two contrasting registers. A lyrical surprise sustains the tension of the first part of the story, when a piece of her child-hood arrives from the past as a moving gift. In the second part, the humorous quarrel with her mother gives room to explore the fine line between honoring the dead and stepping on them. In Rosa's account, the tragic tone gives way to a fully ritual one by the intermediation of plants and flowers. As long as the *siemprevivas* live, a remnant of the father will as well.

We believe that memory belongs to us. Is it not rather the other way round? It comes from the others and goes back to them. Everyone leaves indelible tracks, like Claudia did in her grandpa's wallet. And everyone is touched by others' stuff and belongings, like Rosa by her father's *siemprevivas* and Manuela by her father's shirt. Memory is collective because it can be shared. Their poetic means of evocation and presence offer to those who have gone a last opportunity to stay with us.

NOTES

1. The figure of the tangle is used by Darwin in a famous final paragraph of *The Origin of Species*, sixth edition:

It is interesting to contemplate a tangled bank, clothed with many plants of many kinds, with birds singing on the bushes, with various insects flitting about, and with worms crawling through the damp earth, and to reflect that these elabo-rately constructed forms, so different from each other, and dependent upon each other in so complex a manner, have all been produced by laws acting around us. . . . Thus, from the war of nature, from famine and death, the most exalted object which we are capable of conceiving, namely, the production of the higher animals, directly follows. There is grandeur in this view of life, with its several powers, having been originally breathed by the Creator into a few forms or into one; and that, whilst this planet has gone circling on according to the fixed law of gravity, from so simple a beginning endless forms most beautiful and most wonderful have been, and are being evolved.

Chapter 4

A Visit to IKEA

NARRATING IKEA

The Swedish-founded multinational furniture company IKEA is firmly etched in my memories. In 1996, I visited the store, which had recently opened in Madrid. I had just moved out of my parents' home in Barrio de Salamanca, a well-off neighborhood, to a more modest area downtown. As a student with a limited budget, I learned how to make do with whatever cheap things I could find. I had a couch that I found in the trash and linen made from patches bought at a clearance sale. So, entering IKEA's showroom was an economic and cultural shock. Everything seemed cool but affordable, as practical as it was beautiful. What is more important: things were purposefully designed for a modern, self-sufficient way of life. You could not find those heavy dark *boiseries* like your grandparents had that were built to last forever, nor the faux-leather couches to welcome guests, let alone the pompous cabinets used by more well-off neighbors to show off their bourgeois status. The stuff in IKEA was designed for a clever enjoyment of the present. It conveyed a global flavor from a certain ultra-contemporary nowhere, unequivocally Nordic (with duvets and raw wooden furniture), far from Mediterranean customs. It combined a philosophy of informality, a minimalist adjustment to the scarcity of space, and a do-it-yourself spirit. I paid my first visit to the newly inaugurated store with close friends, and it became a true celebration. The arrival of IKEA heralded a new pedagogy of living in the city, one that I had been an unaware ambassador of with my own bachelor, cosmopolitan way of life.

Many people my age have a memory of this event. "Welcome to the Independent Republic of Your Home" was the catchy slogan with which IKEA presented itself to the Spanish customer. Spaniards still feel complicity with its impertinent self-assertiveness, its declaration of radical independence

129

from any public authority beyond one's threshold. In 2016, IKEA commemorated its twenty years in Spain at the College of Architects with an exhibition of objects donated by customers. Given that IKEA's showroom consists precisely of a museum-like theme park of intimate rooms and ambiences, it was not easy to discern the difference between the commemoration and an actual furniture showroom.

In the early 1990s, Madrid was fully entering the world economy as a global node. Spain had recently become part of the EU; direct investment capitals had grown; Madrid attracted headquarters of transnational corporations; a solid sector of advanced services, with its associated migration flow, had risen (Sassen 2000; Colombo 2016). These structural processes of economic globalization, concentration of wealth, dualization of income, and metropolitan sprawl were accompanied by cultural processes of cosmopolitanization, hybridation, and novelty in daily life consumption. From that time, I remember my mother eating (in front of her six astonished children) the first avocado that entered my home. During the 1990s, we would get used to seeing sushi in the streets and yucca in our markets, even flying abroad on getaways to Caribbean beaches or castles in central Europe.

These two joint processes of economic affluence and opening to the world sparked an inner refurbishing of the whole city. "Totally refurbished" was invariably advertised in apartments for rent. During a real estate bubble that saw prices go sky-high, the savings of many went toward home improvements. Everybody updated their style of furniture and decor. At this moment, IKEA was decisive. Madrilenians swiftly learned to sleep under duvets, to illuminate with low-consumption lamps, and to put children to sleep in Nordic raw-pine bunk beds. Madrid became Sweden's second capital.

The novelty was in the products but also in the mise-en-scène of IKEA showcases. At traditional department stores in Spain, you could look but not touch. At furniture fairs and factories, you would find couches, tables, and dressers piled up in long rows, following a production-chain logic. By contrast, IKEA's showroom captivated with the glamour of entering an inhabited intimate space, by imagining yourself as being a part of it. IKEA inaugurated a new way to shop, a ritual of consumption, and a hyperrealist indoor experience. The company calls it "the visit" (*la visita*) or "the showroom" (*la tienda*) in order to differentiate this moment from the subsequent self-service shopping that comes after in "the store" (*el almacén*).

"The visit" has a strong ritual flavor. It evokes going to a museum or a theme park. Let's put it this way: in the traditional market, customers connect with things by the strong mediation of singular merchants and the public place created by the free concurrence of the many and the diverse (with noise, merchants' cries, added presences of music, street performers, gamblers, beggars, etc.; Bohannan and Dalton 1965; Bakhtin 1990). In the modern supermarket, the capitalist enterprise has swept all that away, taking over the monopoly of mediation, but, paradoxically, it itself fades in favor of the merchandise, which reigns sovereign: nothing must disturb the shopping experience of the customer in their lonely face-to-face relation to the commodity (Martín-Barbero 1989, 99). Objects in a museum are differently mediated. As valuables connected to a sacred reality beyond, things appear as representations of something not visible, whose reality is asserted and honored. Symbols, icons, relics, and works of art have the power to put the visitor in contact with this original and authentic source, be it the sacred past of the nation, the superior values of knowledge and beauty, or some numinous representation of the world. In museums' collections, like in churches, civic monuments, and cemeteries, objects are relics of the past. By contrast, in the theme park, the stress on authenticity vanishes; or it might be better said that it is displaced from the things themselves to the experience of the user, who is invited to manipulate things and fully interact with them in a virtual simulacrum. The controlled situation works "as if": it provides the feeling of an adventure without the risks associated with it. Aesthetics are invariably hyperrealist: more real than real. Objects are declared to be fake, just for fun. Funnily enough, the more alike the fake artifacts are to the originals, the more genuine we consider the adventure to be. In summary, at the shopping mall and the popular market, we look for commodities, although in two very different veins. At the museum, the exhibition, and the concert, we search for the sacred categories embodied in cultural objects. The theme park, like the zoo, is about fun and amusement: diversion as an escape from reality.

What kind of experiences does "the visit" to IKEA provide? This question guided the ethnography of IKEA's showrooms we did a few years ago.[1] The entrance to the shop is organized in a museum-like form, with a predetermined itinerary through a marked aisle that gives access to several rooms arranged and decorated as specific ambiences, called "room settings." To visit them, you abandon the set itinerary for a while, only to return to it later on, to keep following the line.[2] The route begins in the living room and ends with decorations like plants and candles. Other parts of the house, like bedrooms, kitchens, dining rooms, bathrooms, and outdoor terraces and gardens, are placed in between. The sequence is, then, not spatially organized like a real house, but it does provide a realistic feeling of the various atmospheres corresponding to every kind of room. These hyperrealist aesthetics are one of the showrooms' most important values, as you can gather from the visitors' comments. There are shortcuts to move freely along the preset sequence. During peak hours, a steady and orderly flow of people follows the arrows of the itinerary, while groups of people detour from it to enter the ambiences, touch the goods, ask questions, assess the measurements of a cabinet, sit on a couch, or lie on a bed. The visiting group greatly varies, from single individuals to whole families shopping together, groups of young friends, couples with and without kids, and so on. Among this diversity, you can sense that the subject protagonist of a visit to IKEA is people living together, what Kaufmann calls a *group ménagèr* (1997, 81).

Visiting IKEA is not exactly like going to a museum, a theme park, or a traditional furniture store, but it combines components of all three. The attitude of the visitors lacks the respectful relation to symbols expected in the museum. They touch things and interact with them, like they would do in a theme park. Yet there is a concentrated attention on the quality of things as well as a genuine interest in the beauty and inspiration of the room settings. This is reflected in the professional jargon of interior designers when they say that a showroom's function is "to inspire the customer" before the purchase. No matter this aesthetic, contemplative component, the visit is actually a rather tense activity, which involves (1) orientation in a huge place; (2) comparison between the space, needs, and stuff of one's home with the goods present in the shop; and (3) aesthetic evaluation of them. These orientational, parametric, and judgmental activities are frequently shared out loud between the members of the household. A minor scuffle may eventually arise, with spouses arguing about the size of a bed or the correct color of a comforter. You also witness scenes of inverted socialization, when daughters teach their mothers about new styles or children try to actively participate in these negotiations (IKEA embodies our current ethos of full recognition of children's voices and needs in the common space). These are very practical, purchase-oriented actions. Still, the components of fun and aesthetic contemplation add an exciting dimension to the promenade, something less present in the traditional furniture shop. Some people visit IKEA just for pleasure, scheduling a part of the day for it, like when going to Disneyland or a museum.[3]

The global success of IKEA is a narrative one. At the end of the century, IKEA was able to perform a narrative on intimate space shared by vast constituencies around the world, making it both credible and accessible. Of course, economic, marketing, and logistic reasons also exist (cf. Garvey 2009, 2013). This company has fulfilled the aspirations of a broad market niche regarding style and way of life in a modern, comfortable, and practical urban habitat. Moreover, it was capable of building well-designed lines of products and a well-greased global chain of logistics and delivery. However, this would not be sufficient without engaging the imagination of its customers through a successful narrative about metropolitan living. IKEA is about the good life in late modern homes.

The "visit" to the shop is the mediation by which such narrative becomes sensed and embodied. IKEA showrooms function as a theme park of intimacy. The lighting, the spatial solutions, the careful disposition of furniture in every room—all converge in presenting every part of the house as habitable, when not truly inhabited. Aesthetics are not just realist (a *pars-pro-toto* accurate representation of the concept) but hyperrealist: more real than reality itself (Castañares 2006, 14). For example, you may find clues and traces of human presence, like a woman's dress hung in the wardrobe, some books casually open on the couch, or children's toys laying on the carpet. Of course, we understand this is fiction. The customer plays with this trick to imagine what the place would look like when inhabited by someone. As in the theme park, the fiction sets clear limits: all furniture is new, the composition obviously arranged; no one is living there. Unlike at the park, here the purpose of fiction is not the fun of adventure but the imagination of dwelling. How would living in such a place be? The added value of this peculiar modality of showroom lies in the performative actualization of an intimate presence. "Who is dwelling in this store?" I wondered at the end of one of our trips to IKEA. Half serious, half joking, which, by the way, is the proper attitude for an intimacy theme park, we hypothesized that the dweller was a middle-aged, married, learned Swedish woman who had children and a very cosmopolitan taste. We christened her Mrs. Lungren. Once we invented her, we began to find signs and traces of Mrs. Lungren everywhere. You could come across her lipstick on a shelf. You could see photos of her dog on a nightstand. Her presence included others. In IKEA San Diego, her children had been doing their school assignments in the kitchen, leaving open notebooks with drawings made by them. In St. Etienne, Mrs. Lungren's eldest daughter had been listening to heavy metal locked in her room, lying on her bed below a sexy and well-known painting by Gustav Klimt. What Mrs. Lungren reads shows an ample culture: a combination of books in Swedish with treatises about the modern American home.

Freud (1919) popularized the aesthetic category of "the uncanny" as an uncomfortable fear of the unknown, an experience marked by the simultaneous presence of familiarity and the unfamiliar within the same object or character. I find this concept pertinent to understanding the potentials and limits of a theme park of intimacy. As a sacred place, intimacy repels irruptions. Entering uninvited in someone else's space provokes reactions of shame and discomfort in the intruder. A threshold exists that must not be violated without due rituals of hospitality. If taken too far, then, Mrs. Lungren dwelling in IKEA showrooms would probably become an uncanny, monstruous, and uncomfortable presence.

INSIDE STORYTELLING

We invited Manuel, an interior design manager from IKEA Spain, to participate in an educational TV program about home practices (Cruces 2017b). It came as a surprise to discover that storytelling is a key moment in the showroom's production process. During their work, interior designers and decorators make up stories about who dwells in the room, what activities are taking place, and what scene is developing. They support this story with the visual aid of drawings and photographs extracted from image banks. The stories are used as a technique to land abstract guidelines and demands about consumer target, product style, and commercial strategy received from other departments. A good story provides the emotional work that the room settings are meant to inspire in the visitor. The story determines the final products selected and their disposition in the showroom.

Of course, neither the characters nor the actions in such a story are arbitrarily chosen. Before the interior designer decides what room to build, the spectrum of possible stories has been dramatically narrowed down by an exigent work of conceptualization. First, four "macrotrends" frame all the stores at a global scale: urbanism, sustainability, aging, and technology impact. Second, a compilation of international studies (called "insight packages") helps to specify and update those general topics. The resulting clues in dwelling behavior are tested in every country in order to identify locally valid trends. For example, in the case of Spain, surveys indicated that Spaniards attach the highest symbolic value to their living room, that we spend more money on it than on other parts of the house, and that we trace a strong separation between the living room as a public part of the home and the bedrooms as the more intimate ones. These surveys are complemented with "social listening" on social media and other marketing sources that give accurate data about family composition, income, living area, and budget. All this provides a quantitative floor for the stories. Recently they have also adopted interactive methods, like cocreation of home spaces with clients. Third, each season a global catalog sets aesthetic lines regarding colors, materials, and the like. Fourth, "IKEA Tools" contains a fixed catalog of furniture styles that results from a criss-crossing of basic oppositions, such as modern/classic, Scandinavian/international, and urban/popular. Fifth, a *prêt-a-porter* categorization of clients and dwellers called "living situations" classify them according to a basic set of variables: singles/couples, starting out/established, with kids/without kids. In the important target of families with kids, the ages of children are split into babies, toddlers, starting school, and teens. This typology is international and updated every few years. Nevertheless, they adapt it to the local population of each country and region. This population grid is then translated into a list of "long-term priorities" that define the main set of needs of the population group as well as the products associated with them.

This complex of variables results in a matrix that sets the range of possibilities that every team of interior designers and decorators may arrange in a "cluster" or ensemble of "room settings." They try to diversify the ambiences of each cluster as much as possible by contrasting them in terms of target, trends, needs, and style:

> At the cluster we go back to everything that we have seen in the Trends section, and we begin to create stories for each room setting. For example, we say, "In room setting 1, we are going to work with the macrotrend Digital Living; we want to work strongly on the impacts of technology." We have chosen two new needs: "leisure time" and "productivity." And so on for every room setting. In number 2, we are speaking of Urban World, a very strong identity and encounters to socialize. In number 3, we have worked on sustainability, wellness, the reencountering with nature. . . . In cluster 1, for example, we have begun with a family, Living with Children. They have two children. One is a toddler, he may be around three years old, and another will be a "starting school." Then, you need [to set] different needs. Instead, in this other setting, you have a Together Established, an elderly married couple, which connects with the trend Aging World, the aging population. Then, here comes a young couple. Here, a single person. And then over there, a teen. So, we proceed by creating different stories, with different styles, because every room must have a style, like the Swedish modern here. We want a very Scandinavian atmosphere.

The matrix of variables allows for choices in the form of combinations of global trends, IKEA tools, living situations, and long-term priorities. Every story incarnates a set of values of these variables.

> I am going to give you an example. We have chosen the Digital DNA, the new needs of leisure time and productivity, the living situations: here they are going to spend between 1,500 and 3,000 euros—to ensure a price level that is affordable. It is a newly built apartment of around twenty-eight square meters, with pillars—we are going to explore how to maximize the space between pillars. In Design Tendency we have the Scandinavian style—as we said, to enhance our brand image. In this profile we consider the customers who have little knowledge and interest in decoration. The style is Modern Scandinavian, the living situation is Living with Toddlers and Starting School, the long-term priority is Living with Children, and the products and solutions are middle priced.

> Now, here comes the storytelling, OK? We have twenty-seven-year-old Rocío and thirty-eight-year-old Oscar, parents of Laura, who is four, and Matías, who is six. Rocío and Oscar are a young couple; they live near the city center in a recently constructed building. They both run a children's clothing store. They

have a very Scandinavian living room, where they enjoy all their hobbies. They wanted a very flexible space where they could all together play, study, work, and watch cartoons on their tablet. Each one in their corner, but together as a family. The living room is at the center of the home, with the couch in the middle; they have created a big island, where they can carry out multiple activities at the same time. They follow the Montessori educational method, so they have tried to adapt solutions in which their children can be autonomous regarding their own leisure and development. . . .

This [story] is created by the interior designer. I mean, I have worked out the previous part, and now every interior designer in the team begins to create a story like this. I always say, the more real and elaborated the story is, the easier the next step is going to be. Then, this is what we are going to represent in this room setting. It will be a Saturday night. The whole family enjoys the living room. Matías is watching a show on the tablet, in his favorite corner, while Rocío watches TV. Laura is playing with her cellphone, and Oscar is setting the table for his board game time. OK? This is to truly visualize what is going on there.

This storytelling is not a free exercise of imagination; it comes firmly rooted in the company's policies, background knowledge, and commercial strategies. And yet, there is an undeniably narrative artistry in this craft, one that entails an epistemic jump: from abstract trends to concrete people, from categories to contingencies, from numbers to persons. And from all this, its final materialization in the form of a disposition of objects and "solutions." In the storytelling process, a mobilization of local knowledge takes place, which is based mostly—but not only—on the social and personal experience of the professional, in this case, equally acquainted with the Montessori method and with the scarcity of space of Spanish homes. The story is an emotional mediation. It links the abstract marketing of the shop, on the one hand, and the production of a furnished space, on the other. In between, the story carries all the affective power and emotional load attributed to the discourse of things that rules IKEA's showroom.

What do I call "emotional space"? This is very subjective. When you create an emotional link, you have reached people's hearts. It is difficult to reach everyone that deeply. You look, then, for different targets, what their passions are, OK? You look for something emotional, by creating first what we call the storytelling: you search for a passion, then you exaggerate it to the maximum. For example, if you like nature, or children, or music, you exaggerate the story to the maximum, with its solutions and decoration—now we call it the *attrezzo* [props]. You exaggerate this storytelling. At the end this impacts you; it has an emotional link. Sound, we include a lot of sound, video too. . . . This is our work, to tell a story by showing furniture. It is very difficult, because in the end what you are playing with are emotions. And emotions are personal. They are tangible and intangible at the same time. How do we make tools, formulas, to create this emotional link? For me, it is by looking for stories that are real—this is why we do all these surveys, to prevent us from getting lost. To look for real stories and real passions that are also relevant for your market. Stories of people's day-to-day. In the creation process of a room setting, we have a very strong base that begins with the briefing, then goes to the storytelling, then to a powerful visual image, until you arrive at the solution. And then, you ask yourself how to exaggerate it.

So, it was not just Mrs. Lungren and her Swedish family who haunted the showrooms of IKEA but also a plethora of local characters, such as Rocío and Oscar, who populated with their needs and activities what we had imagined to be a para–theme park of intimacy. The narrative hypothesis we had been fantasizing about in our wanderings had firm grounds in the practice that these professionals apply to the material montage of the space.

UNDERNEATH THE TALES

Could our visit to IKEA be over? Of course not. The storage of pieces of furniture and other goods, the cash registers, the food shop, and other services are located on the ground floor. Here, attitudes and activities differ significantly from the ones in the showroom. This is not a place to dream but a place to work. Here you—in IKEA managers' terms—"finish the purchase process": you pinpoint the merchandise, which is stored in gigantic aisles following an alphanumeric code (people often follow a list for doing this); you haul them on top of a heavy shopping cart; you get information about assembly and transport, since the pieces of furniture come disassembled and packaged to the point of unrecognizability; you wait in line and pay. In the last stage, you will face the pieces at home and try to reconstruct them with the help of an instruction booklet and a hex key.

Not stories, but heavy work. Below the intimate narratives of the upper floor, a world of material activities of self-service—searching, hauling, paying—flourishes. "IKEA is like marriage," my wife told me when I tried to explain our fancy ideas about the showroom. "It may have many tales, but the truth is always in the basement." I could not agree more. Any tale of intimacy that neglects the work needed to produce and maintain it would surely be misleading. However, when you ask someone about their impressions of IKEA, it is often the magic of the showroom that prevails.

NOTES

1. This ethnography was made in collaboration with Nuria Esteban and Romina Colombo, between 2014 and 2017, in the showrooms of Madrid (Alcorcón and San Sebastián de los Reyes, Spain), Valencia (Spain), Saint Etienne (France), and San Diego (United States). The ethnography included participant observation in IKEA shops as well as interviews with managers of IKEA in the departments of interior design, communication, and research. We are grateful to Manuel Delgado, Paz Sánchez, and Ana María Figueiras for their kind contribution.

2. The customary organization of the tour has been recently modified toward a model of closed, circular clusters of room settings.

3. This image of the company must be put in a generational perspective. Spanish millennials probably do not agree with the vision of rupturism and global modernity given here, since the very success of IKEA at the end of the century entailed a generalized spread of their low-cost products as well as a routinization of the purchase process. "The customer says, 'You surprised us at the beginning, but then stopped moving forward,'" summarized a manager. "Now we want to reinvent ourselves." The company is aware of this process, which challenges IKEA's market position among the youngest generations and pushes for an update of its product and marketing strategies.

Chapter 5

The Poetics of Dwelling

FORMATIVE PROCESSES IN DWELLING

The IKEA paradox consists of this: an "expertization" of the intimate space comes through experts' appropriation of the practices and narratives of common people. Expert systems have a massive role in giving form to the space we live in. But, ironically, they do so by mimicking the structures of the world of life. We reinvent ourselves with IKEA solutions, and, conversely, IKEA feeds its design solutions with our own passions and tales. There is a circularity here that does not fit well with simple oppositions of classical urbanity, such as public versus private, production versus consumption, or the system versus daily life. Certainly, everyday life is penetrated by structures that come from "outside" (society) and "before" (history). Nevertheless, the subjects' search for autonomy and self-determination is not a mere phantasmagory. The economic and political agencies purporting to affect the intimate realm need to seriously take it into account.

This paradox reveals the reflexive condition of late modern dwelling. In a former study of institutions in Spain (Cruces et al. 2002; Velasco et al. 2006), we focused on the reflexive process we called "repersonalization." Late modern organizations, both public and private, need to repersonalize the bond with their subjects. In institutional jargon: to "reform" themselves, organizations have to be "closer," "more transparent," "participative," and "trusted" by the people they serve (Díaz de Rada 2002). On the one hand, organizations process people as if they were things: they order, number, objectify, and commodify persons by rationalizing tasks, segregating functions, splitting up categories of people, and measuring targets (Douglas 1985). These are requirements of functional efficiency. On the other hand, late modern institutions seek to recover a more holistic and personal bond with their users, clients, and citizens out of what Weber called "the iron cage." This is a requirement of legitimacy and accountability. They must listen to people's voices and needs, build trust, show proximity, enchant the relationship. This process goes far beyond cosmetics: it entails a symbolic investment in building a smiling face for otherwise cold, faceless bureaucracies. The interesting point is that this smiling organization does not cancel out the former instrumental regime. It overlaps with it in the form of a double-binding code (Díaz de Rada, in Velasco et al. 2006, 332). As with any contradiction, you cannot aspire to solve it; you learn to live with it.

The relationship between the intimate sphere and the work of expert systems stands on this kind of paradoxical, circular condition. In the words of our IKEA manager, "To have people [in the visual image of the rooms] is very important, because we work for the people. For me, there have to be people in IKEA, because we work for them. You can never forget this, that [our mission] is to create a better day-to-day for the majority of the people."

How do the stories gathered in this book relate to the reflexive nature of late modernity? In this chapter I will address this question. My stance is that *poiesis*—in the sense of the production of meaning—is integral to the constitution of the intimate space, understood as an order of your own. This order implies a never-ending activity of boundary-work, semantic displacement, personal signature, and semiotic closure. These operations produce such an order. Without them, the joint intervention of experts, reforming policies, and material factors would not create an intimate space as such—just a simulacrum. The stories gathered here deal, in a variety of forms, with those operations. This stance also applies to the storytelling re-created by experts as a means of intervention—like the one performed by interior designers—as well as to the metanarratives that we scholars and analysts produce to describe, explain, and reform this realm.

Following the classical differentiation of language functions by Jacobson (1960, 353), we may properly call this process "poetic" under three conditions. First, the poetic function is not an anomaly—a peripheral misuse of common speech—but a fundamental modality connected with those higher recursive capacities that he called "metalinguistic." In intimacy, language cannot be but poetic. Second, this *poiesis* or search for meaning is never finished, complete, or fully accomplished but is rather tentative and fragmentary. Following Berger's bold metaphor, it is "a rescue operation." Third, these practices never work in a material or sociocultural vacuum. They are strongly overdetermined by other formative processes that converge on the intimate sphere, providing limiting factors, degrees of freedom, and points of orientation. I will mention a few: reproduction, reform, community, commodification, and individualization. By their global, metropolitan nature, these processes represent pervasive, long-term, and large-scale trends. I do not pretend to address them in depth.[1] They set the perimeter for the dweller to act. These processes open and problematize their poetic efforts to build and maintain an order of their own. In the circular interplay between the subject and their environment, these processes provide raw materials, reflexive problems, and practical solutions that ceaselessly open, erode, and modify the order we live in.

Reproduction is the most obvious of all. Let us consider, for example, the paradigmatic situation of the birth of a child. There exists a before and an after to the arrival of the newborn—not only because of the role changes attached to the caregivers but also because of the intense materiality of the work needed to support a life: feeding, cleaning, sleeping, caring, communicating. Any domestic unit performs these formidable tasks routinely and silently. The bias of the conventional opposition between "production" and "reproduction" is the concealment of how productive, generative, and fertile this domestic realm is. And beyond the material conditions for the support of human life, the reproduction process also involves those activities that ensure the cultural continuity of the group. Every individual faces the question of how to handle the legacy received, what to pass down (or not) to the following generation. This collective dimension of the reproductive process was perhaps underrepresented in our corpus of stories from collective exploration workshops since, for many of the younger participants, the challenges of producing themselves—forging a career, a job, a space, a reputation, and a couple—were imperative. The anxieties of the present left little room for this essential question, which involves, beyond the present, a connection between past and future. By contrast, such a dimension was the backbone of interviews devoted to parenting and the management of memory.

A second formative process is community. This is a charged word with a long history in the humanities and social sciences (Amit 2002; Amit and Rapport 2003; Cruces 2007, 7; Sennet 1969). As ideal type, "community" (gemeinschaft) opposes to "society" (gesellschaft), denoting two modalities of the social bond. Community bonds are considered primordial, multifunctional, and holistic, not limited to a restricted dimension of the social role. In the nineteenth century, the opposition was loaded with a strong evolutionist orientation: in industrial societies, community ties were progressively substituted by societal, contractual ones. However, nowadays the presence and importance of community bonds is broadly acknowledged, even in an urban, "post-Gesellschaft" society (Lyon and Driskell 2011). The current problem with the concept is rather the opposite: the idealizing, almost mythological aura that the word tends to carry when used to back any political, racial, ethnic, religious, territorial, residential, or even technological claim. We live in a world of communities: coffee farmers, car buyers, believers in the rapture, transgender runners, ecumenical worshippers, Kardashian followers, booktubers, Real Madrid fans, anti-EU and pro-EU activists, and so on. Any collective cause may sustain the emergence (or return) of its corresponding "community." We may question whether a constituency of people makes a community just because of a true or supposed shared trait; ethnopolitical definitions are contested arenas for culture wars of vast proportions that I will not tackle here. Let us just note that understanding the intimate realm would be impossible without keeping in mind its fabulous potential to grow communal bonds. By living together, people create affections, invent ways to address and name each other, share chores and routines, synchronize their rhythms, pattern their encounters, generate and distribute common goods and services, negotiate their differences, and criticize the rest of the members. They do this because they belong, for better or worse, to a common place. In this deep sense, community means a shared destiny. As someone told me in Mexico, you may detest your neighbors, but they will come to rescue you when an earthquake topples the building. This does not mean that the people you live with, or near to, are necessarily wonderful. It means that they define your daily horizon, play a necessary part in the plot of your life. In our research, the most profound trace of this communal living was the continuous discursive slippage from the "I" to the "we," from "me" to "us," that we have observed in chapter 3. Stories of the self also include others. Alba disguised as her mother; Camilo dinning (and quarreling) with the singles of the Club for Those Who Live Alone; Manuela, Claudia, and Rosa reluctantly accepting to administer their family heirlooms: all are examples of such slippage, which Douglas (1991) and Löfgren (2019b) theorized as a moral economy. Home, family, and household, in their many variations, are the paradigmatic model of a community. This is why they are so often metaphorically projected over the nation, the race, the church, and the ethnic group, in order to enhance the unquestionability of their claims. By virtue of such metaphors, the members of those larger communities can be figured as "brothers" and "sisters" who share the same "house."

Reform, a third formative process, has to do with the intervention of modern agencies to regulate, control, and inform the intimate space. Rationalization, administration, scientization, hygiene, and safety are the civilizing goals of this process, which acts powerfully on the space, the dwelling group, and the individuals themselves. We cannot underestimate the scope and intensity of such a reform. It affects all areas of living: architecture, interior design, furniture, hygiene, personal care, clothing, education, health, food, transport, leisure, sex, mental well-being, telecommuting. Whatever one would consider "just mine" in these areas is actually regulated, designed, supervised, administered, and controlled by some expert system, public or private, to the point that we should rather question whether something that could be properly called "ours" exists. Historians and sociologists have highlighted the long span of this evolution (Elias 2000, 2001; Ariès and

Duby 1985; Dumont 1985; Frykman and Löfgren 1989; Claval 2003; Sennet 1969; Simonet-Tenant 2009). Certain authors shock the contemporary reader, for example, by describing what it was like to eat in England in times when meat was likely rotten, or what it was like to "make your bed" when people lacked a fixed place to sleep in the house (Bryson 2010). There are three critical moments in this civilizing history. One is the triumph, during the second half of the nineteenth century, of hygienic and scientific ideas, with their application to urban planning, the generalization of a modernist standard of house plan, and the incorporation of essential services of air circulation, sewage, running water, and electricity (Eleb and Debarre 1995; Frykman and Löfgren 1989). Nowadays we take these services for granted; they constitute our dwelling common sense. In the nineteenth century, though, they were the focus of entrepreneurial epopees, heated controversies, and social battles (Archila 1991). A second decisive moment is associated with the mechanization of chores during the twentieth century, with the adoption of the stove, the washing machine, and the fridge. This silent revolution in the kitchen announced the progressive incorporation of women in the labor market. Here we can glimpse a knot of complex connections between the public and private facets of this process (Ascher 2001; Hochschild and Machung 1989). Finally, in the twenty-first century, there is a third wave of technological reform going on, with the generalization of screens, electronic devices, and online connections in a wired home.

The digitalization of home life deserves monographic attention, which we cannot provide here. As noted in previous chapters, wireless, mobile, and online technologies have radically changed home landscapes and their inhabitants. By augmenting the sensorial, processing, and storing capabilities of the human brain, these technologies have revolutionized daily routines, tasks, and chores. By allowing synchronic connection at a distance, they have incredibly expanded the network of exchanges of all kinds (from commercial to sexual, from activism to finances, from news to gossiping, from science to soccer, from parochial trifles to planetary crises). Today, a teenager in their room may well be hanging out with their peers while at the same time being "at home."

This overall process of rationalization, scientization, and mechanization is reflected in the stories gathered here in two ways. First, particular objects single it out. Mattresses and clocks, heaters and restrooms, laptops and iPhones play important roles in the stories, facilitating or obstructing the goals of human characters. Second, the reform appears as an unquestioned set of presuppositions about good living, condensed in values of comfort, efficiency, and cleanliness. This older background tends to be left unsaid, while the devices of the last technological generation more vividly captivated the attention of our participants.

Reform is inseparable from commercialization and individualization. The modern nation-state is a principal agent of the reform of dwelling due to its prominence in enforcing regulation, sanitation, infrastructure, technologies, and assistance policies. The other big agent is the market. The argumentative thread of Arlie Hochschild's (2003) work is precisely the commercialization of intimate life: how the market has taken over a growing part of the tasks and competences once attributed to housewives and, more generally, to the household as a whole. In industrial economies, the domestic group has ceased to be a unit of economic production, becoming one of distribution and consumption. There is something ineluctable in this evolution: today few people make their own clothes or furniture, let alone their own medicines or soap. But affective, relational, and bodily activities still exist, which keep occupying the center of daily life—what Beck and Beck-Gernsheim (1995) vividly call "affective work." We generally do not transfer these tasks to strangers if we can avoid it, be it getting a date, feeding a baby, or celebrating the birthday of our child. These things still remain associated with the social space of the home. However, Hochschild (2012) has explored in *The Outsourced Self* the front line of a noticeable process of externalization of functions to providers such as online dating apps, personal shoppers, wedding organizers, family coaches, even a "wantologist" to discover your true wishes. These providers add to traditional ones, such as nannies, babysitters, and housekeepers, whose work has now become normal in middle-class homes. Hochschild sees the process as a form of outsourcing to professionals. The intimate areas where we do things for ourselves is narrowing down. At the same time, home remains an irreplaceable source of value regarding its contribution to the sentimental and psychological well-being of the members of the household.

While *community* sounds attractive and *reform* neutral, *commercialization* sounds like an undeniably bad thing. And yet, if people resort to hiring help, it is because they consider it a betterment in their quality of living. It is unclear how far the commercialization process may or should go. This gray area is the object of heated controversies inside the domestic unit, as well as in the public arena. If people (hypothetically) remove all their time and energies from domestic life, the foreseeable outcome will be poor, miserable intimacies. But the reason to monetize these tasks, outsourcing them to market agents, is because the work on the home is underrated in terms of both monetary and social value. No one wants to bury themselves in something devalued, unacknowledged, and invisible.

This dilemma was heatedly discussed in one of our workshops on kitchens. Everyone in the room recognized the high values of traditional cooking, family meals, and sharing time around food. "All this sounds wonderful," a woman retorted, "but it has been my lifelong wish to leave the kitchen. It is a place I do not want to return to." The dilemma is then a gendered one: for women to leave the kitchen, men have to enter it . . . unless we expect that a hired catering service will come to do the job. Be that as it may, it can also be argued that, with the passing of time, a routinization and naturalization of these services is predictable, as has already happened before with services like the phone, the radio, and the TV. Those inventions were once demonized as invading intruders that would bring about the death of good mores and family life. Following this line of reasoning, anticapitalist critics depict the commercializing process as commodification: a form of alienation in which we trade with ourselves and submit our daily lives to the imperatives of a traffic of goods and money. Regarding our stories, this critique should be reformulated. The home impact of the market tends to be received with a dual and ambivalent approach. True, nobody wants to sell their most precious treasures of intimate life for cheap. But the market is also a useful tool to decide where and how to best invest your time and effort. In a market-driven society, goods and commodities help you discover who you are and imagine who else you could be.

The last process considered here is individualization. While reproduction and community put the dwelling group first, reform and commercialization bring the individual to the fore. Sociological and urbanological literature from the 1990s and after have underlined this individualizing effect as a general trait of post-traditional societies (Beck, Giddens, and Lash 1997; Ascher 2001; Bauman 2001; Lahire 2006). In a "metropolis of individuals," choice is essential. During our fieldwork, the power of choice found expression in the participants' wishes and capacities to decide where to live, with whom, and to what degree to follow or not life lessons from their parents and kin. Choice is always relative to a range of alternatives. But in our times, it becomes mandatory: not to choose is already a choice. Hence, many of our microstories revolve around somebody's assessment of an important life choice: what the circumstances were, how the decision was made, what consequences came, how satisfactory the outcome was. It is important to insist that individuality has to be produced (Beck and Beck-Gernsheim 2001; Kaufmann 2004). There is nothing natural in becoming an individual. Public and private institutions like school, mass media, church, police, and other organizations of the market, state, and civil society are crucial mediators in this process. In our stories, institutional actants may appear personified in the guise of a landlord, a teacher, work colleagues, a boss. Individualization is an ambivalent outcome of reflexive modernity. Bauman (2001, 2003) has warned against its excesses as a radical threat to our life in common. And Beck and Beck-Gernsheim (1995) note the conflictive meanings contained in the idea of freedom, as a "freedom from" old ties and "freedom to" make choices. If modernity impels the subjects to untie themselves from former social determinations of origin, tradition, gender, and class, it also pushes them into making choices, adopting new identities, and trying untrodden life paths. I take a closer look at this dialectic in the following section.

REFLEXIVITY/IDENTITY

Our stories of the self are in line with the "oral accounts of personal experience" of the sociolinguists. In this genre, the perspective focuses on the narrator. In our collective exploration workshops, the stories told in the first person were often introduced through statements like "I am going to explain my case," "this is a little particular," "for me it was different," "this is similar but not the same." This narrative self-centeredness is in line with Goffman's concept of "face" and its relevance in the presentation of the self in everyday life. Every act of storytelling is an opportunity to build a face. The strong, accented "I" results from this insertion of the genre in daily interaction rituals.

In *L'invention de soi* (The Invention of the Self), Jean-Claude Kaufmann (2004) actualizes this analytic tradition, which can be traced back to Erikson and the psychology of the self. His main assertion is that, under late modern conditions, for the individual there is an injunction to become oneself. The very concept of identity is the result of a modern (and problematic) quest that makes of every individual the locus of an open, contradictory search. For Kaufmann (2004, 82), "Identity is a process, historically new, linked to the emergence of the subject, whose key aspect has to do with the fabrication of sense." This process is double-binding. On the one hand, the modern injunction pushes the individual to reflexively overcome origin, class, and tradition—all the objective conditions of social role that Goffman (in Kaufmann, 1004, 94) called "identity carriers" (*porte-identités*): "Objective features are not so powerful with regard to identity. This is so since they are profoundly contradictory, undermined by permanent conflicts. This is a key point: objective features cannot by themselves determine existence, for the simple reason that they lack a stable, coherent universe. They are crossed by all kinds of oppositions, forcing the subject to get involved, whether she/he wants to or not."

On the other hand, the subject looks to glue the pieces together in order to build a coherent totality from the fragmentation and openness that results from the reflexive process: "Identity is a process of closure and fixation, thus opposed to the logic of movement and openness of reflexivity. It continuously creates a unified system of values, working as a frame for the perception of the world that gives meaning to thinking and action" (Kaufmann 2004, 110).

Thus, while reflexivity means a quest guided by critical questioning, choice, and openness, self-identity, by contrast, "never stops gluing the pieces together. It is a system of permanent closure and integration of meanings, having totality as its model" (Kaufmann 2004, 82). Kaufmann's elaboration on the dialectics between reflexivity and identity is pertinent for us for two reasons. First, this theorizing comes from an empirical line of research about domestic mobilization, everyday storytelling, and the system of objects close to the one that inspired this fieldwork. Second, it indicates the intrinsic connections among different dimensions of dwelling. To make oneself, to occupy an intimate space, and to build a coherent story about one's life are three facets of a single modern problem (Giddens 1991). This drama has the self as the main character, struggling to assemble the many fragments of one's relationships, deeds, and biography; ceaselessly reconstructing a meaningful totality where the process of social life pushes to social, geographic, and sentimental mobility; to the multiplication of choices; to rational scrutiny; to the maximizing of goals; to the instrumentalization of affect; and to the compartmentalization of roles and activities. The value of this perspective—in contrast to any spatial, economic, or technological reductionism—lies in bringing the subject's production of meaning to the center of the silent processes that constitute the intimate sphere.

Certainly, intimacy is always entangled with whatever comes "from the outside." Could it be otherwise? The production of one's own order is enmeshed with the processes of reproduction, community, reform, commercialization, and individuation discussed above. Discourse from the political right denounces such a circumstance as proof of the corruption of mores, educational banalization, civilizing loss, and self-destructive license, in a conservative frame where the dwelling heritage is read in purely normative terms: urbanity, tradition, respect, and good mores. The cultural left reverses the critique by setting it on its head, hence interpreting the external entanglements of the self in terms of loss of authenticity, commercialization of human relationships, individualist consumerism, and taylorization of the domestic universe. In opposition to the patriarchal and hierarchical order of the bourgeois nuclear family, they put forward the idealized forces of community, mutuality, and reciprocity. Nevertheless, the fact is that nobody invents their home from scratch. Such space is affected both by the urges of the present and by historical, cultural, and familial heritages that tend to get reproduced in our very personal ways of dwelling.

Be that as it may, the discovery of an everyday order is the central process shown by the bulk of our workshops and interviews. Such an order is open to invention, in the Certeaunian sense of resulting from a *bricoleur*, bustling, and untamed activity by the dwellers. This order is not prefigured in advance—at least among the middle-class subjects we have collaborated with. It is neither determined by external factors nor fixed by the parents' history. It constitutes "the problem" in itself: learning how to live—or, according to the participants, learning how to live *better*. Above all, they want to live "their own lives" in "their own ways." This is so because, as Kaufmann (1997, 43) notes, in modern society there is less a unified compulsory norm about dwelling than a statistical normalcy that everyone struggles to figure out and in which everyone would like—for better or worse—to see themself mirrored. Nothing captures this spirit of the times better than the foundational leitmotif of IKEA in Spain: "Welcome to the Independent Republic of Your Home." Is it not ironic that such a declaration of independence comes from a global business that provides, along with furniture, the new canon of domestic normalcy everywhere?

I owe to my dear colleagues from UAM-I (Mexico)—Miguel Ángel Aguilar, Ángela Giglia, and Ana Rosas—the critical observation that popular or subaltern subjects do not necessarily fit such a description. Extreme scarcity sets limits on the freedom to decide on one's space. In the case of our project, the problem was usually less one of scarcity (in income and space) than one of precarity (in time), since many participants were young people from cultural classes with very uncertain careers and mobile destinies. In the project-made city (Boltanski and Chiapello 2018), life paths are traveled in a sort of expanded, continuous present, and this impedes stability and capitalization.

The injunction to be oneself is compatible with social determinants. Class, education, tradition, religion, gender, and age factors are neither absent nor ignored. They become more or less integrated by the subjects in their idiosyncratic answers to the major problems of openness, unpredictability, and change. The conundrum of late modern dwelling consists precisely of finding ways to combine the reproduction of a given inheritance with the invention of the self. Possibilities seem infinite, but life is only one. Our fieldwork materials are crossed by the invisible thread of a dizziness in front of the vacuum that inhabiting a world devoid of univocal norms and fixed patterns produces. How to fill the house? With whom to share it? When to clean up? And how much? What to buy? How to cook? What to wear? Who to date? When do I stop breastfeeding my baby?

The discovery of one's own order is often narrated as the meditated outcome of a decision: "Then I told myself, I need a space of my own." Other times it comes rather as a revelation. This was the case of Camilo, in the scene when he discovered, after his first dinner living alone, that he had devoured his food in seven minutes. This kind of reflexive estrangement can be projected backward over a whole life in which, finally, it is not easy to recognize oneself.

> I went through different situations, but I never would have imagined that I was going to end up sharing a flat with a woman who is not my fiancée. I would never have imagined it like this. Actually, what I had in mind was the family

type. Supposedly, I was going to have three kids. This was something that at a certain point I must have lost. It came preset, as a somehow inherited decision. But at a certain moment I, apparently, strayed from that path. Now I remember this like it was only a memory. Suddenly, twenty years had gone by. I did not even realize it. And at one point I thought, "Wasn't I going to have three kids, a wife, and all that?" But it seems like I wasn't.

For most people, one's own order emerges or crystallizes. It comes as a result of habit, routine, and repetition: a quantitative accumulation of objects and experiences. Existence deposits its sediments astutely, until the obviousness imposes itself with the force of a fait accompli. This crystallization set the tone of the relationship between ego and their universe, where stuff, affections, activities, bodies, and memories become entangled. The subject weaves and unravels this web, knit from abrupt ruptures (broken marriages, lost jobs, abandoned houses, deceased parents, roommates who come and go) as well as from real and imagined continuities (family customs, life friendships, anniversaries and commemorations, grandmothers' rings, names scribbled in the back of a closet).

The best findings in our research talk about these little inventions. And about the very inevitability of inventing yourself. The mother who raised two daughters around a king-size bed where they used to eat, chat, do homework, and watch TV shows. The living room of five roommates arranged around five easy chairs, one for each. The bachelor who founded a club for singles to have company for dinner once a week. The girl who talks to her neighbor from one balcony to another and dwelled in an old reformed pigeon house. The engineer who reprogrammed the TV remote to prevent himself from getting distracted by zapping through channels. The lesbian couple who liked to indulge in long coffees over breakfast as the most pleasurable time for their morning encounter. The young musicologist who varnished old wooden pallets to make her furniture. The parents experiencing cosleeping with two babies so that the little one would not wake up the rest of the family. The bohemian artist who re-created a public square in his living room with a bench and a streetlight (until his fiancée got tired of sleeping on the bench). The woman who uploaded a photo of her fancy breakfast every day to her blog . . .

SIGNATURE, DISPLACEMENT, CLOSURE, AND REVERBERATION

Living in order produces meaning. It would be wrong to consider that kind of production as an uprooted, immaterial, or solipsistic activity. On the contrary, meaning-making is the craft of a subjectivity in action, relation, and context. These efforts by the dwellers are tentative and provisional, but precisely for that reason they show their ceaseless strategies of cognitive, affective, and symbolic closure and fixation. Living in order is to accept, paradoxically, the ever-latent reality of disorder.

Stuart Hall (1997) and James Fernandez (1986) have insisted on the idea that human culture never stops producing meaning. Nevertheless, even if meaning can never be definitive or closed, signifying practices always aspire to it, since they embody a nuanced refusal of finitude and death (Bauman 2001). In other words, what lies at the bottom of signifying productivity is this agonistic tension of life itself. Such a perspective acutely contrasts with the miserabilism and reproductivism with which everyday life is sometimes approached as a mere "place of reproduction of the labor force," when not a blind object for critique and reform. Everyday life is genuinely productive, open to the eventfulness of time. It is poetic, not in the literary sense of having to do with poetry or other artistic genres but with *poiesis* as a continuous regeneration of the meaning of existence. Following Perec's exercises in listing and inventory, we would say that the everyday is "inexhaustible" (Österlund-Pötzsch 2021, 5).

Let us not mystify things. Daily life may indeed be the scenario for depression, violence, tedium, and nonsense, but indeed also of an enormous display of creation and beauty. The production and maintenance of one's own order counters the dark face of its erosion and emptying. The living character of life manifests in this agonistic, never-ending imperative for any temporary arrangement to be remade, again and again. Reflecting on the effects of domestic ritual, one of our participants put it beautifully: "Repeating something is not the same as doing it anew every time." Constant repetition, which is the mark of the everyday, imprints meaning on life. But it also takes it out. Repeating implies both erasure and renewal. Thus, the concepts of meaning and life are interconnected, as inseparable fundaments of a poetics/politics of life (Giddens 1992). We would not know what a good life is if it were not for the ways we find to communicate it to others. "Intimacy is linked to the art of narrating life" (Pardo 1996, 8).

Intimacy is a creature of language. Beyond poetry as a genre—a "figure of sound" characterized by "projecting the principle of equivalence from the axis of selection into the axis of combination" (Jacobson 1960, 358)—poetics deals with a focus on the message and its form. Jacobson (1960, 359) also differentiated five other language functions, each stressing different elements of the communicating situation: (1) referential—focused on the context and the informative value of words, (2) emotive or expressive—centered on the relationship of the emitter to the message, (3) conative—focused on the addressee, (4) phatic—having to do with the contact between participants, and (5) metalinguistic—focused on the code. In empirical situations, there is no monopoly of any particular function but just a predominance of one over the rest. It is a matter of stress. There is always a continuous flow of emotive information, Jacobson (1985, 19) argues, as every expression also has a poetic side, even if other functions are at play or are predominant. The wide scope of the poetic function is well illustrated by examples ranging from intimate relations to the public arena: the order applied to naming two twins—Joan and Margery. The adjective was chosen for a certain "horrible Harry" and for the paranomasic electoral slogan of Eisenhower, "I like Ike" (Jacobson 1960, 357). The poetic value of these examples lies in that choices of form become matters of meaning. Stylistic transformations have semantic consequences.[2]

The implications of a poetic approach to everyday life are also well understood by going back as far as the *Poetics* of Aristotle (2020), who in one of the most influential treatises on literature of all time applied an organic approach to the understanding of tragedy and epopee. According to him, the common trait shared by all forms of poetry is imitation (mimesis), a general human capacity to be found in child development as well as in daily life routines. "Imitating is connatural in human beings from early childhood, and in this they differ from the rest of animals, for man is very prone to imitation, and he acquires his first knowledge by imitating; and it is also connatural to him to please everyone with imitations" (Aristotle 2020, 42). From this kind of mimetic improvisation, poetry was born. The creation of poetic meaning— *poiesis*—is then not an isolated form of production from scratch but a faculty in continuity with mechanisms such as plot, catharsis, and self-recognition, which are integral to human development and play.[3]

Let us briefly discuss four of these *poietic*, transformative effects of meaning documented in our ethnography. They show the role of signifying processes in intimacy-making. The poetics of intimacy adjust to the Jacobsonian definition of a "projection of the axis of selection into the axis of combination," (1960, 58). I will focus on four effects: signature, displacement, closure, and reverberation. Signature is linked to the intrinsic indexicality of discourse. It marks both the original stories and the mediated stories-about-a-story with authorship. Semantic and physical displacement accounts for the materiality of stuff circulating in the dwelling place as well as for the iterability of meanings—the fact that the meaning of a word tends to subtly change depending on every new context of use. The collusion of these two senses of *displacement* (the topological and the tropological) is responsible for the semantic and affective density of the home. Closure indicates a search for form: a will for style. As I have insisted, there is a mystery in why beauty of traits, round endings, and poetic justice prove to bear moral consequences in a story. Finally, reverberation denotes the dialogical nature of the interpretation. Given its thick intertextuality, the meaning of a story can be fully grasped only as an ongoing open conversation that includes its reverberation in the memories and experiences of the interlocutor. Every tale is a tale of tales. It involves past and future telling of this same story.

SIGNATURE

Whenever we arrived at a new home, I noticed the marks on the walls. This made me wonder who those people were, what was this house like before, who were they, what were they like. I also wanted to leave my name, so the next family could wonder about me. (Norma, twenty-eight, Mexico City)

Signature refers to the marks of ego in the intimate space. As a root metaphor, it points to a written inscription. It must be one-of-a-kind: personal to the point of intransferability and uniqueness. By etching her name on stone, Norma hopes to stop the dizziness of disappearing. No matter the visual predominance of written signature, it is a musicologist, Peter Szendy (2001), who contributed more to the concept. In *Écoute. Un histoire de nos oreilles*, he sketches a fascinating history of musical reception as "a history of the rights of the listener." According to him, whenever someone appropriates and mentally reconstructs a musical work, they are "signing a hearing." The historical contribution of the listeners in the unfolding of works and styles has been overshadowed by the bias that dominates the classical canon, with a privileged attention to composition. But, at the very end, music belongs to the listeners (Finnegan 2003). People sign the music they like. A musicological interest in reception focuses on silent operations and acoustic marks with cognitive, aesthetic, and moral import. At the beginning of his book, Szendy (2001, 17) reminisces how acutely he felt the mandate to share melomaniac discoveries on Mahler or Wagner symphonies—whether his sister was interested in them or not. Where does this moral compulsion stem from? The commitment of ego with the world makes it compelling not only to appropriate it ("from now on, this will be mine") but also to share it ("the way I hear this, it should be yours"). Marks of this kind can also be tracked in a history of readership (Littau 2008; Boyarin 1993), particularly in what Bayard (2012) has called "the personal library" that every reader keeps in their mind. We can also notice the active participation of readers in the authorial process, illustrated, for example, in the troublesome death and resurrection of Sherlock Holmes. Tired of his success, Conan Doyle killed the character of the detective in a purported last episode of the series. The reaction of the public was of such magnitude—from letters of outrage to the scolding of the author by his mother—that it forced him to bring the character back to life in an atypical final mystery, *The Hound of the Baskervilles* (Bayard 2010).

Signature is neither an anomaly nor a theatrical exaggeration. It is rooted in indexicality, a fundamental dimension of language use. Speaking is possible because we position ourselves as locutors in the here-and-now of communication, by self-referential indexes encoded in the persons of pronouns, the time and mode of verbs, and other complements of space, time, and agency (let alone gestures and paralinguistic aids). Although the image of a written signature underscores visual, spatial, and verbal traits, the issues involved are actually multisensorial, temporal, and relational. A soaking-wet towel on a bed carries a strong signature. And the same can be said of the little girl's drawing kept in a wallet; the chili plant that a father had grown in a pot; shirts worn by another father, with his personal style, colors, and odors; the way three people fit in a bed; or the odd enjoyment a certain girl gets out of cleaning her bathroom.

In signature, space and time are tied. The phenomenological concept of the here-and-now of the enunciating situation underlines it. Like a promise, signature is oriented to posterity. The action of signing develops in the present, but it compromises the future in order to warrant the self a place in it. It works like a time bomb. Metonymic powers like those of magic and ritual are mobilized: perhaps you will not be there, but someone will take your name over—or, let's say, your Mahler records; your box of photographs; your skirt at a Roman staircase; your books dedicated by a celebrity; a certain memory of the days you dwelled in a home, had a child, made a trip, mourned someone who passed. Even under the injunction to become oneself, which so strongly uproots the late modern subject from former belongings, duties, and protections, signature is not just a kind of self-referential excess, an egotistic pathology of our times. True, these are times of metropolitan selves, with the complex aspirations and deceptions comprised. But signature is sealed as a possibility inherent to all human communication. The current trend for individualization frees a potential for *poiesis* and self-determination that was already there in more restrained and traditional ways of dwelling.

DISPLACEMENT

Sometimes it happened that when I returned from work, after taking a quick shower . . . and I would put the wet towel on the bed. When I came back, my parents scolded me: "Don't leave wet towels on the bed!" Now, something magical was going on: the towel remained on the bed. There was no scolding. Just a damp bed and a wet towel. No one moving my stuff. This might seem obvious for someone who has already lived alone. For me it was entirely new. Things magically remained in the place you had left them! (Camilo, forty-five, Montevideo)

If a soaked towel can carry a heavy signature, this is so because every day our stuff moves across an intimate space intensely populated with other presences. We become entangled with the persons, actions, rhythms, and feelings around us. Kaufmann has eloquently referred to this domestic choreography as a "dance of things." Nothing is innocent in such a dance. Displacement becomes meaningful, charged with nuances of all kinds. It is at work 24/7, nonstop. Kaufmann's (1998) analysis of the laundry cycle as it travels throughout the different rooms of the house illustrates this. Ego imprints its signature on things, but things bring back both the marks of significant others and the reflections of our own presence. Objects mirror us.

In a recent paper, Löfgren (2019a) presents an eighteenth-century character, Xavier de Maistre, who, imprisoned in his room, tries to register every little movement during the long confinement. Löfgren (2019a, 167) remarks, "The importance to be on the move became a credo of modernity early on: never allow yourself to get stuck or left behind. This also led to a celebration of forward movement, of eyes fixed on the horizon. However, many moves are so small and routinized that they remain unnoticed or are seen as unimportant, but upon closer inspection they turn out to harbor important issues."

What could these important issues be? Löfgren mentions morning habits: getting out of bed, ten minutes in front of the bathroom mirror, getting dressed, breakfast, the exit from the home. All these apparently minor things mobilize the senses, the affects, the body, and the whole mind. They condition whether the day will be a fruitful or lost one, if we will accommodate to the rhythms of the street and the workplace or not, if our mood will be in sync with the occasions to come.

In these moves across the intimate space, two different senses of *displacement* come together. On the one hand, there is displacement in the physical space: persons come and go; objects go in and out of their place; materials are bought, processed, consumed, and disposed of. This sense of displacement has been the focus of sociologies and geographies of the domestic place. On the other hand, displacement is also a key concept in semantics. Poetic language results from displacement of meaning: from literal to figurative. Metaphor and other tropes are "a displacement in the qualitative space" (Fernandez 1974, 124). This second use of the term *displacement* is, thus, derivative with respect to the former. How do these two senses relate to each other? Towels out of place, families in king-size beds, and women at the window reveal that this connection is not capricious. In the context of intimate space, both senses of *displacement* tend to fuse. Movements become meaningful, and meanings are on the move. You can monitor what is going on in the living room from your bedroom, just by hearing the footsteps of the people there: if they are routinary or anomalous, timely or untimely, right or wrong. Unable to find something in my kitchen, I often complain out loud, "Who has been touching my pans?"—just in time to discover it was myself who moved them from the cupboard. The quarreling about trifles that makes couples in crisis feel so miserable (Kaufmann 2009; Beck and Beck-Gernsheim 1995) illustrates this overlap between the occupation of space and the meaning-making process.

Displacement of things and people is the foundation of everyday life. In micromoves new meanings emerge, and the coded, normalized uses of the public sphere may become displaced. Every novelty slightly deviates from former uses of words and practices by adding a variation in form, a contextual adjustment, an unforeseen nuance. This is why people call each other, after decades of living together, by idiosyncratic, affectionate, or absurd nicknames. Conversely, a given frame of meaning (like the narratives by interior designers about a showroom, or the sketch of a house exquisitely drawn on a notebook by a newly married couple) becomes materialized as real space: furniture, decoration, and practical solutions.

The very analytic distinction between signifier and signified tends to get blurred in this process, as we appreciate in the semiotic journey of Camilo's towel: from object in a wardrobe to signal of dampness and disorder (for his parents) to symbol of independence (for him). Intimacy makes the typology of signs collapse. Signals become indexes, indexes become icons, icons become symbols. Home drives the most patient of semiologists crazy. What is at work here is the inexhaustibility of everyday life: the impossibility of the old structuralist dream of fixing meaning in a given place by means of a thorough decoding of its symbols. It is a dead-end. The analytical reduction of complexity into a manageable set of combinations of a limited number of semantic components faces the endless and capricious journey of things, people, and meanings: an unsteady flow of semantic swirls and loops between signifier and signified. The zealous project of exhausting meaning must be substituted by a more modest one: to follow their casual meanders, itineraries, and derives, grasping there some of the meanings-cum-things throughout which the lives of people unfold. The purpose of signature is durability and fixation. The result of displacement is a boiling mutability of the intimate order.

CLOSURE

This drifting character of meaning in daily life makes keeping it at bay through permanent boundary-work necessary (Nippert-Eng 1995, 2003, 2007, 2010). As I insisted in chapter 1, the resulting walls do not become absolute, insurmountable. On the contrary, daily limits need to be flexible, permeable, and transferable. We have to move back and forth between private spaces and public ones. We want to invite others to come into our intimate realm. We carry, as we travel, a fraction of our personal sphere with us. No matter how deep the psychological need for stability and duration at home may be, a compelling need to move, change, and share also exists.

Closures in space are drawn as lines, walls, fences, borders, apertures. In an ampler sense, the idea of closure also projects metaphorically onto time, social interaction, and discourse. Openings, rhythms, repetitions, and endings are examples of temporal closure. Encounters, visits, greetings, farewells, gestures, talks, festivals, commemorations, closing ceremonies, and revivals work as boundary units at the level of social interaction. Stylistic markers, frames, schemata, summaries, common places, and ritornellos are discursive closures. In this book I have been particularly concerned with some prominent bounding traits of narrative: plot structure, round endings, and poetic justice. In chapter 3, I noted how a struggle for style—a willingness to say things beautifully, roundly, or shockingly—could be noticed even in the telegraphic stylizations of Web 2.0. This willingness can be thoroughly appreciated in the agonistic plot of the works of ego, with their often parodic and counterheroic adventures and crashes with (or against) parents, couples, roommates, neighbors, landlords, clocks, umbrellas, and food processors. We showed the narrative artistry with which, in a personal collection of familial memories, Alba interwove life story and photographic image to forge a tunnel through time—a common narrative across generations. We could also appreciate, in a long interview with Norma about her shared apartment, how narrative schemata of diverse scale (flash-images, overarching story lines, and twice-told tales) may be combined to frame the flow of conversation.

Good and round endings—not necessarily happy ones—is what appealed to us more in the oral accounts gathered here. This is consistent with Argentinian writer Ricardo Piglia's (1999) theorizing about the short story as a written genre. According to him, Borges, a universal master of the short story, held that in the writing of a tale, "the beginnings are always difficult, uncertain . . . while the end is always involuntary, or seems involuntary, but is actually premeditated and fatal" (Piglia 1999, 104). The same idea was noted by Kafka: "At first, the beginning of every tale is ridiculous. That this new, uselessly sensitive body, somewhat mutilated and shapeless, may be kept alive seems impossible. And yet, every time you begin, you forget that, if the existence of a tale is justifiable, it carries in itself its perfect form, and you only have to wait until its invisible but unavoidable end can be glimpsed through these shaky beginnings" (quoted in Piglia 1999, 104).

Piglia's (1999, 109) interpretation emphasizes the importance of endings, since they are "ways to make sense of experience." The plot of the story proposes events and actions, but the whole becomes meaningful only at the end. "Without finitude there is no truth." This is the reason why in so many endings we get oracle, fatality, or tragedy, as well as secret, surprise, discovery, and epiphany. "The end," Piglia explains, "allows us to see a secret sense that was ciphered, absent-like, in the clear succession of the facts." The ending gets its results by resources like the twist, the cut, the change of rhythm, the ellipsis, and the tacit understanding. It arrives when nobody expects it, but it was secretly dormant or prefigurated. It waited, invisible, in the heart of the story:

> At the bottom of the plot of a story, the hope of an epiphany is always hidden. We expect something unexpected to happen, and this is also true for the one who writes the story. . . . We only glance the meaning of a story at the very end: there is a detour, a change of rhythm, something from without; something that happens next door. Then, we know the story, and it can conclude. . . . The meaning of a story has the structure of a secret (it points to the etymological origin of the word *se-cernere*, to set apart), it is hidden, separated from the whole of the story, reserved somewhere else for the end. . . . There is something in the end that was at the origin, and the art of narrating consists of delaying it, keeping it secret, and letting it be seen when nobody expects it. (Piglia 1999, 119–122)

As we saw in Berger's theorizing, in Piglia (1999, 117) the importance of the endings is also oriented to show how stories are interwoven with the flow of life itself: "In life, there are crossroads, networks, circulations; while the endings are associated with forgetting, departure, and absence. Endings are losses, cuts, marks in a territory; they draw a frontier, they divide. They scan and split up the experience. But at the same time, in our most intimate conviction, everything goes on."

Unsteady beginnings, definitive endings. Had my informants been reading Piglia, Borges, and Kafka? Why should endings have such significance? In our case, the mystery of good endings consisted not only in the fact that people's daily microstories are so often artful and elaborated. It also and most importantly consists of the hunch that a good ending provides meaning to the story by closing a gestalt, many times unexpectedly, on what had been related before. This wholeness, which the gestalt psychologists called "pregnancy" or good form, carries the moral weight of the story. The artifices of good form have effects of meaning. And these, in turn, support the moral of the story. In our microstories, the good ending was often performed by a parsimonious sentence that recapitulates the intention of the overall story: "Cleaning the bathroom is like therapy." Some stories came to an end with a well-administered rhythm so that the listener is pushed to consider the heart of the experiences confided there—see, for example, Diego's cadenced closure of his Hamletian monologue on having a child: "You see yourself on the chessboard of life: Here I was. A sensation comes over you, like, Whoa, that was it. That was it."

REVERBERATION

Walking around the city has become for me an exercise in personal and collective memory. At this corner, I met a friend. On that street, there used to be a shop. My first kiss was in that park. When you are fiftysomething, everything reverberates in you. Events and places take us back to past occasions and experiences. This path in Avila, with its heavy rocks and its sober pines, resembles another I walked in Colima, or Choroní, or Boyacá. This custard apple reminds me of my mother, the first brave person I knew to eat such a weird thing. Like walking and eating, dwelling has a very recursive quality. The houses you have lived in differ from each other; but, in a deeper inner sense, they are all the same. They call for the continuities of your experience. For example, the other day my wife was at home, putting together a new desk chair. She humorously sent me a photo in which she was doing exactly the same thing twenty years ago, in an identical posture. As in a film montage, one image connects to the other. In the old one, she appeared pregnant for the first time, with the excitement of undertaking a new job. By condensing the contrasting and the identical, this image moved me. It was more than fun.

These flashback effects have emotional power. They are more than accumulated knowledge. They bring the feeling that every action, conversation, flavor, nap, or light makes part of a whole that remains inextricably linked to a certain origin. For a musician like me, resonance (or reverberation) is a good model for thinking about this phenomenon: sounding physical bodies sync up with other vibrating bodies of the same spectrum. Reverberation is a root metaphor. Musicians resort to it when saying, for example, that someone you are singing or playing with "attracts you" to their sound. We also say that human beings are resounding bodies—made mostly of water—and that we move alternatively in and out of sync with the vibes of others. Among the musicological versions about reverberation, I like the one by Charles Keil and Steven Feld on what they called "participatory discrepancies" (Keil 1994). They attribute sounds that are slightly out of tune and sync to be the source of energy and collective connection that we find so appealing in vibrant, catchy music. Much earlier, but in a similar line of argument, Alfred Schultz (1977) promoted the situation of musicians who coordinate the here-and-now of their playing into a metaphor of all human face-to-face interaction—a situation that he called the "tuning-in relationship." Schultz (1956) also used this deep metaphor in his well-informed analysis on Mozart operas. He paid attention, in particular, to the final concertante quintets and sextets that uncover the story line, once the comedy of errors has reached its climax and the characters, each singing their own song, become coordinated in a tutti that allows the public to make sense of the whole. What happens to Figaro and Susanna, to Don Giovanni and Donna Elvira, resembles what happens to us in daily life, says Schultz. Through mysterious ways, we all synchronize the patterns and rhythms of our actions to engage with the patterns and rhythms of others.

This musical metaphor has, of course, other interesting narrative, interactional, and phenomenological counterparts. The most robust and inspiring is probably Bakhtin's dialogism. For dialogue is precisely, for Bakhtin (1981), a "unity of differences in the act of enunciation," a "polyphony of voices" (Holquist 1990). Accent is an act of borrowing from others, handed down dialogically (and intertextually) like the vibrations among strings that share a frequency. The meaning of discourse, written as much as oral, is a highly populated resonance chamber.

In *The Poetics of Space*, phenomenologist Gaston Bachelard (1994) explicitly used this notion of resonance as an essential part of the poetics of dwelling. For Bachelard, dwelling is remembering. Home is not just the place for shelter and protection—although these are basic functions of the home. Nor is it only a place for action and planning, leaning toward the future. Home is a place for daydreaming too. This poetic function has to do with the work of imagination, with the keeping of the old in the new—a conservative drive that is at the heart of dwelling. Regarding reverberation, there is a paragraph in which Bachelard explains why a certain shadowing—not saying too much— is necessary to recover the house of your childhood:

> What would be the use, for instance, in giving the plan of the room that was really my room, in describing the little room at the end of the garret, in saying that from the window, across the indentations of the roofs, one could see the hill. I alone, in my memories of another century, can open the deep cupboard that still retains for me alone that unique odor, the odor of raisins drying on a wicker tray. The odor of raisins! It is an odor that is beyond description, one that it takes a lot of imagination to smell. But I've already said too much. If I said more, the reader, back in his own room, would not open that unique wardrobe, with its unique smell, which is the signature of intimacy. Paradoxically, in order to suggest the values of intimacy, we have to induce in the reader a state of suspended reading. For it is not until his eyes have left the page that recollections of my room can become a threshold of oneirism for him. And when it is a poet speaking, the reader's soul reverberates; it experiences the kind of reverberation that, as Minkowski has shown, gives the energy of an origin to being. It therefore makes sense from our standpoint of a philosophy of literature and poetry to say that we "write a room," "read a room," or "read a house." Thus, very quickly, at the very first word, at the first poetic overture, the reader who is "reading a room" leaves off reading and starts to think of some place in his own past. You would like to tell everything about your room. You would like to interest the reader in yourself, whereas you have unlocked a door to daydreaming. The values of intimacy are so absorbing that the reader has ceased to read your room:

he sees his own again. He is already far off, listening to the recollections of a father or a grandmother, of a mother or a servant, of "the old faithful servant," in short, of the human being who dominates the corner of his most cherished memories. (Bachelard 1994, 13–14)

As if our workshops and interviews had taken place in Bachelard's little room at the end of the garret, resonance made its work in the lively exchange of stories and experiences that has been shown in this book. If their enunciation was marked by signature, their reception was all at once reverberated by the audience. Speaking of cooking and kitchens in Montevideo, everyone laughed at the kitchen stories of the others, as if we were literally sharing a meal together. This empathy equally worked through the solidary silence with which the confession by a recent divorcé in his fifties of the miserable menu of his daily dinners was received: "Some nights, I open myself a can." The principle of resonance (or reverberation) means that the proper floor for interpretation of someone else's stories is not a flat, neutral understanding. It is the pool of memories and vital experiences of the listeners. This also affects the notions of originality and authorship in storytelling. By appropriating stories heard from others, every story becomes a retelling: a re-creation of something already said by someone else, somewhere else. The tales that we have heard live, one way or another, in our own tales.

The principles presented here as poetic devices or effects of meaning—signature, displacement, closure, and reverberation—can be understood as well as "effects of presence" or "intimacy markers." Presence is a central category in Giddens's (1990) sociological theorizing on modernity, as it is too in artistic and literary theories (Keil and Feld 1994, 17). What a signature at the bottom of a closet, a towel on a bed, a beautifully cleaned bathroom, and a well-ended, carefully told story do is bring different kinds of presence to the fore—to begin with, that of the teller. The category of presence derives its power from two sources. First, intimacy is radically about presence (and absence). The movement of the bodies, the thickness of atmospheres, the copresence of people, the synesthetic and multimodal interactions among senses, the assemblages and disconnections of objects, the material and symbolic dimensions of home space: all these things are the bones of intimacy-making. They are also at the heart of the poetic effects underlined here. Second, the category of presence (both in sociological and aesthetic uses) points back to a face-to-face interactionalist frame like the one adopted in this book. This is why I have invoked—in a Goffmanian vein—the paramount importance of everyday encounters, interaction rituals, the construction of face, participations, belongings, and the presentation of the self. What I do not think is that "presence" could be productively opposed to "meaning," not at least for the specific context of intimacy. The entanglement of actions and discourses, affects and materiality, expressions and routines, make drawing a divide neither possible nor desirable. Presence is the carrier of meaning. No meaning comes free from the indexicality of the self.

A MAKING-OF

Characters in a story are good; persons in the flesh can be better. This is probably the reason I became an anthropologist instead of a writer. In one of his last interviews, Berger declared not to feel the need to look for fictional characters for his novels, since he got inspired enough by real stories of people in daily life. The everyday is poetically productive. For Berger (2016), no fiction surpassed the interest of true lives: "I do not understand fiction as a category. If you want to tell a story, you don't go to a category called 'fiction.' What you do is listen to people. The storyteller is first and foremost someone who listens. And he searches for the stories that other people recount, normally about their lives, or the lives of their friends. To me, this is what telling stories is about, not fiction."

Social scientists have become increasingly attentive to the connection between the lives of people and the narratives we build. This route can be walked in two different directions. On the one hand, we must scrutinize how "reality" or "the world" enters a text. In anthropology in particular, from the so-called ethnographic critique of the 1980s—when Clifford, Marcus, and others (1986) underlined, following the footsteps of Geertz's pioneering efforts, the crafted nature of the ethnographic rhetoric—we acknowledge the textual character of the discipline. Ethnography is not fiction, but close: it is narrative about people. The ethnographic experience consists of going somewhere, talking to people, knowing about their lives, and somehow registering histories, places, actions, feelings, and hopes. At the very moment you write that down, they are becoming characters in a story. "Actors," or "agents," we used to say more elegantly (following the deep theatrical analogy that society is a play and we the actors who act it out). Or you may call them "actants" today—to look more stylish. Yet, the transformation of a person into a character makes one feel uneasy, like a kind of treason. A mild one, in my view: a minor sin that is part of our profession, and it does not invalidate our efforts at understanding others' lives. But treason it surely is, as is all translation— *traduttore traditore*. Much of the grace you perceive in the originals becomes forced, frozen, or predictable in writing. In the process, persons may lose part of their singularity, what they try to protect more and convey better in the exchange with the ethnographer.

The route connecting people and texts goes the other way round as well. In writing down stories, you sense the horizons of written tradition, the burden of literacy, the conventions of the genre you are supposed to fit with. A text is a crowded place: there are plenty of people between you and your subjects of study. A plethora of narrative expectations emerge that are, as Eco (2010) put it, the marks of the reader in your writing. Generic intertextuality (Bauman 2004) is also at work. It attracts your characters and their actions to a preset frame of words, concepts, and meanings, which has the inertial power of a bulldozer and flattens nuances from your cherished people. Thus, in this process of persons becoming characters, there are losses and gains. On the former, they lose reality and concretion. On the latter, they get textual pregnancy and good shape. Overall, life stories cease to work for themselves. They are profoundly recontextualized within our own discourse. They become our quote.

This reality is constitutive of the position of ethnographer. There is no escape. If we are still brave enough to translate, we must concede that there will always be gaps in translation, losses in meaning, treasons in the intention. However, there are ways to ameliorate the outcome. One is to engage in collaborative writing and, more broadly, collaborative research. Another is to focus on the added value you can imprint onto the stories you have been handed down. Finally, there is the possibility to follow up the second life of your text when returning to the field, as presented in chapter 2 regarding the screening of our movie.

I conclude this section with a reflexive turn. The poetic processes analyzed here are formative of the intimate sphere but also of the metadiscourses on intimacy produced by mediating agents: the market, the reforming agencies, the arts, the media, and the social sciences among others. Could it be otherwise? This is not surprising, regarding the circularity between the public sphere and the private one that the IKEA paradox illustrates. This observation has important methodological implications. If intimate stories and the accounts we produce are made of the same stuff, we are obliged to pay attention to our own narrative devices.

Table 5.1 presents a few semantic effects of signature, displacement, closure, and resonance that emerged in the process of producing a film out of our corpus of workshops and interviews. Spatial displacement is obvious. Fieldwork in three capital cities entails—beyond the journey itself—the filmic juxtaposition of people, conversations, and atmospheres that took place remotely. Fieldwork is an exercise in spatial (dis)placement. Filmmaking also is, but of a semantic kind: playing with space and time. The transformation of people into characters is a matter of displacement, since excerpts of conversations are selected and disposed in sequential order to produce a story line capable of capturing the attention of an audience. Individual characters are interwoven to build a collective voice, mute until that moment. Selecting,

Table 5.1. Poetic processes applied to film rhetoric

Displacement	Going to the field From selves to characters Weaving stories Series of objects
Closure	Compostion & montage Script, timing, climactic tension "Wording" & titles Silences (rhythm and pause) Subtitles, translation, micro-delay Outtakes
Signature	Authorship, credits Choral voice Me as a character Quotation
Resonance	Remembrance Poetic imagination Unexpected reactions Second life of stories Musical score

ordering, and weaving also applies to objects, rooms, and atmospheres, even to the urban landscape gazed at from windows and balconies. Those series of objects and ambiences played a starring role in our documentary. Trays, beds, accordions, kitchens, dogs, and pans were very dear to the participants. Consequently, we rationed their appearance, playing with the spectator who wants to see the things they are talking about.

Mechanisms of closure are manyfold: visual, narrative, conceptual, and musical. First, the composition of the image on camera focuses on certain elements while blurring others (see figures 5.1 to 5.4). Camera composition awakens the power of the infraordinary. By means of the artistry of Jorge Moreno, the head of a dog leaning out through a hole under a backdoor can be upgraded to the category of "event." By keeping a fresh eye out for little things, the camera makes them significant, as they were for their owners. Second, montage chops up formerly continuous sequences and, conversely, bridges events that were once remote. By juxtaposing either similar or contrasting images, the edit impinges surprising effects of meaning on the singular stories. It is here, in montage, where the power of a filmmaker resides. Sometimes we declined the use of such power, either because the effect of juxtapositions was parodic to the point of insult or because it imperceptibly biased the original meaning intended by the speaker. Many good takes were discarded for this reason. Third, although we began to work without a closed script, soon the need for a story line became clear. We used two conceptual resources to provide the skeleton. Sequences were grouped in six thematic sections so that each character enters in dialogue around a topic with other participants from elsewhere. We also created a transversal line through the figure of the researcher, a traveler between cities in a quest for others' intimacy. Timing is essential. It requires the creation of rhythm regarding not only the dramatical information provided to the spectator but also the visual and musical cadence of sequences. Administering climactic tension is crucial because, as Piglia says, the meaning of a story reveals itself at the end. Fourth, the addition of written words at specific points (opening titles at every main section, final credits at the end) allowed us to conceptually structure the visual discourse, pushing us to read the material in the direction of the hypotheses contained in this book. The quote by Perec from *The Infra-ordinary* that preludes the images works in the same fashion. We also freely invented a literary title for each narrative excerpt, showing them in the credits. Interestingly, it is one of the traits of the film about which we receive more feedback, both from participants and colleagues. Finally, the work of translating and subtitling the original Spanish version was revealing. If the timing of the subtitles was not fully in sync with the speech, any nuances of meaning—especially humor—were lost. Half a second of delay spoils a punch line. Discursive closures are a matter of microtiming.

Figure 5.1. Composing the image (courtesy of Jorge Moreno Andrés).

Figure 5.2. "Sometimes we tidy up." El Parque, Montevideo, 2014 (courtesy of Jorge Moreno Andrés).

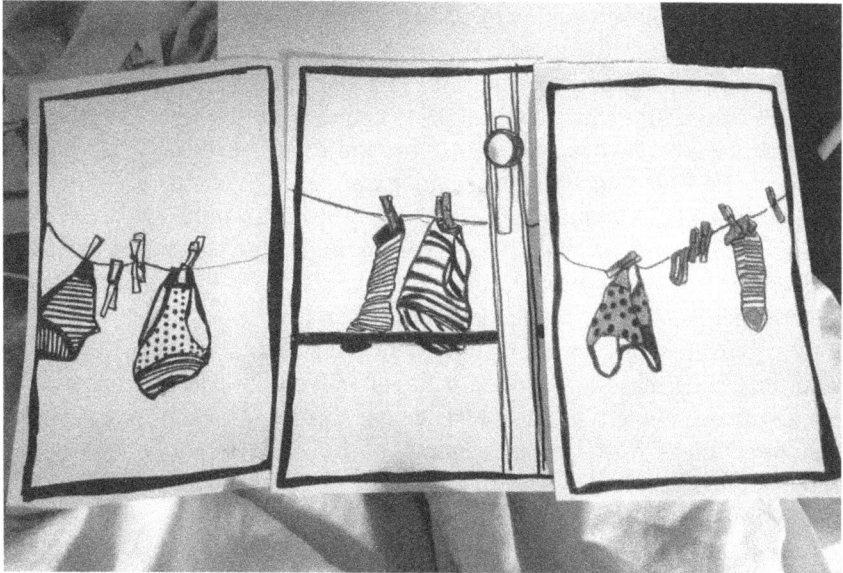

Figure 5.3. Drawings for the flyer of the film, elaborating on figure 5.2 (courtesy of Gloria G. Durán).

Figure 5.4. "From this bed you can reach the ceiling." El Parque, Montevideo, 2014 (courtesy of Jorge Moreno Andrés).

In summary, the principles of choice in the montage process served (a) to sensorily awaken the hidden powers of the infraordinary; (b) to exclude harmful and sensitive information; (c) to avoid effects of critical metacommentary on the informants' voices; (d) to enhance the reflexive insights contained in the monologues, by means of juxtaposition, similitude, and contrast; and (e) to do "emotional editing": cutting and pasting not only texts but also gestures, intentions, and feelings. All these principles would not make up an author's voice by themselves. It is necessary to add the paramount criterium of joining forces with your informants: working in tune with the direction of the argument and the affective tone of their narratives.

What to do with the alternative stories that could possibly be pulled from that large mass of recorded material? Given the potentialities of any narrative corpus for reuse and revisitation, there is no easy answer. I can note three things. First, at the beginning of the research process, you, as an ethnographer, may believe you know what you are looking for. But what finally ends up in a text, be it written or visual, is what you actually found. The best stories. The punch lines. The conceptual revelations. Substantial facts. Emotional peaks. Suspense. Epiphanies. Round endings. Unplausible coincidences. Poetic justice. All this is what your sensibility as a reader and spectator tells you will work best. Second, as noted before, we actually discarded a few preliminary montages of some scenes that looked beautiful and convincing to us but were too humorous or disrespectful. They could be misinterpreted by the public—and the interviewees—as a cruel and distancing gaze on their contradictions and vulnerabilities. In this regard, respect for the informants' public face and their communicative intentions is a priority. Third, at present I am interested in exploring the frailty and precariousness of the everyday, a topic that—for the reasons explained in chapter 2—was not an emphasis in our approach. So, I am returning to the filmed interview material for a closer look at this hidden dimension of the everyday that makes us equal parts strong and weak within the thin layers that protect our homes.

A variety of forms of signature are present. The project was explicitly a collaborative task, but the individual authorship of the documentary appears in the credits too. There would be much to discuss about the gray areas in collective cultural production and the consequent difficulties of collaboration—something I will briefly address in the concluding chapter. Let me note here that the marks of authorship in the documentary are manyfold and subtle. The documentary does not have a voice-over, which we found overly authoritative and aesthetically distasteful. Instead, the authors' voice mutters under the very polyphony of voices that figures as the protagonist. Our subjective visions mediate the whole outcome. This could not be otherwise, even if a lot of naive fantasizing exists around the actual possibilities of collaborative production to generate a voice from scratch. Having a say of our own was as much a responsibility as it was a right, impossible to decline. In our case, the options were either adding a voice-over or fully vanishing as narrators of the story. Both solutions would have killed the spirit of the project. The middle ground we found was to put myself in the movie as a character. Ironically, me-as-character fulfills the process of conversion of persons into characters we are commenting on. Finally, the Perec quote that opens the movie with a fragment of *L'infra-ordinaire* carries an authorial weight. Actually, many of our favorite poems on home, love, and life came to mind throughout the shooting process. We were tempted to bring Pedro Salinas, Luis Cernuda, Octavio Paz, Fabio Morabito, and León Felipe to the mix. In the end, we decided to soberly lighten the filmic discourse from such overwhelming presences. Let the people speak for themselves.

A film is a resonance chamber. Beyond the actual images, wider possibilities for remembrance and imagination are revealed in the reactions of the public, their laughs and silences, their wish to comment on similar experiences and share personal stories. This is the added value that your editing facilitates. It shows the ethnographic capacity to amplify and prolong the life of stories in another medium—to give them, so to speak, a second life. Hence, resounding and vibrating with others' stories is the best service we can offer to reciprocate the gift received from our informants. In my case, the instrument for this reverberation was the music soundtrack, which I composed (see figure 5.5). I got inspiration from *La última noche* by Bobby Collazo, an old Cuban bolero

Figure 5.5. Resounding el barrio for the soundtrack of the film. Ciudad Vieja, Montevideo, 2014 (courtesy of Jorge Moreno Andrés).

about spite and despair: "The last night I spent with you / I would like to forget it, but I can't."

I made three free variations: a barcarole, a bolero, and a Caracas-style merengue. The elaboration on the same melodic material and common instrumentation of clarinets, guitar, Mexican *jarana*, and Peruvian *cajón* gives the movie a unified atmosphere. I searched for a vague Latin flavor, not easy to locate in a specific place. Honestly, I composed it this way because it is the kind of music I like most. I put in music my personal commentary to those deeply moving stories. It was my way of singing that intimacy is too good not to be true.

NOTES

1. For key authors and reviews, see references from the introduction and chapter 1.

2. Of course, much has happened since Jacobson's functionalist scheme, which I introduce here as a hallmark. Goffman (1981) complicates the positions of participants in conversation, with further distinctions that defy any dual exchange between addresser and addressee. For the present analysis, I have relied mainly on a tradition of trope theory in anthropology, in particular Leach (1976), Fernandez (1991, 2001), Carrithers (2009), and Velasco (2003, 2007), as well as its correlates in the field of

cognitive linguistics, particularly Lakoff and Johnson (2003). I also take into account a semantic of critical categories (Lehrer 1982). For a classical deconstruction of the typology of signs, see Eco (1988). The category of *poiesis* has been invoked in various semiotic traditions as well as in biology (Maturana and Varela 2005). The handbook of sociology of culture by Hall, *Representation* (1997), is also of immediate ethnographic use. For poetic approaches based on more recent poststructuralist critiques, see Berlant (2000) and Stewart (2005, 2007). Cognitive narratologies like that of Herman (2009, 2012) and Herman and Vervaeck (2005) are also a good guide.

3. The contrast between two classical references like Jacobson and Aristotle is illustrative of two differing scopes about the poetic function. Through a six-faceted model of communication, Jacobson acknowledges the multidimensional condition inherent to verbal language. But he concentrates his analysis on written and oral genres of poetry, with a formal emphasis. For his part, Aristotle, while focusing on the canonic forms of poetry of his time (the dramatic form of tragedy and the Homeric epopees), had a very organic view of the wholeness of form and its roots in mimesis or imitation, a faculty in common with other creative human activities. According to Aristotle, poetry is a derivative activity that stems from the unfolding of human life.

Conclusion

From Collaboration to Remembrance

Had Borges or Piglia written this book, what kind of ending would they have chosen? If, as they say, the meaning of narrative depends on its ending, now the moment of truth has arrived, when I must think twice about what to deliver to the patient reader. Perhaps Borges would have the main character assassinated. Or would he rather abruptly introduce the figure of a narrator, hidden until that moment? We are not allowed these tricks for abrupt closure in serious ethnographic writing. Nor must I resort—once more—to my informants' nicely crafted endings: signatures deep inside closets, daughters posing on baroque stairs. Regardless, I too keep little treasures of poetic justice. This journey along workshops on intimacy brought about a parallel journey across my own memories.

A friendly critic exclaimed after a screening of *The Order I Live In*, "Is this not much too self-referential?" My first impulse was to reply with commonplaces of reflexive anthropology: you discover yourself by studying others, and there is a moral obligation to signal your presence in the text by showing the backstage. Instead, I simply assented with a smile. It was absolutely true. I had enjoyed the journey so much, the people I met, the homes I visited, the stories I witnessed, that I had to agree with him. Being portrayed through the lives of others? It does not seem a misdemeanor to me but rather the ultimate test for honest ethnography. Certainly, self-referentiality may come from laziness and indulgence on the part of the author. Sometimes it is a result of ideological crusading. The worst cases are a mix of both (partisan stiffness cum heroic self-satisfaction). But self-reference, understood as the presence of an author in a text, can also be a sincere trait that emerges from conversation, deep listening, and shared understandings. My modest assessment is that this is what happened to our collective enterprise.

So, this book ends with a methodological reflection about that big mystery: Why is it that entering others' intimacy may become a reflective understanding of your own? In this concluding chapter, I summarize the arguments in the book, the ethnography offered as evidence, and the cultural processes underlined. Later, I will briefly address a few important questions that this kind of research poses. What does intimacy have to do with contemporary urban changes and with ideas about urbanity and the good collective life? What are the futures of intimacy? What kind of theoretical frames do we need for its study? How can we understand, study, and value intimacy without destroying it? The chapter concludes by singularizing collaboration, reverberation, and remembrance as important faculties mobilized in this search.

This book reports on a research project about the metropolization of intimacy. The project was transurban, collaborative, narrative, and visual in nature. It explored daily life in three Latin cities (Madrid, Mexico City, and Montevideo) between 2010 and 2017, through a system of workshops for collective exploration and a consequent series of in-depth and on-site interviews with collaborators in their own homes. The empirical corpus gathers circa forty workshops, hundreds of participants, and thirty hours of filmed interviews. The resulting documentary was screened in the three cities and a few others in Europe and North and Latin America.

The argument followed is twofold. In the first place, we take the urbanological stance that the rise of the intimate sphere is an epochal phenomenon with deep consequences for contemporary urban life—among others, the visibility, politicization, and universalization of the intimate realm as well as the questioning of its subordination to the public sphere. The right to intimacy has become a crucial claim. It is so in public controversies, in the social sciences, and in the individual pursuit of an autonomous and self-determined life. The increasingly individualized subject of late modern societies strives for intimacy, understood as "an order of one's own." Definitions of intimacy are fuzzy, messy, and slippery. For that reason, instead of cutting off the perimeter of intimacy from the onset, in this book we have chosen to meander the boundary-work and local definitions by which our informants construct the intimate realm. By this method, we came to a working definition that underlines (a) the overlapping of domestic, private, and intimate concepts; (b) its common opposition to the concept of the public realm; (c) its relation to experiences of closeness and familiarity; and (d) its bond with the deployment of the self.

Second, we have also sustained a narratological stance: the centrality of storytelling in the constitution of intimacy. The stories we live by are integral to intimacy itself. In Pardo's (1996) words: intimacy is the art of recounting life. Stories are not an adornment, distraction, or smokescreen that could be set apart from the practicalities of everyday life. They bear cognitive, aesthetic, and moral consequences. We have shown this through an analysis of microstories, either exchanged by the participants in workshops for collective self-exploration or contained in the interviews and takes of the documentary *The Order I Live In.* Even under the compressed and elliptic form that they take nowadays in social media, these "stories of the self" show a striving for form, a definite will for style. Such stylization is noticeable in short flash-images embedded in a wider argument, as well as in narrative frames that provide scaffolding to a whole conversation. The search for style can be documented at its best in the longer twice-told tales and anecdotes that make part of a repertoire of personal narratives (Stahl 1989) and oral accounts of personal experience (Labov and Waletzky 1967). At the structural level, they show an underlying canonical plot that deals with the tasks and works of ego. The plot is agonistic, since the action revolves around the contributions by several actants in favor of, or against, the goals of the self. These actants comprise parents, spouses, partners, roommates, kindred, landlords, colleagues, friends, bosses, kids, pets, favorite objects, furniture, and appliances, and abstract entities like fate; good and bad luck; personal virtues and flaws; hazards; career, job, and unemployment; and lack of time, health, or money. The content of these stories implicitly rests on established conventions of modern living, such as comfort, efficiency, and hygiene. We have stressed the poetic quality at work in many stories: their crafted performance, climactic rhythm, round endings, and poetic justice. A tight connection between good form and moral weight seems to exist. If microstorytelling makes such an essential part of intimacy, it is because of its chronotopical ability to knit together the flow of life and the flow of stories. As Berger (Berger and Sontag 1983) put it, stories are shelter in everyday life, rescue operations to resist loss and oblivion.

This analysis of the narrative of others would be a sterile exercise—a cold dissection of anyone else's life—if it did not allow the glancing of a quantum of the grace and singularity of the persons peeking out from them: Camilo, the architect disappointed with the self-designed house of his dreams; Norma, the woman at the window, paying attention to the noises of the Mexican night; Yunes and Martin, debuting in their brand-new life in common, full of promises but short on frying pans; Claudia, Manuela, and Rosa, who came to learn, to their annoyance, what a burden the inheritance of collective memory can be. These and other people's microstories document things like the mysteries of singularity, the entanglement between the senses, the rejoicing of the self, the emergence of the commons, and the homesickness of the voyager, among other deep processes of intimate life.

The two arguments—the narrative and the urban—meet in one: the significance of poetics in everyday life. By taking *poetic* in the ample sense of *poiesis*—production of meaning—we have stressed the creativity and generativity of daily life. The agency of the dweller is inalienable and inexhaustible as a source of practice, discourse, and meaning. This capacity is entangled with other large-scale metropolitan processes that supply problems, resources, and solutions to the home agency of the dweller. Among them, we have identified reproduction, community, reform, commodification, and individualization. The joint influence of these formative processes results in an entanglement where the dynamic tensions between expert systems and individuals, forces of rationalization and appropriations by the people of the household, can be appreciated. We have also noted, according to Kaufmann (2004), the dialectics governing "the modern injunction to become oneself," between the internal drive for reflexivity and the need to forge and stabilize an identity. The urge for openness, rationalization, and free choice collides with the one for closure, wholeness, and sense. More specifically, the poetics of daily life have been interpreted through the lens of four semiotic devices or effects of meaning: signature, displacement, closure, and reverberation. Their interplay produces not only the discourses and practices of the dweller but also metanarratives like the ones that experts (like IKEA interior designers and the ethnographers themselves) generate to account for it.

TOWARD A NEW REGIME OF URBANITY

How does all this relate to current changes in urban life? The rise of intimacy announces a new regime of urbanity whose traits we are just beginning to conceptualize.

Taking intimacy seriously interrogates the classical notion of the public sphere, which has become eroded and contested but remains central and irreplaceable to our societies. There is an apparent paradox involved here. Studying, caring for, and giving value to the intimate sphere begins and ends with a thorough discussion of the public space. In my view, such a discussion involves three elements: (1) a critique of the techno, political, and economic bias followed by the dominant approaches and favorite tropes that give shape to the emerging public space; (2) remapping many of the classical oppositions (or *couplets*) of urbanity and urbanness; and (3) an assessment of the ambivalent futures of intimacy in a context where the public fascination with, and display of, intimate events, values, and emotions paradoxically threatens to cheapen, devalue, and degrade them.

Néstor García Canclini (2012) argued that, in order to understand contemporary cities, it is imperative to complement the current sociospatial approach prevalent in urban studies, which accounts for the social construction of public space, with a sociocommunicational perspective, which helps to account for the web of mediations, interactions, and forms of agency. I must add the need for an affective, sociosentimental approach, one that should account for the feelings, emotions, affects, relationships, memories, narratives, and structures of sentiment that make life in common possible. This approach brings to the fore dimensions of intimacy, subjectivity, care, and social reproduction—those ordinary things that constitute the stuff that daily life is made of.

These dimensions have been underrepresented either through neglect or mystification, both in urban theory and in the common sense of early modernity. The dominant imagery of urbanism has celebrated the built space with its skylines, towers, emblematic and iconic architectures, megaprojects, highways, and infrastructures. Root metaphors from the industrial nineteenth century onward have represented the city as factory, production chain, road, agora, public square, parliament, government, market, and laboratory. In recent times, the figures of network, flow, project, node, screen, and prototype have been added to this repertoire of images (Cruces 2012). Above all else, the Web! They point to an emergent "new public space" still in its becoming.

However, metropolization has also brought about an increasing visibility, politicization, universalization, and aestheticization of issues of gender, reproduction, domestic life, privacy, subjectivity, and intimacy, which were formerly considered secondary—think, for example, of how domestic life was conceptualized in old Marxian vulgate as "the place for the reproduction of the workforce." We are witnessing the emergence of a new urban common sense in which the very notion of a public sphere—and its physical surrogate, public space—finds itself in a predicament.

The poetics of daily life embedded in the stories presented here springs from this emerging regime. It trespasses limits that would be taken for granted from a classical, canonical perspective of urban modernity, with its eroded oppositions: public/private, production/consumption, home/work, professional/amateur. This remapping of boundaries questions the invisibility, devaluation, and subordination of the domestic, private, and intimate spaces. Whether we like it or not, it will be difficult in the near future to keep defining what is "urban" in terms of a predominance of the public space.

The new regime embodies a contemporary fascination with the creative, the quotidian, the affective, and the intimate. This cultural trend should undoubtedly be welcome. It gives visibility to emotions, relations, and practices that were once hiding in the shadows. It critically questions the formerly prepolitical issues of asymmetries of power at home, among individuals of different gender, rank, and age. It gives value and permanence to cherished traditions, objects, and identities. These things are at the center of peoples' daily lives, in their search for "an order of their own."

Yet, the ethnography also alerts us to potential shortcomings and paradoxes linked to the rise of the intimate sphere—a fascination condensed in the trope of "extimacy." The very forces that give value and publicity to things that were formerly protected in their "islands of privacy" may also be exposing them to the risks of commodification and overrepresentation. This is evident in phenomena such as the popularity of reality shows, the vulnerability

brought about by the spread of personal information on the Web, the growing importance of "show politics" fueled by celebrity revelations and media
scandals, the commodification of love and friendship through online dating
services, and many other issues that push boundaries and defy old definitions.
These dynamics give a contradictory, self-canceling character to the pursuit
of intimacy, pointing to the limits and dangers of this process.

So, the triumph of intimacy also contains the seeds of its potential destruc-
tion. Instead of denouncing this situation as an end of public virtue, or as a
retreat into the private domain—a failure to strive for the common good—we
should explore the possibilities, promises, and threats of this new juncture. In
our times, personal has become metropolitan and vice versa. This may be the
ultimate moral underlying the microstorytelling of our informants. Whatever
results in the near future from this reordering of home/work, public/private,
and so on, the self and its personalizing stories will definitely be at the very
center of what it means to be urban.

WHAT DO WE NEED TO UNDERSTAND INTIMACY?

In chapter 1, I characterized an emerging field where several subfields of
classical disciplines converge: a cultural history of private life, a social psychology of the self, a geography of the domestic space, a sociology of the
everyday, a phenomenology of the life-worlds, an anthropology of the home,
cultural studies on housing and dwelling, folklore studies of personal narratives, and sociolinguistic and narratological approaches to oral accounts of
personal experience. These approaches have been enhanced since the 1980s,
as a fresh reaction against artificial academic compartments that chopped up
the integrity of the dweller's experience. They coincide in their advocacy for
a return of the subject as active agent at the center of everyday life, even if
this agency may be problematized or poured into the jargon of specific theories, like reflexive modernization, sensory ethnography, cognitive linguistics,
network-actor theory, new materialism, or affect theory, among others mentioned in this book.

From the scope of our research, a frame for the study of intimacy can be
suggested based on (a) a constructivist epistemology, (b) an interactionalist
view of the subject, and (c) a noninformationalist theory of language.

A constructivist epistemology recognizes the plurality of forms of knowledge and presupposes the capacity of any subject to build a world of their
own. When speaking of intimacy, everyone is an expert. Therefore, everyone
must have something important to teach the ethnographer. It goes without
saying that a constructive epistemology is also a reflexive one, since it places
the knowledge of the observer in symmetry—not in hierarchy—with regard to

the forms of knowledge of the subjects under scrutiny. This commits the ethnographer to the added exigence of being included in the picture. Of course, in daily life we do not approach others with this attitude, and there are good reasons not to do so. In current life, under what phenomenologists called "the natural attitude," the intimacy of others reaches us as an object of concern, interest, critique, fascination, annoyance, disturbance, resistance, intervention, reform, repression, claim, denounce, or advice—but not of study. It could not be otherwise: it is one thing to understand alterity, another very different one to be willing to live with it. Nevertheless, our research strongly advocates for the scientific, aesthetic, and social benefits of this kind of study, given the values contained in intimate life. For the researcher, the reward we can expect is a fresh discovery of the wealth, power, and beauty enclosed in what Löfgren (2014) lucidly called "the black box of everyday life."

An interactionalist approach is one that considers subjects in relation, not isolated individuals. In line with a tradition rooted in the work of Goffman and Schultz, it contemplates the mutual constitution between the subjects and their physical and social environments. It is only by a continuous give-and-take of material, social, and symbolic interactions that we humans become whoever we may be. We receive our name and our tongue at home, from the hands and mouths of others. In this book, we have made extensive use of the metaphor of the "entanglement" of the subject as a useful image to characterize the web of spaces, actions, people, objects, atmospheres, and emotions in which the subject is embedded. Certainly, the extreme individuation processes of late modernity push in the opposite direction: toward the uprooting of the subject from any former determination of identity and origin. And the modern reflexivity that governs our mobile, changing lives pushes us toward self-making, free choice, openness, and autonomy. But nobody is an island. The self-centered narratives analyzed here show the important role of other actants in this web that—as modern Penelopes—we all weave and unweave. The frontiers of the self come from intensive boundary-work and multiple negotiations, both with institutional agencies and with the rest of the household. We knit the fabric of our life by taking part in the lives of others. The subtle narrative slippage between "me" and "us," the commitment of persons to their participations and belongings, the social structuring of everyday time-space in the form of patterned encounters, social rhythms, collective rituals, and shared memories—all that favors a processual, dynamic, and collective understanding of the subject in intimacy. Intimacy is not the iron cage of individuals but something they mutually create. And the little stories we live by—the focus of our attention here—are just one among the many gifts by means of which such a collective creation emerges, circulates, and thrives. Some of the pleasures you can expect from entering others' intimacies lies here. No matter the worries and hardships they may suffer, people are prone to show chili peppers they grow in pots, recipes from their grandmas, toys and games they plan to hand down to their kids, jokes someone told them days ago, strange heirlooms they have no idea what to do with.

There is no better place than language to keep these treasures of intimacy. In the dialogical engagement of the subject, we find genuine creativity and idiosyncrasy. This was partly the reason why our research strategy has been narratological. We stressed this generativity through the concept of *poiesis*, understood as the production of meaning in ordinary life, not as an adornment or detour from the literal, logical-propositional uses of language focused on its informative, referential, and denotative value. Following a tropological approach, we have assumed the graduality of sign conventions. Our emphasis here was on the speakers' capacity to create worlds, relate to others, position themselves, and keep the conversation alive. Of course, such a conversation embraces the addressee of the storytelling. But there are also untold participants, countless presences in discourse: traces of past conversations, expectations of the audience, generic intertextuality, words of the deceased, and—as in Alba's family photo album—people who might enter the conversation in the future. By following Pardo's critique of any informationalist reduction of language, we have underlined the intimate and hidden—preconventional—side of its use. Intimacy is made with words. And words carry accents, flavors, styles, tones, singular genealogies, ways of saying, ways of listening. This kind of sensibility led us to filming. There seemed to be no better way to respect the singularity of those worlds other than displaying them with their own voice. The reward entailed by this strategy lies in the pleasures of listening, the adventure of recording, and the fun of retelling. In the process of resounding other tales, rewriting them with images and melodies of our own, and projecting them as a collective, I discovered a few personal epiphanies.

FROM COLLABORATION TO REMEMBRANCE

Do you like confidences? Let me end with a few. One: I have been very happy doing this project. Two: collaborative research may sound very nice, but it is riddled with problems. Three: people's stories brought important experiences to my mind that were buried deep in my memory.

Happiness has a bad reputation among academics. As we are supposed to be serious people, this is often wrongly conflated with the torpid step of the camel, who tends to bend (Nietzsche *dixit*) under the heavy weight of knowledge. Other times we choose to adopt the acidic tones of the leftist intellectual, who (as the lion figure in Nietzsche) feels obliged to destroy everything within their reach. Among anthropologists, we have internalized the false idea of being the Jiminy Cricket of social research. We assume all too easily that doing good fieldwork means to suffer woes and hardships and that being critical is to devote our best efforts to amend political flaws, cultural inaccuracies, and inappropriate attitudes of everyone around us. Mission impossible. Maybe I am a dinosaur. I feel more at ease with Gellner's (1990) ironic genealogy of European anthropology when he noted that our craft had emerged from three separate drives: curiosity, love, and guilt; curiosity for the diversity of cultures, love for their national and regional heritages, and guilt for the partiality of Western civilizing pride and the crimes committed under its banner. As I confessed in chapter 2, I did not arrive at intimacy solely for the sake of raw curiosity, much less to redeem Western, patriarchal, modern, or bourgeois misdemeanors. Although the careful reading of Giddens and Hochschild had convinced me of the intellectual promises of the field and its urbanological urgency, I actually went into intimacy for love. Interest in the object, the possibilities of experimenting with it, and the mysteries enveloped in that "black box." I think it is a legitimate drive. In fact, it did not differ much from earlier times when I was moved to ethnomusicology, festivals, oral history, Latin America, street performances, corporate culture, and the practice of reading. They were cool things to study.

In this case, the added element was a wish to share. Urban parenting is an isolating experience. When you have a child, you turn toward your network of relatives and close friends for advice and help. They may not be nearby or available, though. This was our case. Some evenings, during our baby's bath time, I would say to myself, "This is too beautiful to be seen just by me." I would imagine the tiny bathroom crowded with an audience, applauding a fantastic baby bath. Something of this impulse to unveil and share the good things of daily life is behind the current tidal wave of highly private details on Facebook, Instagram, and other social media. I never surfed the new wave of Internet extimacy, but the workshops for collaborative exploration afforded me a fine opportunity to look into the intimacy of others and share my own.

Collaboration is a fancy word, much easier to invoke than to practice. In this book I have presented a methodological process that was, in an overall assessment, satisfactory, considering the ethnographic results, the commitment of so many people, the institutional facilitation in three countries, and the positive feedback received from many persons involved in a process spread out in time and geography. The joys of personal encounters were real. The generosity with which so many agreed to share details about feelings and stories was remarkable. But to get there, it was necessary to overcome plenty of obstacles. I want to mention them briefly, since they were not spurious contingencies but difficulties inherent to the collaborative process.

First, as a concept, collaboration promises egality, horizontality, and symmetry, but today it designs a handful of fuzzily defined situations for working together, whose rules of intellectual and personal appropriation are not written, clear, settled, or known in advance. Nor can they be. Collaborative work is emergent in a variety of institutional contexts within a vaguely constituted group of participants—most of the time, an open network—and full of gray areas. Not everyone in the endeavor understands it in the same terms. Nor are the rules for contribution and appropriation laid out from the onset. Nor is there an authorized arbiter to solve discrepancies and conflicts. Therefore, clashes of various kinds are to be expected. As the reader can easily guess, there will be struggles for the power to lead the task, the right to take the floor, the signature of the results, the payment of the costs, the monetization of the product, the attribution of the merit, and the harvest of prestige and reputation. But there are still more issues involved.

A first source of clashes has to do with the meanings of the gift in everyday life. Emerging techniques and methods for cocreation and collaboration are disruptive. This is commonly recognized with respect to institutional norms, roles, and statuses, as well as with respect to the property and profit regulations of a privative, market-oriented economy. What is less recognized is that these methodologies also usually break or violate commonsense expectations about reciprocity and mutuality, deeply ingrained in everyday life. The give-and-take of the home miraculously produces and sustains the commons, without written nor explicit rules. At home, guests are not expected to behave with cool familiarity—opening the fridge or the drawers in the bedrooms—and the attention given to strangers is differentiated, for better or worse, from what the members of the household receive. Reciprocity has distributive rules. They are not coincident either with the cash economy that regulates the public space nor with the imaginary and solidary economy of the commons invoked by the promoters of social experiments for free cultural collaboration in an open dominion. Consequently, clashes about the give-and-take are to be expected from the onset, among people coming from differing home economies and experiences, where the limits between mine, yours, and ours respond to a huge variety of backgrounds.

Second, collaborative methodologies are institutionally mediated. Although the organizational frame might be hidden in peer-to-peer initiatives, there is always an institutional background framing what happens in the collaborative scene. In our case, it was mainly Medialab Prado from Madrid's city council who had this role, although we also collaborated with a number of other institutions. I had to negotiate with them what could be said or done in our meetings, their length, and their diffusion to the public. Being an organization promoting free culture and open access, Medialab's policies were radical regarding rules of keeping meetings open to participants of all kinds, broadcasting them in real time through online streaming, and licensing them with open access. I did not think this policy was the most suitable for collaborative research on intimacy. To create a sheltered space, where intimacy could emerge among strangers, was what we needed—not putting them out in the open, under the harsh lights of the public dominion. After discussing this with Marcos Garcia, Medialab's director, we found a middle ground. I would stream the beginning and ending sessions of the series, and everything in between would be of the exclusive incumbency of the participants.

In the first stage, collaboration finds resistance and misinterpretations rooted in the common sense of everyday life. In the second stage, it has to negotiate with the universalist horizon of a bureaucratic milieu. The third stage, once a collaborative outcome has been reached, faces the difficulty of finding ways for distribution and appropriation in a competitive world of privative, expert, hierarchical, traditional, or charismatic cultural goods and products. If your film does not receive awards at festivals, it will become difficult to publish it in the market with a Creative Commons license, because most of the distributors work with commercial ones. Islands of cultural collaboration have to make their way in oceans of competence.

My last methodological epiphany is about remembrance. All too often one tends to think that discourse analysis can or should be made from some kind of neutral, objective ground, from which you would decipher, assess, and interpret the meaning of others' stories—like a forensic surgeon hunched over a body on a dissection table. What the concept of reverberation suggests is that listening and understanding do not work this way. As convenor of the workshops and interlocutor with the participants in our film, I was closer to a dancer in a collective dance where, by following the vibes of others, you may get in tune and in sync with them. So, these analyses have been made from a place that resembles more that of Bachelard's childhood room, quoted above, than that of Labov's structural charts and figures, detailed to exhaustion in his classic essay. Sometimes you simply reminisce things. They come back to you triggered by the dialogue and enlightened by the perspective of the informant. This happened to me very strongly in a number of cases, so much so that I did not restrain myself from taking over the starring role and sharing those little pearls with my informants.

Currito, as my mother liked to call me, was a seven-year-old boy who dreamed of finding a hidden treasure. I had watched an educative Spanish TV program in which kids dug up Roman treasures somewhere and received honors for that. I had to find one! So, I devoted my recesses at school to digging in the sandbox. To my fortune, I found a treasure. A tiny, shiny tin medal in the shape of the Virgin. I proudly gave it to my mother as a present. The greatest treasure for the best mother.

When Claudia was telling us about the drawing of her grandpa holding hands with her, how she had given it to him as a child, and how the drawing had been hidden in a fold of her grandpa's wallet for so long, the tin Virgin came to my mind. I told her about it. "And what happened with the medal?" she asked me with curiosity. I was moved. "When my mother died, I was twenty-five. One year later or so, one of my sisters phoned me and told me that she was helping my father to take away the clothes and other stuff that my mother had left. There was a little bit of jewelry—nothing of economic worth, only sentimental value. My sisters were dividing it up, and they wanted me to go and take something. After their insistence, I went to my father's home to choose a memento from my mom. A little jewelry box contained earrings, rings, and necklaces. Somehow, a second, hidden fold under the surface opened. Inside was a tiny, insignificant, apparently worthless Virgin, made of tin." I had to stop, almost welling up. "It seems that the same thing that happened to you happened to me as well." Like Claudia's grandfather, my mother had jealously kept that treasure. People around us are, without notice, secret custodians of our lives.

Poetic justice happens, to everyone.

This undercurrent of invisible connection among life stories is a recursive thread that matches again with Piglia's (1999, 116) concluding remarks in his theorizing on the importance of endings: "All the stories of the world are weaved with the fabric of our own life. Distant, obscure, they are parallel worlds, possible lives, laboratories to experiment with personal passions."

Stories move us because they are made of the same stuff as our own existence. The reverberation with which some participants embrace the micronarratives of the others is also ours. An isomorphism happens between the ways in which stories of daily life are exchanged—in our workshops, as in the day-to-day—and the second life that the analysis purports, by proposing new paths that may resignify them. These stories are listened to and understood from a place that is never the distant and neutral scientific desk, from which its symbolic efficacy could be definitively deciphered and reduced. They have the potential to continue reverberating somewhere else, in other dialogues. Across their vicissitudes, we can recognize traces and memories of our own dwelling.

REFERENCES

Abrahams, Roger D. 2005. *Everyday Life: A Poetics of Vernacular Practices.* Philadelphia: University of Pennsylvania Press.

Adichie, Chimamanda. 2018. "The Danger of a Single Story." TED Talk, March 2018. Video 18:30. https://www.ted.com/talks/chimamanda_ngozi_adichie_the _danger_of_a_single_story?language=es.

Amit, Vered. 2002. "Reconceptualizing Community." In *Realizing Community. Concepts, Social Relationships and Sentiments*, edited by Vered Amit, 1–19. London: Routledge.

Amit, Vered, and Nigel Rapport. 2003. *The Trouble with Community: Anthropological Reflections on Movement, Identity and Collectivity*. London: Pluto.

Archila, Mauricio. 1991. *Cultura e identidad obrera. Colombia, 1910–1945*. Bogotá: CINEP.

Ariès, Philippe, and Georges Duby, eds. 1985. *Histoire de la vie privée*. Paris: Seuil.

Aristotle. 2020. *Poética [Poetics]*. Madrid: Alianza Editorial.

Ascher, François. 1995. *Métapolis, ou L'avenir des villes*. Paris: Editions Odile Jacob.

Ascher, François. 2001. *Les nouveaux principes de l'urbanisme*. La Tour d'Aigues, France: Aube.

Ascher, François. 2005. *Le mangeur hypermoderne. Une figure de l'individu éclectique*. Paris: Odile Jacob.

Auster, Paul. 2002. *I Thought My Father Was God: And Other True Tales from NPR's National Story Project*. New York: Picador.

Bachelard, Gaston. 1994 [1958]. *The poetics of space*. Boston: Beacon Press.

Bakhtin, Mikhail M. 1981. *The Dialogic Imagination: Four Essays*. Austin: University of Texas Press.

Bakhtin, Mikhail M. 1990. *Rabelais and His World*. Bloomington: Indiana University Press.

Balló, Jordi, and Xavier Pérez. 2006. *La semilla inmortal. Los argumentos universales en el cine*. Barcelona: Anagrama.

Barthes, Roland. 1957. *Mythologies*. Paris: Seuil.

Barthes, Roland. 1977. "The Grain of the Voice." In *Image-Music-Text*. New York: Hill and Wang, 179–189.

Bateson, Gregory. 1979. *Mind and Nature. A Necessary Unity*. New York: Dutton.

Bauman, Richard. 2004. *A World of Others' Words: Cross-cultural Perspectives on Intertextuality*. Malden, UK: Blackwell.

Bauman, Zygmund. 2001. *The Individualized Society*. Malden, UK: Polity Press.

Bauman, Zygmund. 2003. *Liquid Love. On the Frailty of Human Bonds*. Cambridge: Polity Press.

Baumann, Gerd. 2004. "Grammars of Identity/Alterity. A Structural Approach." In *Grammars of Identity/Alterity. A Structural Approach*, edited by Gerd Baumann and André Gingrich, 18–52. Oxford: Berghahn Books.

Bayard, Pierre. 2010. *L'Affaire du chien des Baskerville*. Paris: Les Éditions de Minuit.

Bayard, Pierre. 2012. *Comment parler des livres que l'on n'a pas lus?* Paris: Les Éditions de Minuit.

Beck, Ulrich. 1992. *Risk Society. Towards a New Modernity*. London: Sage.

Beck, Ulrich, and Elizabeth Beck-Gernsheim. 1995. *The Normal Chaos of Love*. Cambridge: Polity Press.

Beck, Ulrich, and Elizabeth Beck-Gernsheim. 2001. *Individualization. Institutionalized Individualism and Its Social and Political Consequences*. London: Sage.

Beck, Ulrich, Anthony Giddens, and Scott Lash, eds. 1997. *Reflexive Modernization: Politics, Tradition and Aesthetics in the Modern Social Order*. Stanford, CA: Stanford University Press.

Bellah, Robert N. 2011. *Religion in Human Evolution: From the Paleolithic to the Axial Age*. Cambridge, MA: Harvard University Press.

Bendix, Regina F. 2019. "My Home Is My Castle—My Coat Is My Refuge. Dwelling, Atmospheres and Communicative Arts." *Journal for European Ethnology and Cultural Analysis (JEECA)*, Special Issue, 1: 10–27.

Bennett, Jane. 2011. *Vibrant Matter. A Political Ecology of Things*. Durham, NC: Duke University Press.

Berger, John. 2016. "El silencio no miente." Interview with Juan Cruz, *Babelia, El País*, November 1, 2016.

Berger, John, and Susan Sontag. 1983. "To Tell a Story." *Voices*, Channel Four Television, video 01:03, https://www.youtube.com/watch?v=MoHCR8nshe8.

Berlant, Laurent, ed. 2000. *Intimacy*. Chicago: Chicago University Press.

Berman, Marshall. 1983. *All That Is Solid Melts into Air: The Experience of Modernity*. London: Verso.

Bernaerts, Lars, et al. 2013. *Stories and Minds: Cognitive Approaches to Literary Narrative*. Lincoln: University of Nebraska Press.

Bohannan, Paul, and George Dalton. 1965. *Markets in Africa*. Evanston, IL: Northwestern University Press.

Boltanski, Luc, and Ève Chiapello. 2018. *The New Spirit of Capitalism*. London: Verso.

Bott, Elizabeth. 1957. *Family and Social Network. Roles, Norms and External Relations in Ordinary Urban Families*. London: Tavistock.

Bourdin, Alain. 2005. *La métropole des individus*. Paris: Aube.

Boyarin, Jonathan. 1993. *The Ethnography of Reading*. Berkeley: University of California Press.

Bruner, Jerome. 1997. "Labov and Waletzky: Thirty Years On." *Journal of Narrative and Life History* 7(1–4): 61–68.

Bruner, Jerome. 2002. *Making Stories: Law, Literature, Life*. New York: Farrar, Straus & Giroux.

185

Brunvand, Jan H. 2001. *Too Good to Be True. The Colossal Book of Urban Legends.* New York: Norton.

Bryson, Bill. 2010. *At Home. A Short History of Private Life.* London: Doubleday.

Carrithers, Michael, ed. 2009. *Culture, Rhetoric and the Vicissitudes of Life.* New York: Berhahn Books.

Castañares, Wenceslao. 2006. *La televisión moralista. Valores y sentimientos en el discurso televisivo.* Madrid: Fragua.

Chase, Susan E. 2005. "Narrative Inquiry. Multiple Lenses, Approaches, Voices." In *The SAGE Handbook of Qualitative Research,* edited by Norman K. Denzin and Yvonna S. Lincoln, 651–679. Thousand Oaks: Sage.

Cieraad, Irene. 1999. *At Home. An Anthropology of Domestic Space.* New York: Syracuse University Press.

Cieraad, Irene. 2021. "House and Home: Reconsidering the Anatomy of Houses in Western Societies." *ANUAC* 10(2): 197–214.

Cintron, Ralph. 2009. "Inventions of Hyperbolic Culture." In *Culture, Rhetoric and the Vicissitudes of Life,* edited by Michael Carrithers, 138–155. New York: Berhahn Books.

Claval, Paul. 2003. "Les ouvertures de l'espace domestique. La porte, la fenêtre, le tableau et l'écran catodique." In *Espaces domestiques. Construire, habiter, représenter,* edited by Béatrice Collignon and Jean-François Staszak, 64–76. Rosny-sous-bois, France: Bréal.

Clifford, James, and George E Marcus, eds. 1986. *Writing Culture: The Poetics and Politics of Ethnography.* Berkeley: University of California Press.

Coleman, G. 2010. "Ethnographic Approaches to Digital Media." *Annual Review of Anthropology* 39:487–505.

Collignon, Béatrice, and Jean-François Staszak, eds. 2003. *Espaces domestiques. Construire, habiter, représenter.* Rosny-sous-bois, France: Bréal.

Colombo, Romina. 2016. "Madrid, retratos metropolitanos." In *Cosmópolis. Nuevas maneras de ser urbanos.* Grupo Cultura Urbana, edited by Francisco Cruces, 15–41. Barcelona: Gedisa.

Connerton, Paul. 1989. *How Societies Remember.* Cambridge: Cambridge University Press.

Connerton, Paul. 2009. *How Modernity Forgets.* Cambridge: Cambridge University Press.

Corcuff, Philippe, Christian Le Bart, and François De Singly, eds. 2015. *L'individu aujourd'hui: Débats sociologiques et contrepoints philosophiques.* Rennes, France: Presses Universitaires de Rennes.

Coudreuse, Anne, and Françoise Simonet-Tenant, eds. 2009. *Pour une histoire de l'intime et de ses variations.* Paris: L'Harmattan.

Cowen, Tyler. 2009. "Be Suspicious of Stories." TEDxMidAtlantic, November 2009. Video, 16:25. https://www.youtube.com/watch?v=RoEEDKwzNBw.

Cruces, Francisco. 2007. *Símbolos en la ciudad. Lecturas de antropología urbana.* Madrid: UNED.

Cruces, Francisco. 2012. "Intimidades metropolitanas. La ciudad soy yo." *Telos* 93: 60–69.

Cruces, Francisco, Grupo Cultura Urbana. 2016. *Cosmópolis. Nuevas maneras de ser urbanos*. Barcelona: Gedisa.

Cruces, Francisco. 2017a. *¿Cómo leemos en la sociedad digital? Lectores, booktubers y prosumidores*. Madrid and Barcelona: Ariel Telefónica.

———. 2017b. "Maneras de habitar." CanalUned, La UNED en TVE-2, Video 00:23. https://canal.uned.es/video/5a6f5e55b1111fdb088b458a.

Cruces, Francisco. 2021. "Why Objects Want Stories. And Vice Versa." In "Escuchar a los objetos," by Regina F. Bendix, Dorothy Noyes, Sharon R. Roseman, and Francisco Cruces. *Disparidades. Revista de Antropología* 76(1): e005. https://doi .org/10.3989/dra.2021.005.

Cruces, Francisco, et al. 2002. "Trust, Cosmetics or Suspicion? A Multi-sited Ethnography of Six Spanish Expert Systems." *Focaal, European Review of Anthropology* 40: 35–49.

Czarniawska, Barbara, and Orvar Löfgren, eds. 2012. *Managing Overflow in Affluent Societies*. New York: Routledge.

Da Matta, Roberto. 1994 [1984]. *A casa e a rua. Espaço, cidadanía, mulher e morte no Brasil*. Sao Paulo: Brasiliense.

De Certeau, Michel. 1990. *L'invention du quotidien. l'Arts de faire*. Paris: Gallimard.

De Certeau, Michel, Luce Giard, Pierre Mayol. 1994. *L'invention du quotidien. 2 habiter, cuisiner*. Paris: Gallimard.

De Singly, François. 2016. *Le soi, le couple et la famille*. Paris: Armand Colin.

Díaz de Rada, Ángel, et al. 2002. "The Meanings of the Expression 'Trust in Institutions.'" Unpublished, https://www.academia.edu/40094803/_The_Meanings _of_the_Expression_Trust_in_Institutions.

Douglas, Mary. 1966. *Purity and Danger: An Analysis of Concepts of Pollution and Taboo*. London: Routledge and Keegan Paul.

Douglas, Mary. 1985. *How Institutions Think*. London: Routledge.

Douglas, Mary. 1991. "The Idea of a Home: A Kind of Space." *Social Research* 58 (1): 287–307.

Dumont, Louis. 1985. *Essais sur l'individualisme: Une perspective anthropologique sur l'idéologie moderne*. Paris: Seuil.

Eco, Umberto. 1988. *Tratado de semiótica general*. Barcelona: Lumen.

Eco, Umberto. 2010. *Apostillas a el nombre de la rosa*. México: Lumen.

Ehn, Billy, and Orvar Löfgren. 2010. *The Secret World of Doing Nothing*. Berkeley: University of California Press.

Ehn, Billy, Orvar Löfgren, and Richard Wilk. 2016. *Exploring Everyday Life. Strategies for Ethnography and Cultural Analysis*. New York: Rowan & Littlefield.

Ehrenreich, Barbara, and Arlie R. Hochschild, eds. 2004. *Global Woman: Nannies, Maids, and Sex Workers in the New Economy*. New York: Metropolitan/Owl Books.

Eleb, Monique, and Anne Debarre. 1995. *Architectures de la vie privée, 2. L'invention de l'habitation moderne: Paris, 1880–1914*. Hazan, Archives d'architecture moderne.

Eleb, Monique, and Sabri Bendimérad. 2010. *Vu de l'intérieur. Habiter un immeuble en île-de-France, 1945–2010*. Paris: Archibooks, Sautereau Éditeur.

Elias, Norbert. 2000. *The Civilizing Process. Sociogenetic and Psychogenetic Investigations.* Oxford: Blackwell.

Elias, Norbert. 2001. *The Society of Individuals.* New York: Continuum.

Fernandez, James W. 1974. "The Mission of Metaphor in Expressive Culture." *Current Anthropology* 15(2): 110–145.

Fernandez, James W. 1986. "The Argument of Images and the Experience of Returning to the Whole." In *The Anthropology of Experience*, edited by Víctor M. Turner and Edward M. Bruner, 159–187. Urbana: University of Illinois Press.

Fernandez, James W. 1991. *Beyond Metaphor: The Theory of Tropes in Anthropology.* Stanford, CA: Stanford University Press.

Fernandez, James W. 1994. "Las esencias que celebramos y conmemoramos." *Antropología. Revista de pensamiento y estudios etnográficos* 8: 139–150.

Fernandez, James W., ed. 2001. *Irony in Action: Anthropology, Practice, and the Moral Imagination.* Chicago: University of Chicago Press.

Finnegan, Ruth H. 1977. *Oral Poetry: Its Nature, Significance, and Social Context.* Cambridge: Cambridge University Press.

Finnegan, Ruth H. 1988. *Literacy and Orality: Studies in the Technology of Communication.* Oxford: Blackwell.

Finnegan, Ruth H. 1989. *The Hidden Musicians: Music-making in an English Town.* Cambridge: Cambridge University Press.

Finnegan, Ruth H. 1998. *Tales of the City: A Study of Narrative and Urban Life.* London: Routledge.

Finnegan, Ruth. 2003. "Música y participación." *Trans. Revista Transcultural de Música*, 7. https://www.sibetrans.com/trans/articulo/210/musica-y-participacion.

Finnegan, Ruth H. 2013. *Why Do We Quote? The Culture and History of Quotation.* Cambridge: Open Book.

Finnegan, Ruth H. 2014. *Communicating: The Multiple Modes of Human Interconnection.* Milton Park, UK: Routledge.

Finnegan, Ruth H. 2015. *Where Is Language?: An Anthropologist's Questions on Language, Literature and Performance.* London: Bloomsbury Academic.

Fisher, Walter R. 1985. "The Narrative Paradigm: In the Beginning." *Journal of Communication* 35(4): 74–89.

Freud, Sigmund. 2003 [1919]. *The Uncanny.* Translated by David McLintock. New York: Penguin.

Frykman, Jonas, and Orvar Löfgren. 1987. *Culture Builders. A Historical Anthropology of Middle-Class Life.* New Brunswick, NJ: Rutgers University Press.

Gal, Susan. 2002. "A Semiotics of the Public/Private Distinction." *differences: A Journal of Feminist Cultural Studies* 13(1): 77–95.

Gal, Susan. 2005. "Language Ideologies Compared: Metaphors of Public/Private." *Journal of Linguistic Anthropology* 15(1): 23–37.

García Canclini, Néstor. 2010a. "Las cuatro ciudades de México." In *Textos de Antropología Contemporánea*, edited by Francisco Cruces and Beatriz Pérez Galán, 231–260. Madrid: UNED.

García Canclini, Néstor. 2010b. *La sociedad sin relato. Antropología y estética de la inminencia.* Buenos Aires: Katz.

García Canclini, Néstor, Francisco Cruces, and Maritza Urteaga, eds. 2012. *Jóvenes, culturas urbanas y redes digitales. Prácticas emergentes en las artes, las editoriales y la música*. Barcelona: Ariel Telefónica. https://www.fundaciontelefonica.com/cultura-digital/publicaciones/164/.

Garvey, Pauline. 2009. "Culture Materialised: IKEA Furniture and Other Evangelical Artefacts." In *Lost and Found 11: Rediscovering Ireland's Past*, 53–60. Ireland: WordWell.

Garvey, Pauline. 2013. "'Ikea Sofas Are Like H&M Trousers: The Potential of Sensuous Signs." *Journal of Business Anthropology* 2(1): 75–92.

Gellner, Ernest. 1990. "Anthropology and Europe." Keynote Address, EASA 1st Conference, Coimbra. A modified text of this talk appeared as an article in *Social Anthropology / Anthropology Sociale* 1(1): 1–7.

Giddens, Anthony. 1990. *The Consequences of Modernity*. Stanford, CA: Stanford University Press.

Giddens, Anthony. 1991. *Modernity and Self-Identity: Self and Society in the Late Modern Age*. Stanford, CA: Stanford University Press.

Giddens, Anthony. 1992. *The Transformation of Intimacy. Sexuality, Love and Eroticism in Modern Societies*. Cambridge: Polity Press.

Goffman, Erving. 1959. *The Presentation of Self in Everyday Life*. New York: Doubleday.

Goffman, Erving. 1967. *Interaction Ritual. Essays on Face-to-Face Behaviour*. Chicago: Aldine.

Goffman, Erving. 1972. *Relations in Public: Microstudies of the Public Order*. New York: Harper & Row.

Goffman, Erving. 1981. *Forms of Talk*. Philadelphia: University of Pennsylvania Press.

Guaderrama, Maritza. 2012. "Prácticas digitales en España y México: Un cuestionario online." In *Jóvenes, culturas urbanas y redes digitales. Prácticas emergentes en las artes, las editoriales y la música*, edited by Néstor García Canclini, Francisco Cruces, and Maritza Urteaga, 273–298. Madrid: Ariel Telefónica.

Gullestad, Marianne. 1989. *Kitchen-Table Society: A Case Study of the Family Life and Friendships of Young Working-Class Mothers in Urban Norway*. Oslo: Universitetsforlaget.

Habermas, Jurgen. 1989. *The Structural Transformation of the Public Sphere. An Inquiry into a Category of Bourgeois Society*. Cambridge: Polity Press.

Habermas, Jurgen. 1994. *Teoría de la acción comunicativa. Complementos y estudios previos*. Madrid: Cátedra.

Hall, Edward T. 1969. *The Hidden Dimension*. Garden City, NY: Anchor.

Hall, Stuart. 1997. "The Work of Representation." In *Representation. Cultural Representations and Signifying Practices*, edited by Stuart Hall, 13–74. London: Sage and The Open University.

Hannerz, Ulf. 2012. *Transnational Connections: Culture, People, Places*. London: Routledge.

Harari, Yuval Noah. 2018. *21 Lessons for the 21st Century*. New York: Spiegel & Grau.

Hellesund, Tone, Sasha Roseneil, Isabel Crowhurst, Ana Cristina Santos, and Mariya Stoilova. 2019. "Narrating and Relating to Ordinariness. Experiences of Unconventional Intimacies in Contemporary Europe." *Ethnologia Scandinavica* 49: 92–113.

Herman, David. 2009. *Basic Elements of Narrative*. New York: Wiley.

Herman, David. 2012. *Narrative Theory: Core Concepts and Critical Debates*. Columbus: Ohio University Press.

Herman, Luc, and Bart Vervaeck. 2005. *Handbook of Narrative Analysis*. Lincoln: University of Nebraska Press.

Highmore, Ben. 2002. *Everyday Life and Cultural Theory*. London: Routledge.

Highmore, Ben. 2005. "Unprocessed Data: Everyday Life in the Singular." In *Day-to-Day Data: An Exhibition of Artists Who Collect, List, Database and Absurdly Analyse the Data of Everyday Life*, edited by Ellie Harrison, Jim Waters, and Helen Jones. Angel Row Gallery. Nottingham: Nottingham City Museums & Galleries. https://daytodaydata.ellieharrison.com/benhighmore.html.

Highmore, Ben. 2006. *Michel de Certeau. Analysing Culture*. London: Continuum.

Highmore, Ben. 2010. *Ordinary Lives. Studies in the Everyday*. London: Routledge.

Hine, Christine. 2008. "Virtual Ethnography: Modes, Varieties, Affordances." In *The Sage Handbook of Online Research Methods*, edited by Nigel G. Fielding, Raymond M. Lee, and Grant Blank, 257–270. London: Sage.

Hochschild, Arlie R. 1983. *The Managed Heart: Commercialization of Human Feeling*. Berkeley: University of California Press.

Hochschild, Arlie R. 1997. *The Time Bind. When Work Becomes Home and Home Becomes Work*. New York: Henry Holt.

Hochschild, Arlie R. 2003. *The Commercialization of Intimate Life. Notes from Home and Work*. Berkeley: University of California Press.

Hochschild, Arlie R. 2012. *The Outsourced Self. What Happens When We Pay Others to Live Our Lives for Us*. New York: Picador.

Hochschild, Arlie R. 2016. *Strangers in Their Own Land. Anger and Mourning in the American Right*. New York: The New Press.

Hochschild, Arlie R. 2017. *Strangers in Their Own Land: Challenges Climbing the Empathy Wall*. University of California Television, YouTube, https://www.youtube.com/watch?v=o2flsUT9_QM.

Hochschild, Arlie R., and Anne Machung. 1989. *The Second Shift. Working Parents and the Revolution at Home*. New York: Penguin.

Hodder, Ian. 2012. *Entangled. An Archaeology of the Relationships between Humans and Things*. Oxford: Wiley Blackwell.

Holquist, Michael. 1990. *Dialogism. Bakhtin and His World*. London: Routledge.

Huizinga, J. 2002 [1949]. *Homo Ludens. A Study of the Play-Element in Culture*. Oxon, UK: Routledge.

Ingold, Tim. 2000. *The Perception of the Environment. Essays on Livelihood, Dwelling and Skill*. London: Routledge.

Ingold, Tim. 2010. "Bringing Things to Life: Creative Entanglements in a World of Materials." *NCRM Working Paper Series 05/10, ESRC National Centre*

for Research Methods. https://uncommon.kulturfolger.ch/s/ingold-0510_creative
_entanglements.pdf.

Jacobson, Roman. 1960. "Linguistics and Poetics." In *Style in Language*, edited by Thomas A. Sebeok, 350–377. Cambridge: MIT Press.

Jacobson, Roman. 1985. "El lenguaje común de antropólogos y lingüistas." In *Ensayos de lingüística general*, 13–33. Barcelona: Planeta-Agostini.

Kasinitz, Philip. 1994. *Metropolis. Center and Symbol of Our Times*. New York: New York University Press.

Kaufmann, Jean-Claude. 1997. *Le coeur a l'ouvrage. Théorie de l'action ménagère*. Paris: Nathan.

Kaufmann, Jean-Claude. 1998. *Dirty Linen: Couples as Seen through Their Laundry*. London: Middlesex University Press.

Kaufmann, Jean-Claude. 2001. *Ego: Pour une sociologie de l'individu*. Paris: Nathan.

Kaufmann, Jean-Claude. 2002. *Premier matin: Comment naît une histoire d'amour*. Paris: Armand Colin.

Kaufmann, Jean-Claude. 2004. *L'invention de soi. Une théorie de l'identité*. Paris: Armand Colin.

Kaufmann, Jean-Claude. 2008. *The Single Woman and the Fairytale Prince*. Cambridge: Polity Press.

Kaufmann, Jean-Claude. 2009. *Gripes: The Little Quarrels of Couples*. Cambridge: Polity Press.

Kaufmann, Jean-Claude. 2010a. *Sex@mour. Les nouvelles clés des rencontres amoureuses*. Paris: Armand Colin.

Kaufmann, Jean-Claude. 2010b. *The Meaning of Cooking*. Cambridge: Polity Press.

Kaufmann, Jean-Claude. 2011. *Le sac: Un petit monde d'amour*. Paris: J. C. Lattès.

Kaufmann, Jean-Claude (dir.). 2015. *Faire ou faire-faire? Famille et services*. Rennes, France: Presses Universitaires de Rennes.

Keil, Charles. 1994. "Participatory Discrepancies and the Power of Music." In *Music Grooves*, edited by Charles Keil and Steven Feld, 96–108. Chicago: University of Chicago Press.

Keil, Charles, and Steven Feld, eds. 1994. *Music Grooves*. Chicago: University of Chicago Press.

Kelty, Chris, et al. 2009. "Collaboration, Coordination, and Composition. Fieldwork after the Internet." In *Fieldwork Is Not What It Used to Be. Learning Anthropology's Method in a Time of Transition*, edited by James D. Faubion and George E. Marcus, 184–206. Ithaca, NY: Cornell University Press.

Kundera, Milan. 2006. *La insoportable levedad del ser* [*The Unbearable Lightness of Being*]. Barcelona: Tusquets.

Labov, William, and Joshua Waletzky. 1967. "Narrative Analysis. Oral Versions of Personal Experience." In *Essays on the Verbal and Visual Arts. Proceedings of the 1966 Annual Spring Meeting of the American Ethnological Society*, edited by June Helm, 12–44. Seattle: University of Washington Press. Reprinted in 1998, *Journal of Narrative and Life History* 7 (1–4): 3–38.

Lahire, Bernard. 2006. *La culture des individus: Dissonances culturelles et distinction de soi*. Paris: La Découverte.

Lakoff, George, and Mark Johnson. 2003. *Metaphors We Live By*. Chicago: University of Chicago Press.

Lasén Díaz, Amparo. 2012. "Autofotos: subjetividades y medios sociales." In *Jóvenes, culturas urbanas y redes digitales. Prácticas emergentes en las artes, las editoriales y la música*, edited by Néstor García Canclini, Francisco Cruces, and Maritza Urteaga, 253–271. Barcelona: Ariel Telefónica.

Leach, Edmund. 1961. *Rethinking Anthropology*. London: Robert Cunningham.

Leach, Edmund R. 1976. *Culture and Communication*. Cambridge: Cambridge University Press.

Lefebvre, H. 1991. *The Production of Space*. Oxford: Blackwell.

Lefebvre, Henri. 2004a. *Critique of Everyday Life*. New York: Verso.

Lefebvre, Henri. 2004b. *Rhythmanalysis: Space, Time and Everyday Life*. London: Continuum.

Lehrer, Adrianne. 1982. "Critical Communication: Wine and Therapy." In *Exceptional Language and Linguistics*, edited by L. K. Obler, and L. Menn, 67–80. Boston: Academic Press.

Lejeune, Philippe. 2009a. "Intime, privé, public." *La faute à Rousseau* 51: 9.

Lejeune, Philippe. 2009b. "Le journal au seuil de l'intime." In *Pour une histoire de l'intime et de ses variations*, edited by Anne Coudreuse and Françoise Simonet-Tenant, 117–148. Paris: L'Harmattan.

Lenton, Timothy, Sébastien Dutreuil, and Bruno Latour. 2020. "Life on Earth Is Hard to Spot." *The Anthropocene Review* 7(3): 248–272.

Littau, Karen. 2008. *Teorías de la lectura. Libros, cuerpos y bibliomanía*. Buenos Aires: Manantial.

Lluch, Gemma. 2017. "Los jóvenes y adolescentes comparten la lectura." In *¿Cómo leemos en la sociedad digital? Lectores, booktubers y prosumidores*, edited by Francisco Cruces, 29–51. Barcelona: Ariel/ Fundación Telefónica. https://www.fundaciontelefonica.com/cultura-digital/publicaciones/601/.

Löfgren, Orvar. 2002. *On Holiday. A History of Vacationing*. Berkeley: University of California Press.

Löfgren, Orvar. 2007. "Excessive Living." *Culture and Organization* 13(2): 131–143.

Löfgren, Orvar. 2012. "Material Culture." In *A Companion to Folklore*, edited by Regina F. Bendix and Galit Hasan-Rokem, 169–183. Malden, MA: Wiley-Blackwell.

Löfgren, Orvar. 2013. "Changing Emotional Economies: The Case of Sweden 1970–2010." *Culture and Organization* 19(4): 283–296.

Löfgren, Orvar. 2014. "The Black Box of Everyday Life. Entanglements of Stuff, Affects and Activities." *Cultural Analysis* 13: 77–98.

Löfgren, Orvar. 2015a. "Living in the Past, the Present and the Future: Synchronizing Everyday Life." Keynote opening lecture at the Twelfth International Society for Ethnology and Folklore conference, Zagreb, Croatia. https://www.siefhome.org/videos/sief2015.shtml.

Löfgren, Orvar. 2015b. *Orvar Löfgren's Ethnological Sensation*. SIEF. https://www.siefhome.org/videos/ethno_sensations.shtml.

Löfgren, Orvar. 2016. "Emotional Luggage. Unpacking the Suitcase." In *Sensitive Objects. Affect and Material Culture*, edited by Jonas Frykman and Maja Frykman Povrzanović, 125–152. Lund, Sweden: Nordic Academic Press.

Löfgren, Orvar. 2018. "When Everyday Life Falls Apart. Stories of Precariousness." SIEF 2019 Conference Call Meeting. Incipit (CSIC), Spain.

Löfgren, Orvar. 2019a. "Domestic Journeys: The Importance of Micro-Moves." In *Wohin geht die Reise? = Where Does the Journey Go To?: Eine Geburtstagsgabe für Johanna Roshoven 2019 = A Birthday Present for Johanna Rolshoven*, edited by S. Eggmann, S. Kolbe, and J. Winkler. Akroama. https://www.geruchderzeit.org /loefgren/.

Löfgren, Orvar. 2019b. "Mine or Ours? The Home as a Moral Economy." In *Wirtschaften. Kulturwissenschaftliche Perspektiven*, edited by Karl Braun, Claus-Marco Dieterich, Johannes Moser, and Christian Schönholz, 15–35. Marburg, Germany: Makufee.

Löfgren, Orvar. 2019c. "The Hidden Power of Routines." Personal communication.

Luhmann, Niklas. 1979. *Trust and Power*. London: John Wiley.

Luhmann, Niklas. 1988. "Familiarity, Confidence, Trust: Problems and Alternatives." In *Trust. Making and Breaking Cooperative Relations*, edited by Diego Gambetta, 94–107. Oxford: Blackwell.

Lyon, Larry, and Robyn Driskell. 2011. *The Community in Urban Society*. Long Grove, IL: Waveland.

MacIntyre, Alasdair. 1981. "The Virtues, the Unity of a Human Life and the Concept of a Tradition." In *After Virtue. A Study in Moral Theory*, 190–209. London: Duckworth.

Mallett, Shelley. 2004. "Understanding Home: A Critical Review of the Literature." *The Sociological Review* 52(1): 62–89.

Marcus, George E. 1995. "Ethnography in/of the World System: The Emergence of Multi-sited Ethnography." *Annual Review of Anthropology* 24: 95–117.

Martín-Barbero, Jesús. 1989. *Procesos de comunicación y matrices de cultura. Itinerario para salir de la razón dualista*. México: Gustavo Gili Ediciones.

Martín-Barbero, Jesús, and Gemma Lluch. 2012. "De la necesidad de leer al derecho de escribir." In *Lectura, escritura y desarrollo de la sociedad de la información, 38–44*. Bogotá: CERLALC-UNESCO.

Massey, Doreen. 1999. "Philosophy and Politics of Spatiality: Some Considerations." The Hettner-Lecture in Human Geography. *Geographische Zeitschrift* 87: 1–12.

Massey, Doreen. 2005. *For Space*. London: Sage.

Massey, Doreen. 2013. "Doreen Massey on Space." *Social Sciences Space*, https:// www.socialsciencespace.com/2013/02/podcastdoreen-massey-on-space/.

Maturana, Humberto R., and Francisco Varela G. 2005. *De máquinas y seres vivos. Autopoiesis: La organización de lo vivo*. Buenos Aires: Editorial Universitaria, Grupo Editorial Lumen.

Mauss, Marcel. 1970. *Lo sagrado y lo profano*. Barcelona: Barral.

Miller, Daniel. 2008. *The Comfort of Things*. Cambridge: Polity Press.

Miller, Toby. 2004. "A View from a Fossil. The New Economy, Creativity and Consumption—Two or Three Things I Don't Believe In." *International Journal of Cultural Studies* 7(1): 55–65.

Moreno Andrés, Jorge, and Francisco Cruces. 2018. *The Order I Live In. An Indoor Urban Symphony.* https://canal.uned.es/video/5c07ac67b1111f5b718bb727.

Mossuz-Lavau, Janine. 1991. *Les lois de l'amour: Les politiques de la sexualité en France de 1950 à nos jours.* Paris: Payot.

Murillo, Soledad. 2006. *El mito de la vida privada. De la entrega al tiempo propio.* Madrid: Siglo XXI.

Neruda, Pablo. 2017 [1974]. *Confieso que he vivido.* Barcelona: Seix Barral.

Nippert-Eng, Christena. 1995. *Home and Work. Negotiating Boundaries through Everyday Life.* Chicago: University of Chicago Press.

Nippert-Eng, Christena. 2003. "Drawing the Line: Organizations and the Boundary Work of 'Home' and 'Work.'" In *Managing Boundaries in Organizations: Multiple Perspectives,* edited by Neil Paulsen and Tor Hernes, 262–280. London: Palgrave Macmillan.

Nippert-Eng, Christena. 2007. "Privacy in the United States: Some Implications for Design." *International Journal of Design* 1(2): 1–10.

Nippert-Eng, Christena. 2010. *Islands of Privacy.* Chicago: University of Chicago Press.

Nippert-Eng, Christena, and Alejandro Acquisti. 2011. "Insights on Privacy." *Speakers Series for the Privacy Commissioner of Canada,* Ottawa, Canada. http://www.islandsofprivacy.com/reviews_links.html.

Ochs, Elinor, and Lisa Capps. 1996. "Narrating the Self." *Annual Review of Anthropology* 25: 19–43.

Ochs, Elinor, and Lisa Capps. 2001. *Living Narratives. Creating Lives in Everyday Storytelling.* Cambridge, MA: Harvard University Press.

Österlund-Pötzsch, Susanne. 2021. "Georges Perec, *Species of Spaces and Other Pieces.*" Personal communication.

Pardo, Jose Luis. 1996. *La intimidad.* Valencia: Pre-Textos.

Pardo, Jose Luis, and Amparo Lasén. 2020. "Intimidad y extimidad." *CanalMarch,* January 2020. Video: 59:24. https://canal.march.es/es/coleccion/intimidad -extimidad-23670.

Perec, Georges. 1974. *Espèces d'espaces.* Paris: Éditions Galilée.

Perec, Georges. 1985. *Penser/classer.* Paris: Hachette.

Perec, Georges. 1989 [1973]. *L'infra-ordinaire.* Paris: Éditions du Seuil.

Piglia, Ricardo. 1999. "Nuevas tesis sobre el cuento." In *Formas breves,* 103–134. Buenos Aires: Temas Grupo Editorial.

Pink, Sarah. 2004. *Home Truths. Gender, Domestic Objects and Everyday Life.* Oxford: Berg.

Pink, Sarah. 2012. *Situating Everyday Life. Practices and Places.* London: Sage.

Pink, Sarah, et al. 2017. *Making Homes. Ethnography and Design.* London: Bloomsbury Academic.

Prince, Gerald. 1973. *A Grammar of Stories: An Introduction.* The Hague: Mouton.

Prince, Gerald. 1997. "Narratology and Narratological Analysis." *Journal of Narrative and Life History* 7 (1–4): 39–44.

Prince, Gerald. 2003. *A Dictionary of Narratology*. Lincoln: University of Nebraska Press.

Rebreyend, Anne-Claire. 2009. "Representation des intimités amoureuses dans la France du XXᵉ siècle." In *Pour une histoire de l'intime et de ses variations*, edited by Anne Coudreuse and Françoise Simonet-Tenant, 149–162. Paris: L'Harmattan.

Reyes, Alfonso. 1995 [1956]. "La melancolía del viajero." In *Obras completas*, vol. II., 357. FCE, México.

Reygadas, Luis, Francisco Cruces, et al. 2012. *Empresas de Humanidades. Sectores de Nueva Economía 20+20*. Madrid: EOI.

Ricœur, Paul. 1983. *Temps et récit*. Paris: Seuil.

Roseneil, Sasha, Isabel Crowhurst, Tone Hellesund, Ana Cristina Santos, and Mariya Stoilova. 2020. *The Tenacity of the Couple-Norm: Intimate Citizenship Regimes in a Changing Europe*. London: UCL Press.

Sassen, Saskia. 2000. *Cities in a World Economy*. Thousand Oaks, CA: Pine Forge Press.

Schegloff, Emanuel A. 1997. "'Narrative Analysis' Thirty Years Later." *Journal of Narrative and Life History* 7(1–4): 97–106.

Schultz, Alfred. 1956. "Mozart and the Philosophers." *Social Research* 23(2): 219–242.

Schultz, Alfred. 1977. "Making Music Together: A Study in Social Relationship." In *Symbolic Anthropology. A Reader in the Study of Symbols and Meanings*, edited by Janet L. Dolgin, David S. Kemnitzer, and David M. Schneider, 106–118. New York: Columbia University Press.

Schutz, Alfred, and Thomas Luckmann. 1973. *The Structures of the Life-World*. Evanston, IL: Northwestern University Press.

Sennet, Richard. 1969. *Classic Essays on the Culture of Cities*. New Jersey: Prentice Hall.

Shoshitaishvili, Boris. 2020. "Deep Time and Compressed Time in the Anthropocene: The New Timescape and the Value of Cosmic Storytelling." *The Anthropocene Review* 7(2): 125–137.

Sibilia, Paula. 2008. *La intimidad como espectáculo*. Buenos Aires: Fondo de Cultura Económica.

Simmel, Georg. 1990 [1900]. *The Philosophy of Money*. London: Routledge.

Simonet-Tenant, Françoise. 2009. "À la recherche des prèmices d'une culture de l'intime." In *Pour une histoire de l'intime et de ses variations*, edited by Anne Coudreuse and Françoise Simonet-Tenant, 39–62. Paris: L'Harmattan.

Stahl, Sandra K. D. 1989. *Literary Folkloristics and the Personal Narrative*. Bloomington: Indiana University Press.

Stewart, Kathleen. 2005. "Cultural Poiesis. The Generativity of Emergent Things." In *Handbook of Qualitative Research*, edited by Norman K. Denzin and Yvonna S. Lincoln, 1015–1030. Thousand Oaks, CA: Sage.

Stewart, Kathleen. 2007. *Ordinary Affects*. Durham, NC: Duke University Press.

Straus, Murray A. 1977. "Societal Morphogenesis and Intrafamily Violence in Cross-cultural Perspective." *Annals of the New York Academy of Sciences* 285(1): 717–730.

Szendy, Peter. 2001. *Écoute. Une histoire de nos oreilles*. Paris: Minuit.

Thomas, Frank. 1997. *The Conquest of Cool. Business Culture, Counterculture, and the Rise of Hip Consumerism*. Chicago: University of Chicago Press.

Thompson, Edward P. 1967. "Time, Work-Discipline, and Industrial Capitalism." *Past and Present* 38: 56–97.

Thompson, John B. 2011. "Shifting Boundaries of Public and Private Life." *Theory, Culture and Society* 28: 49.

Thrift, Nigel. 2008. *Non-representational Theory. Space, Politics, Affect*. Milton Park, UK: Routledge.

Tisseron, Serge. 2002. *L'intimité surexposée*. Paris: Flammarion.

Tisseron, Serge. 2011. "Intimité et extimité." *Communications* 88(1): 83–91.

Tournier, Michel. 2004. *Journal extime*. Paris: Gallimard.

Valenzuela, Hugo, Luis Reygadas, and Francisco Cruces. 2015. "My Job Is my Life. Overlap between Life and Work in Spanish Companies." *Revista Española de Investigaciones Sociológicas* 150: 189–208. http://dx.doi.org/10.5477/cis/reis.150 .189.

Velasco, Honorio M. 2003. *Hablar y pensar, tareas culturales*. Madrid: UNED.

Velasco, Honorio M. 2007. *Cuerpo y espacio. Símbolos y metáforas, representación y expresividad de las culturas*. Madrid: Centro de Estudios Ramón Areces.

Velasco, Honorio, et al. 2006. *La sonrisa de la institución. Confianza y riesgo en sistemas expertos*. Madrid: Editorial Universitaria Ramón Areces.

Weber, Max. 1969. "The Nature of the City." In *Classic Essays on the Culture of Cities*, edited by Richard Sennet, 20–34. Englewood Cliffs, NJ: Prentice-Hall.

Winocur, Rosalía. 2015. "Prácticas tradicionales y emergentes de lectoescritura en jóvenes universitarios." In *Hacia una antropología de los lectores*, edited by Néstor García Canclini, 243–281. Ciudad de México: UAM-I/Ariel/Fundación Telefónica.

Wirth, Louis. 1969 [1938]. "Urbanism as a Way of Life." In *Classic Essays on the Culture of Cities*, edited by Richard Sennet, 143–164. New Jersey: Prentice Hall.

Zafra, Remedios. 2010. *Un cuarto propio conectado. (Ciber)espacio y (auto)gestión del yo*. Madrid: Fórcola.

Zafra, Remedios. 2017. "Itinerarios del yo en un cuarto propio conectado." In *¿Cómo leemos en la sociedad digital? Lectores, booktubers y prosumidores*, edited by Francisco Cruces, 79–102. Barcelona: Ariel/Fundación Telefónica. https://www .fundaciontelefonica.com/cultura-digital/publicaciones/601/.

Zerubavel, Eviatar. 1991. *The Fine Line: Making Distinctions in Everyday Life*. New York: Free Press.

Zerubavel, Eviatar. 1996. "Lumping and Splitting: Notes on Social Classification." *Sociological Forum* 11(3): 421–433.

196

INDEX

Page references for figures and tables are italicized.

ABOUT THE AUTHOR

Francisco Cruces is professor of anthropology at Universidad Nacional de Educación a Distancia (UNED, Spain), where he teaches social and urban anthropology. His ethnographic fieldwork in Madrid, Mexico City, Bogotá, and Montevideo has focused on a diversity of forms of expression: rituals, music, festivals, demonstrations, expert systems, ways of reading, and the making of intimate space. He coordinates Cultura Urbana, a team of a dozen scholars studying emerging practices in global cities. He has published *Símbolos en la ciudad* (UNED, 2006), *Jóvenes, culturas urbanas y redes digitales. Prácticas emergentes en las artes, las editoriales y la música* (with Néstor García Canclini and Maritza Urteaga et al., Ariel/Fundación Telefónica, 2012), and *Cosmópolis. Nuevas maneras de ser urbanos* (with Cultura Urbana group, Gedisa, 2016). His recent work on the poetics of intimacy has produced the documentary *The Order I Live In*, coauthored with Jorge Moreno Andrés and premiered in Madrid, Montevideo, and Mexico City.

www.ingramcontent.com/pod-product-compliance
Lightning Source LLC
Chambersburg PA
CBHW022313280326
41932CB00010B/1085